Praise for Randi Minetor's
Breadwinner Wives and the Men They Marry

"Here is a book for women who are committed to their success, to their families, and to their marriages–smart women who are ready to succeed in all aspects of their lives. Minetor shows them that breadwinner wives really can have it all."

> – David Bach, bestselling author of *Smart Couples Finish Rich* and *Smart Women Finish Rich*

"Randi Minetor has earned more than her husband for as long as they've been married, 11 years. She went looking for a book on the subject–and found there was none. Through interviews for her book, Minetor learned the pros and the cons for families with a breadwinner wife."

> – *Newhouse News Service*

"Randi Minetor's book gives us hope that someday in the twenty-first century it will no longer matter who earns the most money in a relationship, but rather that each one finds work they enjoy along with the other partner's acceptance and respect of that choice."

> – Priscilla Y. Huff, author of *101 Best Home-Based Businesses for Women* and publisher of the e-zine *A Self-Employed Woman*

"According to the U.S. Department of Labor, one-third of wives earn more than their husbands. As a result, they must fight to maintain what Randi Minetor calls a 'new, marital dynamic.'"

> – *Daily News*

"Three cheers for *Breadwinner Wives and the Men They Marry*–referring to both the book and to the people it addresses! Randi Minetor is helping millions of people understand their lives better; she is also helping raise society's awareness of this important change in the very structure of our culture."

> – Gregory P. Godek, author of *1001 Ways To Be Romantic*

BREADWINNER WIVES
AND THE MEN THEY MARRY

BREADWINNER WIVES
AND THE MEN THEY MARRY

*How to Have a Successful Marriage
While Outearning Your Husband*

Randi Minetor

New Horizon Press
Far Hills, New Jersey

New Horizon Press
P.O. Box 669
Far Hills, NJ 07931

Randi Minetor
    Breadwinner Wives and the Men They Marry: How to Have a Successful Marriage While Outearning Your Husband

Cover Design: Robert Aulicino
Interior Design: Susan M. Sanderson

Library of Congress Control Number: 2001089173

ISBN: 0-88282-215-2
New Horizon Press

Manufactured in the U.S.A.

2006   2005   2004   2003   2002 / 5   4   3   2   1

AUTHOR'S NOTE

This book is based on my survey results and extensive personal interviews with breadwinning wives and their husbands as well as research in the fields of psychology, sociology, family dynamics, gender issues and financial demographics. Fictitious identities and names have been given to all characters in this book in order to protect individual privacy.

A portion of the author's proceeds from this book will be donated to the Women's Foundation of Genesee Valley, managers of an endowment fund for programs that explicitly benefit women and girls.

TABLE OF CONTENTS

PREFACE
Why I Wrote This Book

I have a confession to make. I started the research for this book in a quest for personal validation.

The disquieting sense that I was some kind of superwoman oddity came to me when I found myself, a married woman, at the top of my career, yet strangely alone. I was vice-president of an advertising agency, I had the respect of my professional peers and a salary that proved my worth. I had a beautiful home on the "good" side of town, a new car, an upscale wardrobe and a loving husband—all the conventional symbols of personal success. However, according to those around me, that success was deeply and irrevocably flawed, because I dared to earn more money than my husband.

My husband, Nicholas "Nic" Minetor, found his calling early in life as a theatrical lighting designer. Highly skilled both technically and artistically, he earned a consistent income that put him through college at the University of Minnesota and brought him to a full-time position at a theater in Rochester, New York in the early 1980s. Had he not met me, he might have continued on to the ultra-competitive theatrical whirl of New York City. We met, however, and created a home together in upstate New York and Nic chose our comfortable lifestyle over a frenzied quest for professional advancement. While he built a thriving business as a lighting director for corporate film, advertising and the arts, the choice to stay in Rochester imposed an upper limit on his earning potential. Thus, over time, I became a breadwinner wife.

It's not easy to find yourself at the forefront of a trend, especially when you have no idea the trend exists. I had no way of knowing that I was *not* the only woman in my social circle, in my town, maybe in all of America whose income exceeded her husband's. I felt alone, isolated and different from the women around me. I told myself that I carried the weight of all the positives and negatives of thirty years of feminism—and that somehow, my own feminist drive had gotten me to a place I wasn't supposed to occupy.

If you listen to conversations at parties and watch television or movies or view media stories on any network station, you will soon realize that our society continues to believe it is distasteful and socially incorrect for a wife to be the primary breadwinner or the more successful partner in the family. "If your husband is healthy, skilled and able-bodied," we are told, "he'd better be the one putting bread on the table—and *your* income, you overachieving wife, had better be ancillary."

Everyone from my mother to my employer to my best friend suggested to me that my husband—my greatest emotional supporter, my best buddy, my constant source of encouragement—would be embarrassed, even destroyed, if I let on to a single soul that my income exceeded his.

Yes, I had succeeded in life, but I had just better shut up about it. Because my success would *humiliate* my husband.

After a period of time, I began to chafe under such restrictions and decided to look into research and studies on wives who earn more. When my preliminary research disclosed I was not alone in the role of breadwinning wife, I undertook the task of explaining the issues that arise when a woman earns more than her husband and talking to the men and women who cope on a daily basis with this new marital dynamic. This book is the result of my discoveries about breadwinner wives and their husbands. It offers insights to those already part of, entering into or contemplating such unions, as well as recommendations from the many couples with whom I have spoken on the satisfactions and the pitfalls these pioneering men and women have encountered as they build fulfilling, equal relationships.

ACKNOWLEDGEMENTS

First, to the 120 wives and husbands across America who shared their stories freely with me over the course of my research: From the bottom of my heart, I thank you for your generosity of spirit, your enthusiasm for my work and for your absolute candor in telling me about the challenges you face every day.

I approached more than sixty national professional women's associations for their assistance in helping me find breadwinning wives across the country. I would like to thank Women in Technology, the Association for Women in Computing, the Association of Black Women in Higher Education, Financial Women International, Women in Cable & Telecommunications, the National Association for Women in Education, the Society of Women Engineers, the Association for Women in Mathematics, the American Association of Women Podiatrists, the National Association of Women Business Owners, the American Association of Black Women Entrepreneurs and the Association of Women Geoscientists for their particularly effective assistance.

Writing is a solitary process, even with a research project of this magnitude. Yet a few individuals stand out as absolutely key to the completion of this book. I could not have succeeded in my research or my writing without Daniel O'Donnell, who took the transcripts of my interviews, built a powerhouse of a database and turned my information into solid, credible quantitative results. Never allowing me to ignore the importance of pure, unsullied data, Dan kept me honest and on track until the last percentage point went into print.

Dr. Julie Brines of the University of Washington at Seattle provided me with citations of sources I had not discovered on my own. Her insights sent me in new, fruitful directions as I searched for sociological research that would contribute to capturing an accurate and comprehensive picture of breadwinning wives and their relationships with husbands, children, family and friends.

Dr. Arthur Goldberg and Clay Woomer helped me formulate my research model and proceed with the collection of information. In particular, Clay's expertise as a market research specialist was invaluable as I created my initial survey.

Nancy Rees probably has no idea that she was an inspiration to me. I thank her for her honesty, her trust and her unwitting place as a role model as this project began. In addition, my thanks go to Marilyn Schicker, Joan Nobeling and my friends in the Thursday night group, for teaching me to turn a vicious cycle into a vitalizing cycle.

This book might still languish in the bottom of a drawer had it not been for the motivational force of Mary Ann Shew, my Friday morning writing buddy, who locked me into a three-hour weekly date with laptops, café mocha and ever-effusive encouragement while we worked on our respective books. For that matter, my thanks to the entire staff at Starbucks at 12 Corners in Brighton, a suburb of Rochester, New York, for providing me with the perfect atmosphere for concentration and composition.

A cadre of teachers shaped my writing and my critical thinking skills from the beginning, both in academic and professional settings. My thanks go to former Brighton School District teachers Tony DeFusto, Kay Marvin and John Mehrenger, SUNY Buffalo professors Anna Kay France, Marcus Klein, Ray Federman and Miles Slatin, and colleagues Gary Stockman, Audrey Saphar and Adele Fico for their leadership and guidance.

Needless to say, I am grateful for the enthusiastic encouragement and literary insights of Dr. Joan Dunphy and everyone at New Horizon Press, in moving this book from manuscript to publication.

Many friends have cheered me on over the last three years as I approached my publication goal. I could not possibly list them all, but those to whom I owe a tremendous debt of gratitude include Martha and Peter Schermerhorn, Ruth Watson, John King, Jen Wheelock, Stacey Michaels, Jim Sulanowski, Anita Jones, Paula and Rich Landis, Elouise Oyzon, Jim McMurtrie, Martin Winer, Ken Horowitz, Rose-Anne Moore, David S. Cohen, Margery Kimbrough, Bruce Barton—and above all, my best friend for thirty-five years and most likely for forty-five more, Debra Weiland.

Finally, four people stand out as the most critical to the completion of this book: Marlene Dohr, friend and counselor, whose clarity of understanding revealed the exit I so desperately needed from the corporate world, sending me into this new life as a full-time writer.

My father, "Big Al" Bassow, my biggest fan and the greatest dad a breadwinning wife could ever hope for, whose unshakeable faith in me kept me moving forward in many uncertain times.

My mother, Annette Bassow, my most influential role model and a breadwinning wife in her own right, who not only transcribed every single one of my taped interviews (God bless her), but listened to my endless vocalizing about this book for three solid years.

And most of all, my husband, Nic Minetor, my great romance and the greatest love of my life, who swallowed his own pride to allow this book to happen, encouraged me, praised me, gave me space to write on countless evenings and weekends, opened his cherished bottle of 1976 Chateau Lafitte Rothschild the day I signed the publishing contract, believed in me and loved me every single day, even on the days when I was decidedly unlovable. No words are adequate, Nic, so know that I thank God every day for giving me the great gift of your love.

CHAPTER 1

THE ROAD LESS TRAVELED
Becoming a Breadwinner Wife

When Nic and I met, I had just taken the job of public relations assistant at the same theater at which Nic was master electrician. I wrote news releases, handled special events and served as the conduit between the media and the theater's technical and artistic staff, while Nic was in charge of all lighting installations and equipment maintenance for the theater's annual seven-show season. It was 1984 and I would turn twenty-five later that year, while Nic had just turned thirty. My income just barely scraped the $14,000 mark for that season; Nic earned about $15,000 a year.

Nic was unlike any man I'd dated before then. Mild-mannered, excruciatingly polite, soft-spoken and filled with genuine Minnesota friendliness, he was as comfortable dicing vegetables in the kitchen as he was on a catwalk thirty feet in the air, running miles of cable from one lighting instrument to the next. Charming, good-humored and ever positive, Nic stood in sharp contrast to the flamboyant, self-involved men of my past.

Nic surprised me again and again with his interest in my work. He went out of his way to read pieces I'd written years before; he rejoiced when I convinced the media to write or tape feature stories about the theater; he grinned when I took his tuxedo-clad arm on opening night and greeted guests as his date. Nic's delight in just being with me won me over for life. I never gave a thought to his earning potential; here was an intelligent, attractive, charming man who loved me without reservation.

Yet very early in our relationship, Nic made a point of telling me that he never expected to earn enough to support a family. "I'm good at what I do and I've chosen a profession that just isn't very profitable," he said, with the characteristic frankness I had already learned to appreciate. "My wife, whomever she may be, will have to be able to contribute to the household—if I'm lucky, maybe she'll even make more money than me."

At that moment, I had never considered the possibility of earning more money than my future husband earns. When I thought about it, however, I was relieved at how comfortable I was with the idea. Never had I expected a man to support me, mainly because I felt that I wanted a more equitable relationship with my husband. Life experience had already taught me that money is power—so if my husband didn't want the implicit power he would hold as family breadwinner, I might actually have a chance to share some of the power myself. Maybe, just maybe, we would have a true partnership. Maybe our marriage would be something different, something new, something better. That was my fantasy as I moved into this uncharted territory—a journey that would prove to be treacherous.

Marriage would be a long time in coming, however, as Nic and I shared an apartment and struggled to eke out a living in the arts. By 1987 I had reached the upper level of my tolerance for life in the theater—I'd become the theater's marketing director and my income had inched upward to a paltry $18,000 annually. Even in 1987, that was just barely over the poverty line. I applied for and landed a copywriting position at a well-respected downtown advertising and public relations firm—and nearly doubled my income overnight, to just under $30,000.

While we enjoyed an almost instantaneous difference in our combined lifestyle—graduating from fast food drive-through lines to diners, making modest furniture purchases and upgrading my wardrobe to include tailored suits—neither Nic nor I paid much attention to the fact that my income now exceeded his by about a third. Later that year, Nic made the same exit from the theater to launch his freelance lighting business and within a year his income once again matched mine. My breadwinning status had hardly registered as a blip on our household radar screen.

Nic and I married in September 1990. Then, very suddenly and very quickly, everything began to change.

Less than a month after our wedding, my employer took me to lunch and handed me a new set of responsibilities and a new title, boosting me to middle management—with a salary increase to $50,000.

"How much did you say?" Nic asked, dumbfounded.

"Fifty," I replied. "Thousand."

We rejoiced over dinner at a fine establishment we could not afford the day before, swallowing our innate frugality to order a bottle of wine at an exorbitant restaurant price.

Never did I sense any discomfort from Nic because my income was nearly double his own. I immediately volunteered to take over monthly payment of the utilities and other small household bills, expenses we scrupulously had split down the middle during our six years as cohabitants. Within a few weeks, we engaged a real estate agent and began the search for a home of our own.

As we settled into our 1917 American foursquare house on the trendy side of the city, something began to change for me. The more money I made—every year, another promotion would bring me a high percentage increase—the more I resented the fact that Nic made less.

I paid the household bills while we continued to split the mortgage. I socked money every month into mutual funds and retirement savings, while Nic's earnings seemed to be "fun money" for his own personal use. I worked long hours every week, while Nic had entire seasons off when his business was slow. I did what I considered to be my wifely duty and managed all the cooking, laundry, dishes and most of the gardening, while Nic puttered in his workshop and played games on his computer. Nic had the life of Riley, while I smoldered like Vesuvius. Real life was very different from my early dreams about pioneering a new, fairer version of marriage.

Six years into our marriage, the volcano finally erupted. By this time, I'd become a vice president; I managed six people and led the company's new business prospecting efforts. Business had never been better—until one winter day, when one of our biggest accounts abruptly fired us and hired a top New York City firm with global connections. The sudden disappearance of this account cut my workload by two-thirds. Almost instantly, my ability to bury my personal problems in overwork vanished. No longer could I suffuse my anger over my home situation in long hours at the office. I had to face my distress head-on.

Face it I did, nearly tearing my marriage asunder in the process. I railed over the drudgery of monotonous, repetitive household tasks. I chafed against the drastic imbalance between Nic's free time versus my own and the inequity of our responsibilities at home. I fumed as my savings—*our* savings—grew and Nic contributed little. Deciding that his comparative lack of ready cash signaled a lack of respect for me and for my contribution to the household, I felt used, unappreciated and taken for granted.

Our battle for change and consensus lasted three tense months, during which Nic moved from bafflement at my unchecked rage to a new understanding. Over this period, he began to participate in housework, taking over the daily dishwashing and the weekly laundry. Gradually, he absorbed the substance of my argument: It's not the task or the chore—it's the *attitude*. I was angry over Nic's assumption—a direct result of his upbringing in a traditional home—that everything involved in maintaining our lifestyle was *my* job, requiring no active participation from him.

We established a truce, but my bad days and restless nights continued. Despite Nic's increased contribution to household chores, I burned with the injustices of life as a breadwinning wife.

At the time, I didn't fully realize Nic was not the problem. Ever the loving and dutiful husband, Nic had not changed a hair throughout our twelve-year relationship except to become even more supportive of me and even more considerate as a husband. I, on the other hand, had changed considerably. Always the driven, career-focused achiever, I found myself approaching my late thirties and desperately frustrated at work, pulled taut by the rigors of managing people, exhausted by the constant quest for new business and farther away from the writing I enjoyed. I had not yet recognized that what I felt was not only anger, but also jealousy—because Nic could make *choices* in his life, choices I made possible for him by earning a high income. I, on the other hand, felt utterly trapped by that big paycheck, locked into a job that seemed destined to destroy me.

Never had I felt so alone as I did then. I didn't stop to notice that Nic and I had formed a circle of friends and coworkers in which many of the women earned more money than their husbands. I didn't look around to see that I was not alone at all; in fact, I was part of a growing population of women who had the opportunities to shine, but were hiding their own lights for fear of overshadowing their men or were struggling to find their ways in what had become a new relationship dynamic.

One day I found myself sitting across the desk from a woman of considerable corporate power, as she described her own nontraditional marriage as if it were the most commonplace thing in the world.

It was a blustery December morning and I'd arrived slightly early for a 7:30 A.M. meeting with Janice, a vice-president of a Fortune 100 manufacturing company. She had engaged the services of our agency and I had just become her speechwriter.

When I arrived, Janice was nowhere to be seen. I waited a full twenty minutes until she blew in, flustered and disheveled, unwinding a huge challis scarf from her head and neck and shaking snow from her long, black coat. "I'm sooo sorry," she gasped, still catching her breath, "but I had to get things straight at home. I really blew it last night with my husband."

Janice and I were hardly on intimate, personal terms, but sometimes a speechwriter is like a stranger on a train to a client. I said nothing and waited.

"I had to work late last night and I forgot to tell Hal," she said, dropping into a chair. "I didn't get home till half-past nine. Man, he was angry! He's home all day, every day, with the kids and he had dinner on the table right on time—and I just didn't show. I didn't remember until I was on my way home that I hadn't called him. So I stopped at the supermarket and got flowers—but it didn't help."

"Your husband is...home all day?" I immediately assumed he was disabled or between jobs. I was wrong.

"Oh, yes. It is important to us to have a parent home with the kids until they're in school. I can certainly support us all. So he stays home and he takes care of the house and the kids." She smiled ruefully. "Usually it's great. But sometimes I really screw up."

Janice supported her husband and children. I gulped before I spoke. "I know how that is. I'm the breadwinner in my family, too."

"Really?" Janice leaned forward, suddenly a co-conspirator. "Don't you just feel like such a *man* sometimes? Like you just want to go home and sit in front of the television with a cold beer and let them do everything else? But that's exactly what women hated about men supporting them—so we have to do better. We have to be participants, too."

It was as if she'd opened me up and read the writing on my soul. Janice knew the constant struggle for balance in the relationship, the conflicting need to compensate for our success by succeeding as a homemaker as well, the minimizing of our achievements so that other people (not necessarily our own husbands) would not see us as unfeeling or overconfident or, God forbid, ambitious.

If she knew and experienced all these conflicts...how many other women did, too?

I spent a Saturday in the library and perused endless magazine articles on-line, searching for some evidence that the media had discovered a trend. What I found stunned me. Only two short articles, "Women, Men and Money" in *Fortune* and "The New Providers" published in

Newsweek nearly two years earlier, even acknowledged that some women's earning abilities might exceed their spouses'. "Couples attempting to adjust to a shift in economic power often find it too touchy to talk about honestly," said the August 1996 article in *Fortune*. "Men don't talk about it when their wives earn more, because they're afraid other men will sneer at them and women don't talk about it, because they don't want to embarrass their men."[1]

These articles supplied the statistic that made my head spin: According to the Bureau of Labor Statistics, by 1996, *more than 29 percent of all married, working women in the United States made more money than their husbands.*[2] By 2000, the *Washington Post* would upgrade that statistic to a whopping 33 percent.[3] That's *one in every three married working women* in America—an estimated 10.5 million wives.

Who are these women? How do they deal with their situations? Such a high percentage can't all be the wives of unemployed men—especially with the rate of unemployment relatively low throughout the country. And only a tiny percentage can be "powerchicks" as defined by Matt Towery's book of that name, the women who have shattered the glass ceiling and risen to the top of major corporations and professions.[4] No, the rest of them are the rest of *us*—women who work hard, earn the rewards we deserve and apply ourselves in such a way that we secure a comfortable living...one that happens to be larger than the income supplied by our husbands.

That night, I described all of this to Nic. And it was he who said it: "There's a book in this somewhere."

Here is that book.

This is a book for us—the women who do well professionally and who deserve to enjoy the rewards of this success with their husbands and families. This also is a book for men who find themselves husbands of achieving wives and who want to be as happy, secure and open about the situation as they would be if the tables were turned and they shouldered their traditional role as principal breadwinners.

Can such a marriage work? Certainly! But it's a balancing act—and in this book, we explore that balance. We'll talk about everything from who pays for dinner to who does the dishes; from sharing the child care responsibilities to praising each other's accomplishments.

The more I learned from the wives and husbands who shared their lives with me, the more ideas I could apply to my own marriage. Now, I want to share the enlightenment this quest brought me with the 10.5 million breadwinning wives in America who face the same challenges, doubts, discoveries and resolutions I did, the husbands of breadwinning wives and those men and women who are contemplating embarking upon this twenty-first century relationship dynamic. The perceptions and ideas of my interviewees and respondents worked for me. They can work for you.

Research Methods

The couples profiled in the pages that follow are real people. Names, locations and situations have been changed to preserve their anonymity. The women range in age from twenty-three to seventy-three, while the men range from twenty-three to eighty-four.

Wives interviewed reported incomes from $25,000 to $250,000 annually, while men either had no income or lower earnings, ranging from $5,000 to a high of $90,000 per year. My research couples were of many races and ethnicities; most couples were parents, others were not.

I located these couples by placing my call for volunteers in the newsletters and on the Web bulletin boards of more than sixty professional women's associations across the country. In all cases, wives and husbands were interviewed separately and I endeavored to arrange the interview times so the other spouse was not in the house or nearby. While I always asked to interview the husband, some wives were adamant in their refusal to allow this. Other husbands simply declined to be interviewed. In only two cases, the husbands were willing to talk with me, while their wives were not.

Breadwinning Backlash: Buck's Logic

As I neared the completion of this book, I happened to meet a man in a fairly high-level position in a major upstate New York non-profit organization. I introduced myself to this man, whom I'll call Buck, after a conference in which we were both participants.

I'd received some media attention for my work on *Breadwinner Wives and the Men They Marry*, so our brief conversation led inevitably in that direction. "Tell me again about the premise for this book you are writing," he said, raising an eyebrow. Like many men who engaged me in discussion of my work, he was poised, ready to debate. "I don't think I understand."

"It's about women who make more money than their husbands," I began, but he quickly cut me off.

He let out an unrestrained guffaw. "Oh yeah?" he laughed. "I've got the title of the first chapter for you. Chapter one: Marry a Loser."

Unless he reads this—which is highly unlikely—Buck will never know just how much he told me about himself with this one little zinger. I call this from-the-gut reaction "Buck's Logic."

Buck's Logic flows like this: *I judge the world based on what goes on in my own home. All women must make less than I do, because I've never met a woman who did otherwise. A man who makes less than his wife must be a low-paid man indeed. Not only does he make so little that his wife must support him, he makes less than a* female. *That must be astoundingly poor pay. What kind of man would allow this to happen to him? Only some kind of pathetic loser.*

It would never occur to Buck that many women are extremely successful and outearn their husbands simply because their incomes are so high. Buck would never understand that some men choose lower income positions, because they love the work they do or because such jobs afford them the freedom to spend more time with their children. Buck would assume that such men don't deserve comfortable lifestyles, because they don't have the drive to get themselves high paying jobs like Buck's.

Buck's Logic can be found everywhere. This book is a guide to repudiating this skewed logic, setting the record straight and bringing breadwinning wives out into the open, where we can shine together.

Breadwinner wives, you are no longer alone.

CHAPTER 2

SUCCESSFUL WOMEN, SUCCESSFUL MARRIAGES
Breadwinner Wives
Shatter Marriage Conventions

Zoe and Paul met through the modern equivalent of a matchmaker—a personal advertisement Paul placed in a small newspaper in their upstate New York hometown. Zoe, thirty-two, had just accepted the assignment of chief resident at a prominent hospital in the area, where she would complete the last year of her medical studies to become an obstetrician. In another year, she would begin pursuit of an associate's position in a private practice. Paul, at thirty-three a moderately well known professional choreographer, enjoyed an artist-in-residence position with a local university.

Somehow they skipped over the expected awkwardness of a traditional first date, finding immediate comfort in one another's company and a mutual understanding of the grueling schedules that came with their chosen professions. "I knew before dinner was over that Zoe was the woman for me," Paul said. "She was intelligent, articulate, funny and she would never take my working until 2:00 A.M. personally. If anything, her schedule was worse than mine. We hit it off on a very fundamental level."

Zoe's eyes still sparkle when she talks about that first evening with Paul. "We laughed about being two accomplished people in our thirties who had to resort to a personal ad to find companionship," she said. "But considering how hard both of us worked, how were we supposed to meet people? I never wanted to be married to another doctor. Imagine the competition in our house over whose work was more important. That's not the life I wanted."

It was on their second date that Paul decided to broach a dangerous topic head-on—the relationship-busting issue he'd run into with women on many other occasions. "I just came out and said it," he remembered. "I said, 'Zoe, you realize that you will always make more money than I do.'"

He held his breath, knowing he'd stated the obvious, but fearful that he'd just blown it with this fascinating woman.

To his amazement, she began to laugh. "Yes, of course I know that," she said. "That's not an issue for me. Is it a problem for you?"

Paul smiled. "I thought it would be a problem for *you*," he told her. "For me, it's...sort of a relief."

It was a relief for Zoe as well. In fact, she was delighted with the prospect—a man who would not only be comfortable as the secondary breadwinner, but would support her own professional pursuits and be part of a home in which she, the primary wage-earner, could enjoy emotional security and comfort.

How could this be true? Were Zoe and Paul kidding themselves? What self-respecting man would willingly marry a woman who would consistently and predictably outearn him, presumably for the full duration of their marriage?

Furthermore, what woman would consent to such a marriage, knowing that the burden of breadwinning responsibility would rest on her shoulders? What benefits could a woman possibly find by taking on the role of primary financial support for her family?

When they met in the early 1980s, Zoe and Paul were an anomaly—statistics show that in 1980, only 11 percent of all wives made more money than their husbands.[1] But by the year 1998, Zoe and Paul had become almost commonplace. As the twentieth century ended, *one in every three wives held the primary breadwinning responsibility for her family.*

Can such marriages be happy and successful for both spouses?

There's no doubt that in some of these households, the wife has taken on the breadwinning responsibility because the husband has lost his job, is suffering from a physical disability or is underemployed. However, in the majority of marriages in which the wife earns more, *she does so by choice.* Many couples are finding a level of comfort, contentment and fulfillment made possible, in part, by the wives' higher income—and many others are just beginning to adjust to this nontraditional arrangement in their own homes.

This book is for the couples who are learning to understand the new dynamics they find between husband, wife and children when the wife brings home the larger side of bacon. It's also for those couples who don't understand what's happening between them at all—and for the parents, friends, coworkers, employers and associates who believe, out of a lack of understanding and an adherence to decades of stereotypes and societal pressures, that these marriages are headed for disaster.

First, let's get some socioeconomic perspective. Dozens of media and statistical sources tell us that the breadwinning-wife phenomenon grew steadily over the last decade, as our nation's workforce achieved gender balance and our definition of "family" gradually altered.

Wives making more? Since when?

Our nation has long accepted the idea that most families require two incomes to make ends meet, as more than fifty-six million working women over the age of twenty now make up nearly half of the American workforce.[2] It is only recently, however, that wives' incomes have begun to exceed husbands' earnings in significant numbers. Dr. Richard Freeman of the National Bureau of Economic Research noted in a recent paper, "It is now normal in about three in ten American dual earner families for women to be higher paid than men."[3]

Yet breadwinning wives remained the nation's best-kept secret throughout the 1990s, even as women began to outearn their husbands in ever-growing numbers. The earliest public acknowledgement of this trend may have been a 1993 article in the *Wall Street Journal*, "Playing Second Fiddle Tough for Many Men." Writer Joann S. Lublin observed that about 18 percent of corporate relocations in 1992 were female employees—which, if they were married, meant that their husbands became "trailing spouses." Lublin wrote, "...many American men feel torn between traditional social values and some demands of modern life, but few are torn more brutally than those who are following their wives as these women ascend the managerial ladder.... The strain tends to intensify when a relocated husband can't find a new job and must depend on his wife's paycheck."[4]

I couldn't help but be dismayed by Lublin's choice of "brutally" as a descriptor for the effect of a wife's relocation on her husband when wives have traditionally been expected to relocate their families as their husbands climbed the corporate ladder. Lublin went on to discuss several couples who had made the move, with the husband's unemployment as its apparently inevitable result. "Increasingly, employers are going to great lengths to retain a female transferee and help save her marriage," she reported, noting examples at Monsanto, Ameritech, Sprint and Marriott in which the company provided assistance in finding employment for the husbands of their transferred female workers.

The tone of this article is jarring—and the fact that it was written in the early 1990s reminds us that even in the third decade of women's move *en masse* to the workplace, the concept of breadwinning wives is still a new one indeed. In Lublin's article, we find an attitude that still prevails in many pockets of current society: Wives who outearn their husbands risk victimizing these men, turning them into powerless individuals and robbing them of their self-esteem.

The same concept was echoed in 1996, when reports by the Current Population Survey of the Bureau of Labor Statistics first revealed that wives' incomes rose above their husbands' in nearly one in three American married couples. In the *Fortune* article, "Women, Men and Money," mentioned in chapter 1, it was suggested that wives who make more could not and should not talk about their elevated earning status, lest they humiliate their husbands. "The New Providers," an article in *Newsweek* a few months earlier, made the same inference. Wives who made more were essentially in the closet, afraid to cause marital conflict by admitting to the success they had trained for, worked for and earned.[5]

Two years would pass before the national media acknowledged the trend once again. An April 5, 1998 issue of the *New York Times Magazine* contained an article by Peggy Orenstein, "Almost Equal" which described a series of nontraditional couples, including a wife, Doreen, who held a high-earning position with a Web development firm while Michael, her husband, finished his doctorate. The writer's day-long observation of the family spared nothing in describing their seven-year-old son's afternoon moodiness with the baby-sitter, a pan of cookies that burned because Doreen forgot they were in the oven, Michael's insistence that his education is also a full-time job—just not a paying one. Later, Doreen assured the writer that she was looking forward to Michael resuming his breadwinner position when he completed his degree.[6]

Finally, on February 27, 2000, breadwinner wives became front-page news. The article, "Breadwinner Wives Alter Marriage Equation," appeared on page one of the Sunday *Washington Post*, announcing that breadwinning wives were here to stay—and weren't automatically making their husbands miserable and humiliated or hiding their own accomplishments. The article described several couples who found equity, comfort and even fun in their nontraditional arrangement. The *Post* discussed the challenges as well, however, planting more seeds of doubt about the central issues in these marriages. "The financial attainments of this army of U.S. women—some 10.5 million earned more than their husbands in 1998—are, in turn, testing traditional gender roles in ways far more concrete than the feminist movement of a generation ago. According to economists, sociologists and couples themselves, wives' heightened wages have unbalanced other aspects of the equation of marriages: housework and child care, economic power, egos and expectations."[7]

Has the breadwinning-wife phenomenon further unbalanced these aspects—or has it simply brought the established, long-existing lack of balance between marriage partners into sharper focus? This is the question we will answer in this book, as we talk with people who live in these relationships every day.

Whether or not the media is ready to embrace breadwinning wives, we are here to stay. We're part of a revolution in women's equality in the workplace, as more and more corporations open the top-floor doors to female CEOs, presidents, vice-presidents and senior managers. We're part of the newest, most innovative endeavors as well, as women in their twenties secure lucrative positions in Internet companies and in the nation's technology centers. We're also the workers in the field, in home offices, in hospitals and professional specialties and in retail establishments across the country, earning more by following our instincts, working industriously and making the most of our abilities.

How did we get here?

Most of the women I interviewed did *not* say that they had set out to be breadwinning wives. But as they began to succeed in their career paths, they found themselves earning more than even they would have imagined—and making the necessary adjustments in their own households to buoy that success.

These women credit many forces with the rise in female earnings at companies of every size. We can see indications of these within the changes in our society's economic and social structure.

Education. Women are graduating from colleges and pursuing advanced degrees in greater numbers than at any other time in our history. With higher education comes the opportunity for higher level, better paying employment. For example, the Association of Medical Colleges reported in March 2000 that women now make up the majority of first-year medical students in almost one out of three United States medical schools. Women represent 46 percent of entering medical students nationwide.[8]

More women than men are earning undergraduate degrees and master's degrees, noted the *Monthly Labor Review* in reports in July and December 1999. In 1998, 938,000 young women were in college, while only 906,000 men were enrolled. This is particularly significant because there were 100,000 more male high school graduates in June 1998 than there were female: 1.5 million boys graduated from high school, compared to 1.4 million girls. The December article noted that more than 75 percent of women aged fourteen to twenty-four expect to be working at thirty-five, up from 28 percent of women in this age group in 1968. "Young women want better jobs than their mothers might have had, because they expect to remain in the labor force much longer," the *Review* said.[9]

Taking this further, a February 1999 article in *US News and World Report* explored the whereabouts of men who did not choose college after high school. With 57 percent of all bachelor's degrees going to women in 1999 and a projection by the United States Department of Education that by 2008, women will outnumber men in college degree programs by 9.2 million to 6.9 million, *US News and World Report* went looking for the men who chose to pass up college in 1999. "Armed with better grades, better resumes and a clearer sense of future goals, many females reach the senior year of high school primed for the college admissions game. Males, meanwhile, have been tempted by fast cash in the recent economic boom, preferring $30,000 starting salaries in such fields as air-conditioner maintenance and Web design to four years of *Beowulf* and student loans."[10]

These are all very recent measures of enrollment, so it will be years before we know if men who skipped college for the immediacy of wage-paying jobs actually reached their earning goals. However, we *can* attribute the increase in higher paid professional women in American society to the last three decades' growth in the number of women earning college degrees.

This focus on education directly affects the expansion of the number of families in which the wife is the principal breadwinner as well. Thomas Mortenson, senior scholar at the Center of the Study of Opportunity in Higher Education, observed in a July 2000 article in the *Denver Post* that as educated women increasingly move into top business and political leadership roles, they'll have to settle for marrying less educated men—if they marry at all. "There are at least 125,000 college-educated women now who won't find college-educated men to marry and in a decade it will be a quarter million women," said Mortenson.[11]

Technology. The information management sector now makes up more than 55 percent of the nation's total employment,[12] so one would expect to find more women working in positions that require technical or computer-related expertise.

To truly understand the impact of the new economy on women's success, however, we need to separate the statistics into *information technology*—those who create computer and electronic products and services, representing only 1.3 percent of total United States employment—and the *information management* workforce, or those who use computer-related products and technology. Information management professionals—that 55 percent of our total workforce—reside in every industry, every large corporation and nearly every small business in the country.

In this ubiquitous segment of the workforce, we see women's participation increasing. The United States Department of Labor reports that the number of female information systems (IS) managers has grown from 2 percent in 1985 to 22 percent in 1997.[13] Nearly 30 percent of all systems analysts and 33 percent of all computer programmers are women, reports the Equity Equation, a study by Cross University Research in Engineering and Science.[14]

Some analysts note that women actually have achieved parity within the ranks of IS users: According to a February 1999 article in *Computerworld*, 13.3 million women hold managerial and professional positions in IS fields, or roughly 49 percent of all IS positions. "There are more influential positions available to women in the huge (55% of total employment) 'IT-using' information management sector than in the smaller (1.3%) 'IT-producing' sector," the article noted.[15]

Many of the women I interviewed for this book hold positions of responsibility and authority at dot-coms, information technology consulting firms or at companies that provide outsource services, equipment and supplies to these Internet empires. However, outside of the IS world, women still are not moving into more traditional technical fields. For example, women still hold only eight percent of engineering jobs.[16]

Corporate responsibility. Many of our leading corporations have made it a priority to move women into higher positions within their companies. The 1999 Catalyst Census of Women Corporate Officers and Top Earners reports a 37 percent increase in the number of female corporate officers at Fortune 500 companies: a total of 11.9 percent of these officers are women, up from 8.7 percent in 1995. Meanwhile, women now hold 3.3 percent of the top-earner spots in these companies, a 175 percent increase over 1995 figures.[17] While women's representation at this high level still pales in comparison to men's near-total dominance, more women are rising to the top than ever before—and their numbers climb steadily every year.

A study by Runzheimer International, a consulting firm specializing in information about corporate executive relocation, noted that in

1996, women made up 26 percent of all corporate relocations nation-wide—up from 16 percent in 1993. More women are accepting high-level positions that require them to uproot home and family—and more hus-bands find themselves the trailing spouses.[18]

In a 1996 study, Catalyst asked a sample of female top execu-tives about the qualities that propelled them to such high positions. Above all, the female chiefs cited two critical elements that led to their successes: their ability to consistently exceed expectations and their development of a style that made their male managers comfortable.[19] We will see that the ability to adapt, to make others comfortable and to build partnerships also help create harmonious marriages for bread-winner wives.

Small business. More women than ever before are starting their own businesses. The National Foundation for Women Business Owners (NFWBO) noted in a recent report that in 1999, women-owned firms accounted for 38 percent of all firms in the country, an increase of 103 per-cent since 1987. This adds up to 9.1 million women-owned businesses—and they're not all in traditionally pink-collar industries: Construction, wholesale trade, transportation, communications, agribusiness and man-ufacturing are the leading growth areas for women business owners.[20]

In managing their own destinies and taking control of their future growth, women who own their own businesses have developed an entirely new style of business management. According to NFWBO research, women entrepreneurs are more likely than male business owners to place a high value on business relationships as well as on fac-tual information. Women who own businesses are more willing than their male counterparts to seek out others' input and opinions, the study notes, and are more reflective than men in making business deci-sions. The success of these approaches is clear—1999 figures show that women-owned businesses generate close to $3.6 trillion in annual sales and employ 27.5 million people.[21]

A decline of male achievement. In her 1997 book, *Beyond Gender*, Betty Friedan points out that the rise in women's earning power is not the only reason for this shift in wives' status as family breadwinners. She highlights the decline of the male—specifically the white male—in our working society as an important element in this societal change.[22]

Indeed, while I do not subscribe to the idea that success for one gender must lead to the victimization or failure of the other, dozens of stories in 1990s media suggest a significant dip in male achievement in the workplace. Most short newspaper and magazine articles don't explore the causes of this trend, but they point to the leading indicators:

a downswing in men's enrollment in college and estimates that as many as 4.6 million employment-aged men are not working and not seeking employment.[23]

A growing body of research suggests reasons for this male work-force decline. One reason has to do, at least in part, with public grade-school education and a built-in bias against boys. This relatively new theory flies in the face of the more prevalent view that girls are getting the short end of the educational stick.

Decades of study and the enormous outcry against treatment of girls in elementary and high school peaked in 1992 with a report by the American Association of University Women (AAUW), "How Schools Shortchange Girls." AAUW researchers observed that teachers called on elementary school boys several times more than girls, and that boys received opportunities to excel in class that were not made available to girls.[24]

In 1998, AAUW completed an examination of research to assess the nation's progress toward gender equity in the public school class-room since 1992. Within this context, AAUW discovered that more girls enroll in math and science courses than ever before, although more boys take all three core science courses—biology, chemistry and physics—than do girls. The largest gender gap is in physics, where girls' enrollment lags substantially behind boys'. However, girls now lead boys in biology enrollment and they enroll in chemistry and calculus nearly as frequently as boys.[25]

Today, some researchers claim that the tables may be turning—favoring better-behaved, more studious girls over their more rambunctious, more aggressive male counterparts in the classroom. Kathleen Parker, a columnist for the *Orlando Sentinel*, summed up the argument: "More and more young men are rejecting higher education because 'lower' education rejected them long ago. For many boys, school has been a punishment, where boy behavior was pathologized and girl behavior was sanctified. In our noble attempt to elevate girls and women, we've denigrated boys and men and, no gluttons for punishment, they've had enough. Meanwhile, for two decades, we've heard only that girls are being 'marginalized' by teachers who cater to boys, by biased teaching methods and by unfair testing practices. Anyone with sons knows otherwise."[26]

As disturbing as this point of view may be, it is born out by actual statistics. The National Urban League's annual report, *The State of Black America*, introduced evidence that black women now vastly out-number black men in higher education: Among African-Americans in college, approximately 63 percent are female. In addition, nearly five times as many black women as men pursue master's degrees. The Urban League report notes, "The disparity in higher education among African-American men and women is a long-term problem that begins in junior high school."[27]

Researchers are only beginning to explore this trend. In her book, *The War Against Boys*, Christina Hoff Summers reveals that girls are out-performing boys in elementary, junior high and high schools across the country. She cites a trend toward in-class discrimination against boys by their teachers—rather than against girls, as researchers have cited in the recent past—as a leading cause for boys' underperformance in school. "The national phenomenon of male underachievement has remained almost invisible, because those who shape discussions on equity in education have deftly played down the plight of boys," Summers wrote in an August 2000 editorial in the *Washington Post*. "Gender experts...and advocacy groups such as the American Association of University Women regard any advantage boys enjoy (e.g., more participation in sports, slightly better scores on math tests) as evidence of unfair discrimination to be aggressively combated. They regard any advantage girls enjoy (more college attendance, dramatically better scores on reading tests) as a triumph of 'gender equity.'"[28]

Even if the theory of public school bias against boys does not prove valid, young American men are struggling to achieve their predecessors' success. The reasons for this decline are not clear.

In his 1999 book, *The Decline of Males*, Lionel Tiger provides a series of interconnecting theories that begin with the obvious—the growth of feminism and resulting legislation of everything from labor conditions to sexual harassment and discrimination—to more subtle influences of morality shifts and biological changes throughout our culture. Noting tacitly that men are in danger of assuming the role of "second sex" in our culture, Tiger emphasizes that the change in men's status is in essence biological, as women grow in their ability to produce children without a man's active, personal involvement and raise these children through a "bureaugamy" involving a mother, a child and an institution (such as day care—or welfare). This change in the fundamental structure of the family system then translates to changes between genders on the professional level, as women take advantage of opportunities to support themselves and become high-earning professionals—and as the laws and rules of the workforce change to accommodate the redefinition of gender relations in the world of work.[29]

Susan Faludi takes a more sociological stance on the decline of opportunities for men in today's society in her 2000 book, *Stiffed: The Betrayal of the American Man*. She cites four implied promises made to young men by politicians, by societal messages and by their own fathers in the post-World War II era: Space, a frontier to be claimed; a clear and evil enemy in the threat of Communism; an institution of brotherhood in work as engineers, middle managers and bureaucrats; and finally, home and family, for which men would be responsible for providing leadership, security and protection. As the baby boom era developed and one promise after another was broken—the space program offered little true exploration, Vietnam dragged soldiers into a war they could not win, women fought their way into men's domain at work and the traditional home and family pattern altered—men's perception of their place in America changed.

"When I talk with men who grew up during the baby boom, this mission to manhood shows up in their minds not as promises met but as betrayals, losses and disillusionments," Faludi writes. "It is as if a generation of men had lined up at Cape Kennedy to witness the count-down to liftoff, only to watch their rocket—containing all their hopes and dreams—burn up on the launchpad. There had been so much antic-ipation, so much excitement, so many assurances that nothing could possibly go wrong. But somehow, it all had."[30]

Undoubtedly, all of these factors have a hand in changing the way millions of men view their opportunities in the current United States workforce. Match these disturbing trends with the surge in opportunities for skilled women in all kinds of professions and we can see that it was only a matter of time before a significant number of wives' incomes began to surpass their husbands' earnings.

What do we do now?

Now that significant numbers of women make more money than their husbands, how do we adjust our ideas about marriage, family, work and gender identity to accommodate this new concept?

In the next chapter, we'll explore the theories about husbands and wives and how husbands and wives in traditional marriages found their own identities within the family unit. We'll also begin our explo-ration of today's breadwinner-wife couples in our quest to understand what can and must change if we are to enjoy the advantages of life as a higher earning wife or as a lower earning husband.

CHAPTER 3

CASTING AGAINST TYPE
Throwing Out the Rules of Gender Identity

Jeanine is a high school principal in a rural Mississippi community, earning about $40,000 annually and taking time off for the better part of every summer. She uses these summer months to work with her husband, Mack, tending to their family farm in hopes of increasing Mack's annual income from crop sales.

"When we first started dating, my sister knew Mack and kept telling him that I was the youngest child in our family and spoiled and that he wouldn't want to go out with me," Jeanine said. "Meanwhile, she kept telling me that Mack's family was blue collar and I should look at their house and decide if that was the lifestyle I wanted. Naturally, that just made us both all the more interested in each other. So here we are."

Married for seven years, Jeanine and Mack have two preschool-age children who spend their days at home with their father. Mack's seasonal work on the farm makes it possible for him to see to the children's daily care several months out of the year. He arranges for additional child care help from his family during his busiest times. "We wanted to make a go of the farm full-time—that was our intention when we got married, to run this business together, have a family together and raise the kids together," said Jeanine. "But we just found it wasn't economically possible."

Part of the financial hardship came from the condition of their home, a ramshackle farmhouse built in the 1920s and sorely in need of extensive repairs. Buffeted by hurricanes, bleached by the sun and weakened by wood-eating insects, the house cost almost nothing to buy—even with its surrounding acreage—but instantly became a yawning pit that swallowed all of Jeanine's and Mack's savings and ate away at their meager family income.

College educated and fully expecting to translate her skills into additional income someday, Jeanine gave in to the inevitable and returned to the profession she'd entered before marriage: teaching elementary school. As higher level positions opened before her, she took advantage of opportunities and moved into school administration, closing the gaps in the family's needs by surpassing her husband's $25,000 annual earnings.

The boost in household income made a big difference for her husband and children—but it didn't satisfy Jeanine's mother, who couldn't believe her daughter had chosen the farm existence over the stylish life she'd planned for her. "Mom didn't want me to marry Mack, because she likes the suit-and-tie type," Jeanine scoffed. "I had a college degree and Mack didn't. She feels I married down. You'd think I'd committed a mortal sin." She softened. "But Mack's parents never made an issue of the differences between us. My parents have more money, but they are selfish with it. When people have less, they tend to pool their resources and work together. Things can be shared and you draw closer to these people."

True poverty had never been part of Jeanine's plans, however—and its reality proved even harsher than she expected. "Mack and I fought in the past, when we didn't have enough money," she said. "When I got the first job, it was a big deal when I could buy a hamper for the bathroom. It was a fifteen-dollar item, but before I returned to teaching, I couldn't afford it or the other little things that make life nice. We are still climbing out of debt from our last bad season, but business is picking up. Mack has new accounts that are buying more from him. We're adding a tent next fall, so we can sell the Christmas trees we grow. Things are getting better."

From the outside, it looks like Jeanine chose a difficult way of life when she could have picked a much easier one. She married a man whose income depends on one of the world's most challenging and backbreaking professions—and whose earnings are at the mercy of land and weather. She lives in a fixer-upper farmhouse with repair needs that exceed the family's available resources for the foreseeable future. She had dreamed of a totally traditional lifestyle, in which she would stay home and raise her children while she helped her husband tend to the crops and the livestock, but this dream quickly soured when their income thinned and their debts piled sky-high. On top of all this, her husband spends every weekend during the growing season at the market, selling his crops to customers, thus limiting their time together to weekday evenings and the occasional Sunday night. Jeanine made choices that made her life tougher than she had ever anticipated.

But when Jeanine talked about her life with Mack, I heard no hint of bitterness or unhappiness in her voice. "Mack's been so supportive of me going back to work and he's been great taking care of the kids. He is the most sensitive man I ever dated—that's why I married him. He can pick up on things. I get mad at him when he's right, because he's always right! He puts things in perspective for me. I'm a control freak and Mack teaches me to let go of things. I can't tell you how much I value that."

Jeanine shook her head as she continued. "We got a lot of negative comments when the kids were born and I went back to work. People would say, 'Females are the only ones who can raise children. Men can't do it.' That's just really weird. People still say to me, 'What do you mean, your kids are home with their daddy?' At first that was hard to deal with, until I realized that's just the common response. Now I don't tell them my husband is watching the children. I tell them that a family member is watching the children. It's not that I care what they think. I just don't think it's everyone's business to judge what's right for my life."

As we talked, the children raced in and out, alternately squealing, shrieking and demanding Mommy's arbitration over one emergent issue after another. Jeanine paused repeatedly to quiet the children, resolve the dispute, raise new issues—"You can't touch that cookie with your hands looking like that!"—and shoo them back into the sun-drenched front yard.

Back in her chair, Jeanine pondered for a moment. "You know, it's funny. I noticed something about my friend Sue's family. Her husband, Joe, comes home in the evening and does nothing. I come home in the evening and I take over the child care. On Sue's husband's Saturdays, he goes out and plays golf. On my Saturdays, I do things with my kids. To me, it just seems backwards that Joe wouldn't want to spend more time with his children. What Mack and I have may not be a traditional family life, but it's much more balanced than what my friend and her husband have.

"Sure, it would be easier if we had more money," she added. "But really, I just wish that Mack could work five days a week instead of seven. That would make a much bigger difference in our lives."

A glimpse of the future
It's difficult for Jeanine's and Mack's neighbors, family and friends, used to traditional couples, to accept the role reversal in Jeanine and

Mack's relationship—especially in the tradition-steeped rural community they call home. Other people's acceptance, however, is not high on this couple's list of priorities. Like so many wives and husbands I interviewed, Jeanine and Mack have found ways to strengthen their family, improve their lives and provide for their children while not compromising their core values. One of the many tools they utilize to maintain happy lives just happens to be Jeanine's higher earning power.

What does Jeanine get from the relationship she chose over the affluent husband and fine suburban home her parents wished for her? Jeanine effusively lists the benefits of marriage to Mack, plusses that far outweigh the minuses of low income: moral support, lessons in letting go, complete understanding and his loving care of their children. In the end, she sees herself as happier and enjoying a greater balance at home than her less cash-strapped friend down the street, whose high-earning husband regularly chooses his own recreational pursuits over time with his family.

In her 1995 book, *Kidding Ourselves: Breadwinning, Babies and Bargaining Power*, Rhona Mahoney provides a picture of future marriages based on a new type of relationship: "If...millions of women choose to marry down, as a few women do today, and they find partners who consent, then in millions of marriages the wife will earn more than the husband. The husbands may be as intelligent, healthy, attractive and competent as the wives. They simply choose not to maximize their incomes. They might be men who would enjoy an upper-middle-class style of life, but who aren't prepared to make the bruising competitive effort that earning that kind of money requires. They might vaguely or explicitly imagine a future in which they focus on taking care of children. They might work in a low-paying field, such as music, counseling or community organizing." [1]

By the time Mahoney published these prescient words, millions of couples all over the country already fit her description. A year later, the media would begin to acknowledge that a substantial percentage of wives were outearning their husbands—and that these marriages were *not* all doomed to disaster.

You mean we're "marrying down?"

Fundamental changes have taken place in professional women's attitudes. Throughout the first twenty to twenty-five years of our lives (and longer, for those of us who waited until our thirties or forties to marry), most women are encouraged by parents, friends and other role models to find a man who will provide financial support—even in twenty-first century America. Our families expect us to marry someone who will make more money than we do, because they follow Buck's Logic, the twisted method of viewing a wife's higher income as a sign of a weak husband. Women predictably made less than their husbands for as long as our parents can remember, so our mothers and fathers don't stop to take their daughters' high earning potential into consideration. They simply hope and pray that we will marry men who make more. While we no longer feel the overwhelming pressure to adopt full-time home-making as our role, we still know that our mothers and fathers would be "pleased" if we found a professional spouse with a good income.

Of the one in three married women in the United States who out-earn their husbands, we can assume that a certain number are wives of men with disabilities or men who are involuntarily unemployed or under-employed. Studies bear this out: According to the Bureau of Labor Statistics, nearly 37 percent of all breadwinning wives in America per-sonally earn less than $25,000 annually.[2] "Nontraditional couples are especially common among dual-earner couples with low-wage hus-bands," noted Anne E. Winkler in a 1998 issue of *Monthly Labor Review*. Winkler used data from the 1993 Annual Demographic File of the Current Population Survey to complete an extensive study of couples in which both husband and wife work. Her study revealed that wives earned more than their husbands in nearly 60 percent of the couples in which the working husband earned less than $10 per hour. In the vast majority of these cases, the higher earning wives made less than $20 per hour.[3]

This dispels the myth that wives who make more are wealthy superwomen, a chosen few who have reached the pinnacle of personal and professional success. On the contrary, breadwinning wives exist on all economic levels, with far more of them in the lowest-earning wage bracket than in the highest. Winkler reports that a little less than 14 per-cent of women who outearn their husbands are in the highest income bracket she measured (up to $100 per hour).[4] The far greater share of breadwinning wives exist in the lower to middle class range—in my study, more than 50 percent of the responding wives earned between $25,000 and $75,000 annually. Only 19 percent of my sample earned $100,000 to $200,000 annually, with a mere 8 percent earning above $200,000.

Statistics also tell us that many of the low-earning men may have chosen to maximize the value of their non-professional time to pursue other avenues. In a May 1995 article in *American Demographics*, writer Cheryl Russell notes that eight in ten men aged twenty-five to fifty-four who were not working or job-hunting in 1994 reported to the Bureau of Labor Statistics that they do not *want* a job now. These men are busy with other activities—college, early retirement and housekeeping. Russell goes on to report that in 1993, 325,000 men in this age group were full-time homemakers, up 26 percent since 1990. At the same time, the number of women who reported themselves as full-time homemakers *declined* by five percent. [5]

The key concept here is *choice*—the choice of women to reach their full earning potential and the choice of their husbands to do otherwise.

We can guess that most involuntary breadwinning wives—those whose husbands are disabled or otherwise unemployed—would choose to be in the more flexible position of sharing the income responsibility with their husbands, even if they have found happiness within their current situation. In my sample, I spoke with wives whose husbands were permanently injured in accidents or who were "downsized" by corporations. These wives had seen their share of sorrow and frustration over their sudden move to breadwinning or single-income status, but many had come out on the other side of strife and found a new, positive way of looking at their relationships.

The wives who have become the main breadwinners in their families because of their husbands' misfortunes are in the minority, however. *The greater number of today's breadwinning wives made the decision to marry men who would never match their own earning potential.*

This larger group of women placed a lower priority on their husbands' incomes and a higher priority on the men's characters and values: an emphasis on home and family, a love of the arts and creativity, a desire to help others, an ability to create a relaxed home, a remarkable instinct for child care. While most did not intentionally seek men whose income was less than their own, such wives do not see the discrepancy as an obstacle to happiness.

What's more, their husbands are in agreement with them. The opportunities this untraditional life affords them are very much all right with them.

Is this what Mahoney calls "marrying down?" Strictly speaking, for the women, it is—because the husbands earn less than their wives. However, in virtually all cases, these women married men whose level of education matched or nearly matched their own: for example, women with bachelor's degrees married men who also had completed four-year degrees. The women I interviewed married men who are their equals intellectually, spiritually and in their personal beliefs and value systems. These women sought men with qualities that would nourish their souls, instead of husbands with incomes that would fill their cupboards and bank accounts.

So these high-earning wives have the power now...right?

By all theories and studies that measure the balance of power and control within the institution of marriage, wives who make more should be in the drivers' seats. Research by many venerable universities, psychologists and sociologists have told us that the spouse who brings home the money is the spouse in charge. Ever since the groundbreaking book *Husbands and Wives: The Dynamics of Married Living* emerged in 1960, the "resource theory" of marital power has been the generally accepted rule for balance and decision-making in the American family. "The sources of power in so intimate a relationship as marriage must be sought in the comparative resources which the husband and wife bring to the marriage, rather than in brute force," wrote authors Robert O. Blood, Jr. and Donald M. Wolfe. "A resource may be defined as anything that one partner may make available to the other, helping the latter satisfy his needs or attain his goals. The balance of power will be on the side of that partner who contributes the greater resources to the marriage."[6]

Whether we take "resources" as a euphemism for income or as a combination of money, intellect and skill, in 1960 the power in the marriage almost always belonged to the husband, because he brought all of these resources into the household in presumably larger quantities. "As one partner is able to contribute more than his share to the marriage, he acquires the basis for a more than fifty-fifty say in decisions," Blood and Wolfe continued. "Thus, a wife may not only depend on her husband for 'bringing home the bacon' but recognize that in his work he becomes familiar with some of the complexities of life outside the home. Therefore, she may defer to his superior knowledge in decisions about politics, taxes and cars."[7]

While the details of this quaint point of view are now anachronistic at best, dozens of researchers tested and studied this theory over the ensuing decades. Many found that the dynamic bore considerable weight in the traditional home, in which the husband took the role of principal breadwinner while the wife either stayed home full-time or held a job with a lower income. Studies showed that as the wife's earnings increased, however, the balance of power shifted so that she became more of a partner to her husband in making major decisions about home and family.

If we take these theories to the next logical step, we would conclude that when the "gold" belongs to the wife, she automatically becomes the head of the household and makes the major family decisions. Money, after all, is power...right?

Wrong.

I interviewed husbands and their breadwinner wives in households across America, expecting to find a shift in the balance of power. I thought that these women would manage the household finances, provide their husbands with allowances, demand that their husbands share in housework and child care, make the major family decisions and, overall, play the role that traditional, breadwinning husbands have played for as long as most of us can recall.

The fact is, very little of this is happening.

Instead, I found a different kind of marital schematic—one that involves exactly the traits that now attract major corporations to female executives: collaboration, consensus-building, trust and empathy. These marriages come closest to the dream of a fifty-fifty split between husband and wife as any described by researchers and reporters. Within such marriages each spouse knows his or her responsibilities and takes these commitments seriously.

I also found marriages in which no gender role shift has taken place beyond breadwinning status. The wives in these marriages still carry the full load of household chores and child care, while their lower-earning husbands put their feet up at day's end. These couples know that they are trapped in a cycle of resentment and imbalance, pouring out their hearts to me as if I were a stranger on a bus: Husbands described embarrassment they felt about their wives' dominant income, while wives expressed their frustration with husbands who seem to take advantage of them.

All of these wives, happy or unhappy, contribute the greater share of the household income—in some cases, even ten or twenty times more than their husbands. So why aren't they in charge at home?

The reasons are as varied as they are fascinating.

Men and women are different.

This is a statement that is absolutely polarizing in feminist, sociological and psychological circles. In fact, even as I suggest that men and women view the world in different ways, I know that some of my readers are leaping out of their chairs with vociferous objections, insisting that there are no differences between genders beyond the obvious biological ones.

In my search for the "truth" about gender differences, I examined dozens of theories and studies by some of the most prominent and respected researchers of our time. I explored the more visible and popularized transaction-by-transaction manuals on husbands and wives, men and women and (of course) Mars and Venus. I sifted through accounts of counseling sessions, results of psychological testing, studies focused on one aspect or another of marital relationships and countless other journal articles and reports. I also took a hard look at the transcripts of my 120 interviews with men and women across the country to find the similarities and differences in the way these individuals viewed their worlds.

The one premise on which virtually all of the experts agree is that men and women *are* different—in the way they approach problems, in their observations about their own relationships, in the way they handle money and in their approach to the restrictions and liberties involved in marriage. These differences come, in part, from decades of conditioning and responses to the expectations of various microcosms of society—their own families, their friends, their coworkers and their employers as well as the general norms of our culture. The differences are particularly apparent as wives take on the role traditionally assigned to husbands, without buying into all of the assumptions that go with it.

"In the beginning, there was sex and there was gender," wrote Candace West and Don H. Zimmerman, two California sociologists whose 1987 article, "Doing Gender," was the first to fully explore the concept of gender-specific behavior. "Sex...was what was ascribed to biology: anatomy, hormones and physiology. Gender...was an achieved status: that which is constructed through psychological, cultural and social means."[8]

West and Zimmerman saw gender as a set of learned behaviors, rather than an accident of birth or an instinctive response to situations. Therefore, they determined, gender is something we *do*, not something we are. While all preceding research suggested that human beings act out their gender roles as a part of their essential nature, West and Zimmerman offered a different perspective: "Doing gender means creating differences between girls and boys and women and men, differences that are not natural, essential or biological.... Accordingly, virtually any activity can be assessed as to its womanly or manly nature. And note, to do gender is not always to live up to normative conceptions of femininity and masculinity; it is to engage in behavior *at the risk of gender assessment.*"[9]

Our gender roles are dictated by decades of these learned behaviors. For instance, dividing household responsibilities into "men's work" and "women's work" is a common but artificial construction. We learned from birth that there are specific expectations of men and women within every marriage—if not from our parents, then from teachers, role models, neighbors, friends, television, movies and books. We learned that women are frequently judged by the cleanliness of their houses and their exterior attractiveness, while men are often judged by the size of their paychecks and their ability to support a family. Like it or not, we relate to this gender delineation on a baseline level we developed as children.

When we begin to subvert these roles, flipping the household income responsibility to the wife while giving the husband more household responsibilities, we can't help but squirm. Even the most progressive, gender-reversal families chafe against the constant, nagging itch of self-doubt, wondering if they have upset some fundamental balance in the sanctity of marriage. Every wife I talked to expressed some semblance of self-recrimination for her messy living room or her insistence that her husband share in the housework; every husband spoke defensively about choosing a lower-paying profession or leaving a job to become a stay-at-home dad. Even in their righteousness and self-confidence in the decisions they have made, these couples still wonder if they have made choices that can fit into the real world of narrow, one-way gender paths.

The majority of couples who spoke with me, however, have embraced the challenge of breaking with gender norms. They battle their own tendencies to fall back on comfortable patterns of "men's work" and "women's work," each holding onto just enough gender-specific behavior to maintain a sense of femininity or masculinity within their relationships. They work hard to bridge the gender gap in housework, in their handling of finances, in sharing big family decisions and in raising their children. Only a few of these couples have truly approached the dream of a gender-neutral household environment—but those who are close to this goal seem to be the most contented couples in my research.

Commanding respect and equality by making more

As women begin to outearn their husbands in significant numbers, we have the opportunity to rewrite the rules of "doing gender"—or to throw out that rule book entirely.

Before breadwinning wives were a significant reality, working wives whose income supplemented their husbands' higher earnings responded to all manner of research across the country in the 1980s and 1990s. These wives noted that they still carried the lion's share of the household responsibilities, working a "second shift" after their full work day by taking on all the cooking, cleaning and child care at home. Even when their incomes rose to nearly equal their husbands' earnings, the majority reported that their husbands chose a couple of chores around the house, but generally did not participate in running the homestead in any major way.

Now, when wives make more than their husbands, they have the opportunity to change the picture. The wives in my research treat their husbands as equals, *but not as superiors.* They engage their husbands in discussions about the household, they encourage them to become equal child care providers—and even to take over that responsibility altogether. They open and maintain clear lines of communication with their husbands. And they command their husbands' respect, partly because of their earning power and partly because they know they deserve it as individuals and will accept nothing less.

Yet to finally enjoy a relationship as equal partners, working through the challenges and celebrating the joys of marriage together, these wives first had to outearn their husbands. And even then, not every breadwinning wife has achieved the status of an equal partner in marriage.

I did not speak with a single woman who wished to dominate her husband and family. As twenty-first century wives who grew up in the 1950s, 60s and 70s, we've had all the role models we need to show us what *not* to do as breadwinners. Endless sitcom reruns featuring Ward Cleaver, Ricky Ricardo, Mike Brady and Ozzie Nelson show us how breadwinners are supposed to act: coming home to a clean house with the children lined up to greet us, sitting down to a dinner that magically appears before us, leaving the dinner table without clearing our places, settling down with the evening paper or with a pile of work in the study and shutting out the din of home and family. We know that this is exactly the kind of breadwinner against which wives rebelled with all their hearts, embracing *The Feminine Mystique* and its revelations about unhappy housewives.

We wives with higher incomes are not taking over and becoming the disengaged, distant spouses and parents our male predecessors often were, because we saw firsthand the dangers of that in our childhood homes. The anger and frustration bred of enforced homemaking are still fresh in the memories of many of today's breadwinning wives, as we recall the discomfort, disappointment and despair of our childhood female role models. We know that the model of one dominant spouse and one subservient spouse is wrong, even destructive. That's not what we want in our homes. That's not what we want for our husbands—or for ourselves. That's not the example we want to set for our children.

Naturally, we feel the pull of the traditional breadwinner lifestyle. Many wives who make more told me that they wished they could just come home and relax "with a drink and the remote control, like a man," but they know they could not feel comfortable actually doing it. It would not occur to these breadwinning wives to subjugate their husbands and turn them into servants. On the contrary, these wives are willing to participate in running the household—but as partners, on equal footing with their husbands.

The women I interviewed went out of their way to avoid making unilateral decisions that affected the entire family. Only a few consciously undermined their husbands' positions as partners by taking their contributions for granted or refusing to acknowledge their participation. Wives in happy marriages did not choose to keep important information about the household secret from their husbands—financial accounts, cash flow, family records or any other business aspect of the relationship. And at the end of the work day, not one of the wives expected to come home and relax every night while her husband prepared dinner, tended to the children and cleaned the house without her involvement—even if her husband was a full-time homemaker.

The life of the married female breadwinner provides a range of benefits, but household domination is not one of them. Essentially, these women chose breadwinning status for reasons other than power.

- Most seek financial independence with or without a husband, and the assurance that they can and do support themselves so that they will never be forced into total dependence on another human being.
- Nearly all of these women report that they enjoy the challenges, praise and rewards they receive on the job far more than the repetitive chores of household management.
- All of these women seek something more fulfilling than dominance in their relationships with their husbands. They seek *equality*.

An equal share. An equal footing. An opportunity to achieve the fifty-fifty partnership that is the holy grail of marriage. The battle that women are finally beginning to win in the workplace—equal opportunity, equal pay and equal recognition for equal work—is finding its way into our homes. Never did we seek *superiority* over men, even in the earliest and most passionate days of the feminist movement. We have always sought *equality*—and as breadwinners for our families, we finally have the bargaining power at home to achieve this hitherto unattainable goal.

Inside and outside the laboratory

Undertaking this research, I felt the need to compare my own findings with those of sociologists who may be examining the same trend. However, my exhaustive search produced precious little on the topic of wives outearning their husbands. I was nearing the end of my literature review when Dr. Julie Brines, assistant professor of sociology at the University of Washington in Seattle and one of the few individuals who have published on this topic, provided me with a citation that stunned and delighted me.

As I was conducting my own research, it seems Veronica Jaris Tichenor of the University of Michigan was conducting a very similar study, with a smaller sample of twenty-two couples and a control group of eight traditional couples. Tichenor's work, published in the *Journal of Marriage and the Family* in August 1999,[10] produced results that were virtually identical to my own in terms of each spouse's responsibilities at home, wives' expectations of their husbands' involvement (versus their actual involvement), wives' decision-making power in the family relative to their higher incomes and the continued link to "gender stereotypes" within the relationship.

The discoveries I made in my own anecdotal research and a clinical study conducted in a university setting provided the same results. These conclusions provided factual, useful insights about the ways in which breadwinning wives and their supportive husbands make their marriages work.

Let's explore what makes breadwinning wives and their supportive husbands come together, stay together and construct new standards for partnership in their marriages.

CHAPTER 4

CAN *YOU* TAKE IT?
Are You Cut Out
To Be a Breadwinning Wife?

Who are the wives who make more?

We are *not* a tiny subculture of superwomen—the famous, the workaholics, the brilliant leaders.

Generally, we are *not* wives who saddled ourselves with dead-beat, non-earning husbands who mooch off their careworn spouses.

Some of us find ourselves supporting our homes and families after our husbands are "downsized" by big corporations, but this still doesn't include the greatest share of breadwinning wives.

Breadwinner wives frequently are a new and different breed altogether. Only a handful of the wives who told me their stories would describe themselves as ultra-ambitious, victimized or soldiers of bad fortune. Instead, these women have found a new way to define marriage and lifelong partnership while making the most of their own abilities and talents and simultaneously empowering their husbands.

Most of the couples I met described themselves as happy. Some had come through periods of struggle and conflict to find a sense of comfort in their situation. Some were standing on the brink of that struggle. And some, bless them, had never struggled at all.

The more we talked, the more I saw patterns emerge. Eventually I was able to plot the characteristics of *happy* marriages in which the wives outearn their husbands. These content couples mirrored certain patterns of behavior, shared a belief system about themselves and their spouses and found common ground within their marriages in similar planes of understanding.

Breadwinner Wives

To fully understand what's going on in these marriages, let's first take a look at the women who chose this path. While all of the wives I interviewed were strong individuals, many similarities between them came to light as well—and not necessarily the similarities conventional wisdom might dictate.

1. *Breadwinner wives were raised from birth to be independent.*
The wives I met who make more money than their husbands are painfully aware of the potential need to support themselves exclusively. Many of them have spent their lives preparing to do so, whether or not this would prove to be necessary in the end. In fact, many of these wives expected to be self-supporting throughout their lives, even after they married.

"When I was two years old, we were at my grandparents' farm and I was holding an egg and a large cat," said Adele, a corporate communications executive whose income often exceeds her artist husband's by ten times or more. "My grandparents were trying to get me to put down one or the other and I was screaming at the top of my lungs. I was furious that they would dare think that I couldn't do both."

Born to think and speak her own mind and raised by liberal, intellectual parents, Adele always knew she would earn her own livelihood. "My parents always believed in women's rights and equality. My father once stood up in a PTA meeting and told them that he thought it was ridiculous that they had boys taking shop and girls taking home economics. Because of his protest, they said, 'Fine, if your daughter wants to take shop, we'll let her.' I was definitely taught these ideas about what I could and should demand in my own life."

A veteran of several relationships in which her high corporate rank placed her in the position of principal breadwinner, Adele's experiences only reinforced her commitment to maintain a substantial, stable income of her own. "I cannot imagine not being financially independent," she said. "Whether my husband makes more than me or not, I can't imagine not making enough to support myself on my own. If I was married to someone who was a millionaire, we lived in a penthouse and we owned boats, cars and a house in the country, that wouldn't be for me—I still would need to have my own money and be independent."

Not all breadwinning wives are the daughters of "liberated" mothers, however. A significant number of the women I interviewed described homes in which their mothers experienced the frustration of unbalanced, traditional marriages, putting aside their own aspirations to devote their energies to their husbands' advancements.

"I grew up without having a lot of money," said Kaye, a forty-two-year-old high-ranking supervisor in a Silicon Valley technology firm, whose husband works in construction. "My mother dropped out of school to support my dad, to keep him in school and keep him from being drafted. She never finished her degree and my dad did not make a considerable amount of money. When I grew up, there were two things I wanted. One was to be able to buy *what* I wanted *when* I wanted—I never did that when I was in high school. All the other kids got the right clothes or the 'in' shoes and I didn't get those things. And the second was to not owe anybody anything. When I'm financially secure, I don't have the feeling that I owe anybody. I pay my own way."

The substance of her words, *I don't want to owe anybody anything*, were echoed by nearly all the wives I interviewed. Their discomfort with indebtedness is a driving force behind many of the women's needs to establish their own financial independence, either before they married or within the context of their marriages.

"My dad was an alcoholic," said Brianna, the owner and founder of a personnel agency in downtown Minneapolis, whose husband currently stays home with their preschool-aged children. "I saw a lot of things in my parents' relationship that I didn't want repeated in my relationship. My mom had five kids and no income and was in a really bad situation. My father was pretty abusive to her and my brothers. I just remember growing up thinking, *I am never, ever, ever going to be in the position where I don't have financial independence, ever*. I know that has motivated me and driven me over the years. It didn't matter to me whether the man I got involved with had money or didn't have money. It was not an issue for me—I would always have my own."

The imprinting for financial independence came early to many of these women, often through observations of one parent's dominance over the other—determined by whose hand held the purse strings. Yet only a few of the women with whom I spoke described childhood homes filled with strife or disadvantage. Patricia, a partner in a law firm in Albuquerque who is married to a manufacturing supervisor, described the behavior of her father, a corporate vice-president with earnings well over $300,000 annually: "My father's role was to go to work and my mother's role was to take care of the home. I didn't really know my father until I was over thirty—I never saw him. When I was in high school, my mother got her real estate license. After that, the home was still her job, even though she was working full time. Literally, when my father is done with dinner, he will just leave the dishes on the table. He won't walk the two steps and take them to the counter. I'm sure he doesn't know what's underneath the counter—he has no idea there's a dishwasher in there.

"I think my current lifestyle is something of a rebellion," she continued. "I had an issue about authority—nobody was going to tell me what to do or how to live and I wasn't going to do something unless I wanted to. I'm sure that's because my Dad ruled with an iron hand."

Rhonda, a graphic artist in Napa Valley who is married to a man who works in public television, had the opposite experience. "Mom was the principal breadwinner in our family. This was in the 1970s, when that was just unheard of," she said. "My father is a decent, honest, hard-working man who just never made a lot of money, while Mom rose in the ranks of one of the area's largest corporations. At no point in my growing up did I ever really believe that I was supposed to have a man support me. It truly never occurred to me, even though all of my friends were in traditional homes in which their fathers made the bucks. I was raised to make my own way in the world—anything a man might provide in my home would be ancillary to my income. Maybe that means my expectations of men were low—or maybe that gave me a wider horizon of potential husbands to choose from. I didn't want a hard-charging doctor or lawyer. I wanted someone more like me."

2. Breadwinner wives have histories of breaking with convention.
The flip in the traditional marriage income structure is not the only unusual thing going on in the homes of wives who make more. Many of these women have tossed the traditions of married life, the American suburban dream and the world of work to the winds in their reinvention of their own lives and their relationships. Nearly all of the married couples who were interviewed described one or more of these unconventional choices.

- **None of the breadwinner wives have chosen to stay home with their children beyond the first few months of a child's infancy.**

"I don't know if I could do it—be home all day with the baby," said Sarah, an oral surgeon in Nebraska. "It's very tough. It's physically and emotionally draining—it's really hard work. I work hard at my job all day, but raising children is different. I would like to have more time with my family, but I need the to go to work everyday."

Sarah's point-of-view echoed through a large number of the interviews I conducted with breadwinning mothers. Many of these women feel a burning desire to raise children—but this need does battle with their equally strong desires to achieve status in the workplace.

"I wouldn't be able to do the things that I do in my career if I didn't have someone else to care for my children during the day," said Billie, the owner of a human resources consulting agency in central New York State. "Occasionally I feel guilty about that. I'm out here getting recognition and traveling all over the United States and sometimes it just feels awkward. But we turn my trips into family vacations whenever we can—if I have to go somewhere for a consultation or a conference, I tack on a couple of days and bring everyone along."

The constant juggling of work and family places considerable strain on these hardworking wives and mothers, yet only a small fraction of the women I interviewed wished they could give up work or cut back on their hours to spend more time with their children. The practical need for household income, the personal desire for recognition of their many talents and the absolute certainty that full-time motherhood would make them miserable—all of these factors come together to keep breadwinning wives in the workplace and out of the house.

"I was in a very nurturing environment growing up," said Nancy, a corporate executive in the Phoenix area. Nancy earns about $150,000 annually. "I loved having my mother at home and both my parents were very supportive of any interests I had. Growing up in that situation gave me the confidence to have dreams and pursue them. Consequently, both my husband and I felt very strongly about having a parent home with our children. If you have children, you should work very hard to meet their needs."

Nancy's nine-month-old son is home with his father, Walter, instead of in a day care facility. Walt gave up a mid-level corporate position to stay home full-time with the baby. "My friends are a little bit jealous that Walt is there and does so much for me and our baby," she said. "If the situation were reversed, I don't know if I could do what Walt does. I would be miserable staying at home all day taking care of the baby. It's such an exhausting, daunting responsibility. My job isn't easy—in fact, it's incredibly hectic and stressful at times—but I love the challenge."

Nancy considered for a moment. "Although if I could change one thing, I would opt to have more time at home. If I could work three days a week and make the money I make now, I would do it."

- **Many breadwinner wives are self-employed, working from home or building start-up companies into profitable enterprises.**

The self-confidence and high self-esteem so characteristic of breadwinner wives leads many of them to take professional risks, leaving well-paying jobs to pursue higher dreams as entrepreneurs. These women have found new levels of success—exceeding their husbands' earnings in the process.

"I worked for another company as a sales manager and I had an idea," said Wendy, the owner of a firm that specializes in digital imaging for the Web and other high-tech applications. "The company I worked for didn't want to do it. Now I have a company with eight people and I'm also running someone else's company with another fifty people. It's a huge undertaking. But it's profitable."

Indeed, Wendy's venture earns her an income that exceeds her husband's technical writing salary by more than three times annually. She is one of more than 9.1 million female business owners in the United States and one of about 20 percent of the women I interviewed who have increased their earnings and found new satisfaction in business ownership.

"I'm a member of the corporate diaspora," said Debbie, a highly specialized management consultant with a home office in Oregon. "I was laid off from a major corporation with great delight, because I had been planning this transition for some time. I have been successful in every way so far. I love what I do and I am disgustingly proud of it. I was in the corporate world for twenty-seven years and I watched big companies do things just totally wrong. I knew that I could teach people how to do those things better."

The family breadwinner since her wedding day, Debbie married her husband, Jeff, when they were both in their forties. "He was disenchanted with his career and he had tried a bunch of different jobs. He wanted a fresh start," she explained. "When we met, I was making $60,000 and he was making nothing. He wasn't threatened by my business strength or by my independence. He thought it was hot stuff!"

Laughing, Debbie continued, "Jeff was not only capable of dealing with my success, he welcomed the idea that he was involved with a woman who had a ferocious intelligence and a drive to do well. He is not ambitious; he doesn't care. I got so much respect and so much emotional support from Jeff that I didn't give a damn about financial support."

- **Many breadwinner wives chose professions that number few women in their ranks, including high technology, medicine, corporate management, engineering and geology.**

As women who are not afraid to take the tougher road to success, many of the breadwinning wives I spoke with are pioneers in high technology fields or the first females in the corporations that employ them to reach the highest levels of the organizations.

To these women, the battle against public opinion, gender bias and well-meaning but insensitive observers is a daily ritual. Not only do their high earnings almost inevitably place them among the ranks of women who outearn their husbands, their success has readied them for the judgments that come their way as women who "married down." They know how to play in the big leagues—and how to grin and ignore those who would criticize their choices of paths to earnings that far exceed their husbands' abilities to match them.

"Five percent of the people in my profession are women," said Georgia, a mechanical engineer whose husband works for the same firm in a different department. "Especially when you get into the higher levels, where I am. I hate to say it, but I am quite sure that part of the reason that I have been afforded more opportunities than my husband is because I am a woman. But if that's how it has to be done, that's okay with me."

For Georgia, working in her profession means that she some-times needs to "be one of the guys" to maintain her position and con-tinue her advancement in the company. "If the guys are all going out golfing and I don't go with them, it is not that they will hold it against me—but they just remember that I am not with the guys," she explained. "I am really competitive and I want to stay completely equal in every-one's mind. The reality is that men very easily can classify you as some-one different, because you are a woman. I think I may go overboard to dispel that myth of gender difference in my workplace."

At home, Georgia is the mother of a two-year-old in addition to her role as stepmother to her husband's grown children from his first marriage. "Sometimes I miss her," said Rich, Georgia's husband, whose work schedule is far lighter than his wife's. "I don't have any problems with her making more money than I do. She spends more than I do on clothes and things like that, so it's only right that she make more. And she earns it. Initially I was making twice what she was, but we put the money in one pot and we decide together what to do with it and how to spend it. I don't think her success has changed much between us—and as my job progresses, I may make more than she does again."

- **In more than 25 percent of the marriages, the husband is the principal child care provider. Many are at-home dads.**

Even though statistics show that more men than ever before are taking over the primary child care responsibilities in their homes, the at-home dad phenomenon is one that arouses amusement, incredulity and even suspicion among many outside of the relationship. Fathers as full-time child care providers are still an anomaly, even as they become the objects of television commercials for household products and the premise for films and sitcoms. Still unusual enough to be funny, the higher visibility of at-home dads is comparable to the rise in awareness of minority cultures in the 1970s, the mainstreaming of the gay community in the 1980s and the heightened visibility of people with disabilities in the 1990s—growing populations whose existences are suddenly validated by their appearances in popular entertainment, in advertising and in mass-market media.

Stan, a masonry contractor with a thriving New England freelance business, made a bold move in the early 1990s when he chose to take several years off to stay home with his newborn son while his wife, a corporate executive, continued to bring in a greater income. "It's amazing how little society values a husband who takes care of his children," he lamented, looking back on the five years he spent at home before rebuilding his business. His younger son, Chris, is now eleven years old; Stan and his wife, Diane, have an older son who is nineteen. "Negative comments came constantly from my friends and my father, asking why I couldn't get a part-time job," Stan remembered, "But Diane was grateful I was there. She knew the children were safe and someone who loved them was watching them. I'm like a lot of people in that I need strokes from people outside telling me that what I'm doing is worthwhile. Unfortunately, except for Diane, I wasn't getting any of that."

"Did you find something yourself that made your choice okay?" I asked.

Stan nodded. "Oh, yes," he said. "The look in my son's eyes."

- **A significant number of couples have chosen not to live up to their means, even though in many cases their combined earnings are quite substantial.**

Instead of living life to the hilt and spending the higher dollars of a two-income household, these couples often seek and find unusual means of keeping household costs down. Some are renovating old homes they bought well below market value, building child care relationships with neighbors or friends instead of with institutions or even bartering goods for services to maintain low expense levels at home.

"We have a lifestyle that is deliberately under-consuming," said Frances, a Wisconsin psychiatrist whose husband runs his own counseling practice for recovering drug abusers from their Madison home. "We have the flexibility that at any given time we can switch responsibilities and Keith can make a lot more money and I could shift to a different pattern. It's a function of our career paths, but it also has to do with having a mortgage that's only $500 per month. There are few people who have houses that cost as little as ours. That was a deliberate decision—to have a very conservative financial structure. It gives us the opportunity to make choices."

- **Approximately one third of the men and women who spoke with me do not participate in or practice any organized religion.**

Many described chosen spiritualities of their own definition or senses of morals and values gained from their upbringings, but said they had chosen not to join churches, synagogues or mosques or practice their religions in group settings.

One husband described himself as removed from even these settings. "I'm practically an agnostic," he explained. "Not even; I don't believe there is any higher force at all. I believe that the universe will grind to a halt one day and all electronics will revert to their elemental cores. I don't think there is any cosmic force that is going to change things."

This unconventional answer to a basic demographic question was unusual, but I heard many other unconventional attitudes—women and men who were raised within religious contexts, but have found different ways of looking at the spiritual world. Only a few of the study's respondents mentioned attending church or involvement with a spiritual congregation, while others noted that they practice a religion "in our own way." In addition, several who do practice a religion named groups beyond the standard Judeo-Christian tradition: Ba'hai, Mormon, Universalist and others.

3. *Breadwinner wives are motivated, but not obsessed with career and financial success.*

Not a single one of the happily married, breadwinning women with whom I spoke described a situation in which they pinched pennies, worked excruciating hours or put their careers before family or home life. While many of them talked of long work days or challenging jobs, they emphasized the importance of their marriages, their children and their families above all else.

This trait more than any other separates the wives who are happy in their role as principal breadwinners from those who are not. The happiest breadwinning wives sincerely feel that all income is a shared benefit for the household, regardless of where it comes from or who earns it. The concepts of "mine" and "yours" truly have been discarded by these women—sometimes after years of internal and external conflict, but discarded nonetheless.

Once they could adopt the attitude of a monetary "ours," the women who today have achieved happy ways of life managed to overcome whatever resentment or discomfort they may have felt toward husbands who make less money. This opened the door to many other ways their husbands could contribute to their homes—if not by virtue of income, then through child-rearing, supervision of home renovations, emotional support or by tending to the house while their wives bring home the bacon.

"My husband never went through the jealousy thing," said Devora, an entrepreneur whose architectural firm now employs nine people. Devora's husband, Matthew, lost his position as a technical draftsman and moved into a part-time position in Devora's business three years later. "It's our money and it goes into one pot. But Matt has picked up a lot of the maintenance around the house. He does the laundry, otherwise I'd be going out to Wal-Mart every week to buy underwear. We still haven't worked out the cooking, but he takes care of the house, pays the bills and makes our yard look nice. He also picks up some jobs at the office as well."

Matt's layoff had an actual benefit for the couple—it coincided with the beginning of the renovation of their Midwestern farmhouse. "I spent the last two years finishing that up," he said. "Now I handle most of the housework, because it needs to get done. I feel I contribute that way."

"I call him my rock of Gibraltar," Devora added. "To the outside world, I am this really hard, tough person. I've actually had clients that I've worked with say to Matt, 'She must be difficult at home.' To the outside world I'm all business, no fooling around and very, very focused. Then I come home and all I want is a hug. That's when I appreciate Matt the most."

4. Breadwinner wives have strong senses of themselves and the directions they have chosen.

With only a few exceptions, the wives who make more are women with clear heads and keen eyes. They believe in facing and overcoming obstacles and they apply many problem-solving methods to keeping their personal and professional lives on track. There are few shrinking violets in this bunch! The happiest of the wives who make more are those who can spot a conflict, sort it out with the help of their husbands and replace it with a solution that works for both of them.

Sam and Janet are North Dakota residents who have chosen a life of comparative independence within their own marriage. Janet owns a counseling practice, while Sam spends his time running their household—not as a househusband, but as contractor and construction foreman. Building their new home from the ground up with his own hands, Sam has become an expert at bartering for materials and learning the additional skills he needs to handle plumbing, heating, electrical work and all the other complexities of home construction. Sam works on their house between professional commitments, so the project was in its twelfth year at the time of our interview.

"Sam has always fixed things for friends and relatives, so he continued doing that and then did it for a living," said Janet. "When we met I was just breaking into my field and for a while I helped him paint houses for extra income. At that point, he was earning more than I was. But now my business has gradually improved to the point where I am making more per hour than he could, but I couldn't do it without him. He is doing more of the house building than I am and I am doing more of the money-making."

When it comes to paying the bills, Janet takes full responsibility. "I just pay everything," she said. "I even pay him an allowance—about two hundred and fifty dollars a month. That's money for him to do anything he likes with. It doesn't matter."

Their unusual relationship began when they met in an organization called a skills exchange. "It's where people in the community contribute time and talent and barter from each other, rather than exchange money," Sam explained. "Janet and I discovered that we were the ones putting in all the time and we weren't spending our credits. After a while, we realized that we could do this for each other, instead of all these strangers. It seemed like an obvious thing to have our own projects and contribute to each other. And we haven't stopped.

"I guess I was always into the idea that you have to do it yourself and you don't need money," Sam continued. "Janet was raised as a gifted type kid, so she was always saving money to go to college—and as it turned out, she never really needed it because she got scholarships. To her way of thinking, money was always something to be saved for the future, so it was not an issue for her. And me, I never thought about money."

Throwing away the conventions dictated by popular culture, Sam and Janet have created their own formula for marital happiness. In talking with Janet, there's no question that she feels she owes no one an explanation. "What we do works for us," she said. "I don't care if Sam makes money and I don't care if he doesn't. What's more, if I quit my practice tomorrow and choose to do something else, he'd be 100 percent behind me. That's what a partnership is all about."

My interviews showed that the happiest breadwinning wives are women who make their own rules for marriage, family and lifestyle. Already confident in their own abilities to make money and support themselves, these women actively seek men who complement their strong characters and who can see the benefits an unconventional lifestyle can bring to them. None of these women could be happy with husbands who regard their successes with jealousy, who resent their long work hours or who expect their wives to fulfill the traditional housewife role in addition to full days at their offices.

It stands to reason, then, that the most contented husbands of breadwinning wives are a unique group, with characteristics that bend or break the rules of gender-specific behavior. In our next chapter, we'll look more closely at these men and the positive qualities many of them share.

CHAPTER 5

WHO *ARE* THESE GUYS?
The Unusual Husbands of Breadwinning Wives

Once committed to the role of principal breadwinner, many wives who make more adamantly defend the lifestyle and the benefits it brings them.

However, the staunchest defenders of this new marriage dynamic are their husbands.

Conventional wisdom tells us the opposite. Aren't these husbands supposed to be humiliated by their lesser role? Don't they feel as though society looks down on them for not being the responsible, competitive breadwinners they are expected to be? Or are these the deadbeat men who won't lift their fingers to support their wives and families?

I spoke with many husbands who have heard these arguments and accusations hurled at them. One of them is my own husband.

Recently, an article about my book research in our local paper mentioned my husband's and my financial arrangement:

> It's a topic near to her since Randi has always been her family's primary breadwinner, earning about twice as much as her husband. Nic Minetor, a freelance lighting designer, also works from home.[1]

A few days after the article appeared, a coworker of Nic's approached him at a job site. "Boy, if I were you, I'd be really angry," the coworker said. "That article makes you sound like some kind of free-loader."

My husband was stunned. Whatever subtext his acquaintance had found in the article was entirely lost on Nic. "I didn't know what to say to him except, 'I don't have that problem with it,'" he said to me at the time. "He's clearly got issues I just don't have. It's never occurred to me to see our relationship his way."

Nic's observation is echoed by husbands of breadwinner wives across the country—hardworking men who contribute to the stability and happiness of their homes and are delighted that their wives have higher earning potentials than their own. "I love it," said Ted, the manufacturing supervisor married to Patricia, whom I described earlier. While Patricia earns about $200,000 annually, Ted earns about $70,000. "The more she can make, the better. She works a lot of hours and she earns everything she makes. It really doesn't bother me at all, because she gets what she deserves. She has a Ph.D., so she should be making a lot of money. That's just what's fair."

Some people are shocked that these men aren't offended by the idea of being the secondary earner in their homes. Others feel why *wouldn't* they be thrilled with their wives' high income? They're living the good life, aren't they? They have all the benefits of a great home without the sole responsibility of paying the mortgage, the car loan and the college tuition out of their own paychecks. They can goof off! What a deal!

I did encounter husbands of breadwinner wives who also thought like this. These are the men who not only bring home the smaller paycheck, they also expect their wives to carry the lion's share of the daily household responsibilities. I also encountered wives who *believe* that their husbands fall into this category—while the husbands see it entirely differently and believe they are contributing equally to the household.

In her landmark book, *The Second Shift,* Arlie Hochschild writes at length about the differences in perception between husband and wife about the amount of responsibility they share in the household. Her central premise is that even in households in which wife and husband earn comparable salaries and work similar hours, the wife carries the greater burden of household management—whether or not her husband believes this or realizes it. The wife comes home at the end of a professional workday to a "second shift" of laundry, dishes, cleaning and child care, while the husband makes a much smaller contribution to household duties by mowing the lawn or tinkering in the garage.[2]

Hochschild was one of the first researchers to explore the two-income marriage and the ways the second income changes the balance of power in the relationship. In all of the case histories she describes, the husbands see the wives' incomes as ancillary or less important than their own—and they assume that their wives will continue to supervise the households as part of the women's basic responsibilities.

How does this change when the wife is the principal breadwinner? For some men, it does not change at all—and we will explore such situations in a later chapter, where we will see that this attitude creates friction, bitterness and resentment in the husband-wife relationship. And we will discuss what couples can do to work beyond this problem.

There's no question that having a wife who outearns him is not a satisfactory arrangement for every man. A recent study on this subject conducted by Prudential Securities in New York, as quoted in the *New York Times* on August 1, 1999, noted that 34 percent of husbands interviewed said they would find it a problem if their wives made more on the job than they did.[3] This means that for every two couples with breadwinning wives who described their satisfaction with the household income arrangement, there is a third couple in which the husband is entirely unhappy with it.

It takes a certain kind of man to be contented with this new form of marriage—a man who can see the benefits without taking advantage of his wife's earning potential or feeling diminished and who can share a happy home by contributing to its harmony. The men I interviewed who were successful in this regard were remarkable in the traits they shared, whether they were high-income professionals, stay-at-home dads, entrepreneurs forming new businesses or men pursuing their dreams in non-profit or low-income fields. The following are the similarities I noted and the perceptions I gleaned from talking to these men.

1. *Money and power are not these men's primary motivators.*
In fact, money and power may not even be in the top five motivations for the men who are contented marrying women who outearn them.

The men who are most comfortable in this kind of marriage are those to whom family, personal enrichment and lifestyle choices are more important than money. The world is full of such men—artists, musicians, teachers, actors, leaders and employees of non-profit organizations, social workers and a host of others—those who choose to make a different kind of contribution to their community and their household than with a large paycheck.

Many of the men I talked with have made *conscious choices* to reject the stereotype with which society has saddled them. They know themselves well enough to understand that they don't want the long hours, high stress and constant expectations of a life in management or a high-paying, fast-paced profession. While others around them continued to push them toward "a job that will support a wife and family," these men took the road less traveled, leading them toward careers that would bring them the personal fulfillment they longed to achieve.

"I never really thought much about money," said Paul, the part-time choreographer we met in chapter 2. Paul is now an at-home dad, whose wife, Zoe, is an obstetrician. "I mean, I knew I needed money to pay for the necessities of life. But it was never the main reason I existed. It was always more important to me to choose a profession that used my talents, one that I would enjoy. If it meant I would never be a millionaire, then that's the way it would have to be."

Paul and Zoe met later in life, when he was thirty-three and she had just turned thirty-two. "It was clear that by thirty-three years old, short of a miracle, I was not going to make a lot of money," he said. "I had pursued a career in performance and there would just never be a lot of money there for me." After more than a decade of working as a dance instructor in an upstate New York city, Paul had no illusions about his future as a professional dancer. He had just made the transition to choreography when he and Zoe met through a personal advertisement.

Why would Zoe, a highly motivated professional woman, readily accept this arrangement with the man who would become her husband? "It really made it easier for me," she said. "When we started to make geographic decisions based on my being the primary wage-earner, we could have run into some significant problems. And at first, we certainly had conflicts."

Zoe was offered an associate position with a thriving practice outside Los Angeles. Paul was happy to make the move with her, even though he was then thirty-six and it meant leaving his university position and starting all over in a disadvantageous situation.

"We went to California and lived in a place that was inconvenient for him, because I had to be near my practice," she said. "Living sixty miles outside of the city was tough for him—when he got choreography jobs, the commute was long and miserable. Then moving to central California—where I was offered a partnership—made him essentially unemployed. My income, however, was several times the size of his, so my career dictated the geography."

Paul was shaken by the need to move away from the wealth of opportunity Los Angeles offered. His choices were limited in the new location—teaching dance didn't interest him and there were no performance venues nearby. He could either travel for work at distant dance companies and theaters—leaving his wife behind for weeks at a time—or he could choose a new career altogether. Meanwhile, the years had continued to pass and he was now forty-two.

"Not doing anything was just not an option," he said. "What kind of person would I be then? I need to contribute something—I'm not interested in being a slug around the house. It wouldn't be fair to either of us if I didn't pursue some kind of career."

Finally, after months of introspection and consideration, Paul put aside his stage aspirations for a completely different career, taking courses in Web site design and development and launching a business from home. Then when Zoe became pregnant, Paul found it easier than he expected to put his emerging career on hold to stay home full-time with his long-awaited daughter. "This is the area in which Zoe is the most supportive of me—emotionally as well as financially," he said. "There wasn't any big discussion about my staying home. We had no interest in a day care or nanny situation for our child and it made no sense to live off my $18,000 a year when Zoe is a partner in a medical practice. Most of all, our daughter is just more important to me than some job."

Paul's experience was echoed by dozens of men with whom I spoke, all of whom told me stories of realization, revelation and great satisfaction with their marriages and financial arrangements.

Steven, an insurance company claim adjuster, received a wonderful and unexpected gift from his wife, Becky, two years before I spoke with him. Becky also had a corporate job, working as a manager of a financial department and earning upwards of $80,000 annually. "I was working full-time and my hobby was music," said Steven. "But all I ever wanted to do was record a CD. Becky's job got more and more taxing and she was out of town often. She knew that what I really wanted to do was make music and she was trying to decide whether or not she really wanted to rise within this huge corporate structure and take the next step to senior management, because it takes so much time and is a such a huge personal sacrifice."

Then one day Becky had an idea that would work for both of them. "She says she was in an elevator in Chicago," Steven described, "and it just hit her that I shouldn't be working forty hours a week, because I know what I *really* want to do with my life. She came home that day and said, 'Look, you know what you want to do. Why don't you stay home a few days a week and do it? You can take care of the house and have the domestic responsibilities.'"

Until that moment, Steven truly had not considered this as an option. "I needed a couple of weeks to think about that. It wasn't something that I was ready for. Going part-time at work was a big adjustment—not having those big paychecks that you can use to pay a bunch of bills. But Becky has been really supportive of everything that has to do with my musical career."

Becky well remembers her rationale for offering Steven the opportunity to pursue his dreams. "This job was not a career for him," she said. "This was a place to work and to use some of the skills he had acquired, but he never really aspired to build a career in business or to get promotions or increase his responsibility. That's just one of the things that's well balanced for us. My job takes precedence and that works for us, because his job isn't that important to him. We're not competing for the same things and we don't have the same goals in terms of employment. I think it works out very well."

They made the switch, with Steven working two days a week for the insurance agency and Becky continuing her climb up the corporate ladder. But even while Steven records and mixes the tracks on his all-instrumental jazz CD, he looks forward to the day when he can return the favor and give Becky the opportunity she has given him. "We are also in the middle of making some big decisions about what direction our lives are going in and whether we want to stay on this fast track," he said. "There's high reward, but also high risk. It's very stressful for Becky to be in a high-powered, corporate environment all day. So we are trying to decide if we want to stick with this, get everything we can and make a lot of money, put it away and go do something that we would both really like—move to Maine and run a lighthouse, maybe—instead of this hectic lifestyle. Depending on what happens with my music, maybe Becky and I can do a little role reversal here."

It is Steven's focus on their quality of life together that Becky appreciates the most in their relationship, she said. "Steven sort of marches to his own drummer—he has a very here-and-now kind of perspective," she noted. "He has a vision of the future, but he really wants every day to be a great day. I used to be much more future focused. He's also not very materialistic at all—I was much more materialistic. Owning things and having just the right bedspread or just the right set of plates was more important to me. Steven would still wear the same jeans he wore in high school if they hadn't fallen apart."

For Steven and Becky, their joint focus on the quality of everyday life meant the opportunity for each of them to pursue their dreams, as disparate as they were. While Becky took the corporate promotion route and worked her way to the top of the organization, Steven chose the less conventional career path with a longer wait for the payoff—if it comes at all. Steven keenly feels the need to contribute in some way to their marriage, both financially and emotionally—and his contribution is enough to engender Becky's good will.

Each of these couples found their way to a positive relationship in which the wife outearns the husband, chiefly because Paul and Steven are not driven by their desire to earn big money. Neither of these men ties his personal identity and self-worth to the size of his paycheck. Instead, they seek personal fulfillment and they work to support their wives *emotionally*, rather than financially.

2. *Men who are satisfied in this relationship are basically non-competitive.*

This is not to say that these men are not interested in doing good work, accomplishing a great deal in their lives or earning a good living. They are simply more likely to choose independent pursuits and to measure themselves against their own personal bests—*feeling no competition with their wives*, whose incomes exceed their own.

Competition between husband and wife can not only taint the pleasure of achievement; it can turn success into disaster for a married couple. Liesel, a divorced woman in her late forties living in Atlanta, describes the miserable situation she and her then-husband, Dan, encountered when her career advancement demanded a relocation for them. "Dan was a manufacturing foreman, with good skills and managerial experience. We were told that it would be no problem, that my spouse could work for the same company," she said. "We asked this question a number of times and the replies sounded like it would be fine. So we decided together that taking on this new position was the right thing to do."

But when they arrived in Tampa, the city that would now become their home, they discovered that Dan's opportunities were not as they had been described. "I was the first and only woman the company had ever relocated," said Liesel. "The human resources staff had never seen a woman with a husband in tow. They held special meetings and they finally came back to us and said there was no job for Dan in the company."

Dan, who had left a good corporate job to make this move with Liesel, was devastated. "He wound up finding a low-level job with another corporation," Liesel said. "He became very depressed. Meanwhile, I got a promotion and another pay increase with a more responsible job. Dan just became more depressed. He was never able to gain any level of confidence on his own."

When Liesel became pregnant, Dan decided that the best thing he could do was to stay home with the child. But two months after their daughter was born, Dan selected a day care facility and placed the child there for eight hours every day. "He did nothing around the house," said Liesel. "He didn't do laundry, shopping, cooking, didn't help with the child. I had a full twelve-hour day with the commuting and I had a second job taking care of my baby and my husband. I realized there wasn't any partnership here."

Liesel desperately tried to hold the marriage together. "The payoff to me was a family, a home, a stable environment for a child. I believed in an ethic that you try to work out your marriage problems. But this was not a healthy relationship. It was not going to change."

Now, several years past her divorce and well into her next relationship, Liesel has learned to look for signs that her high income will not pose a threat to her potential spouse. "I am involved with a man now who is ten years my senior and he would love to retire if we stay together. It could be exactly the same situation, but a different scenario. I would be the breadwinner and he would be retired. He would have his own income and his own money, but not as much as I would have."

In her rocky marriage, Liesel's success became a direct reflection on Dan's failure. Even though he had agreed to a move that would benefit his wife's career more than his own, Dan could never make the adjustment in attitude that would allow him to enjoy the personal choices this new arrangement afforded him. His identity was in his job and his work—both of which were denied him through circumstance.

Men who do not define themselves by the power in their title or their rank within an organization are far less likely to object to a relationship with a woman whose income exceeds their own.

"I started out living the bush life in Australia," said Jonathan, a thirty-seven-year-old stay-at-home dad and part-time research geologist. "Just being out in the bush and being real self-sufficient—that is what I love the most. But of course, there wasn't any money in it. So I returned to the States—and that's when I met Rebecca."

Jonathan's wife Rebecca, a paleontologist, is the only woman in a corps of government-sponsored researchers performing an archaeological excavation in Utah. While they met on the job and their professions are very similar, their aspirations took them in entirely different directions—which suited both Jonathan and Rebecca just fine.

"The thing that is hard to describe to people is that my mom and dad were professionals and burned the candle at both ends," he said. "They essentially drove themselves to the grave very early because of it. Mom impressed on me that I should do what I love. That is more important than making big money or climbing the corporate ladder, because it's pretty empty when you get to the top."

Jonathan's career concentrates on the study of rock formations that occur in the state's most remote regions, often taking him 120 miles from the nearest store, telephone or electricity. "I'm not cut out to be a nine-to-five person," he said. "The people that I am involved with out here are pretty much the same. We settled very happily for Rebecca being the nine-to-fiver—she loves it—while I work the stranger hours and do the domestic stuff."

Rebecca, who manages a specific research project, finds herself in an office environment most of the time. "I have always had a full-time job," she notes, "and Jonathan hasn't, because his jobs are seasonal. So I think it took a long time for me to get used to the fact that if I was going to have the kind of income I was used to, plus stability and benefits and that sort of thing, I was going to be the one to do it."

While Jonathan feels no competition with Rebecca because of her career success, Rebecca is surprised to find that she also feels no competition with him for the attentions of their daughter. "I guess the biggest benefit that I never would have known until we had our child is that Jonathan is so good with her," she said. "I think he's a better stay-at-home parent than I would be. And I'm totally free to enjoy my work. I can't imagine being married to a man who is really invested in his career," she went on. "I think I would see that as being in conflict with me."

3. *These men choose to be more engaged in the daily lives of their wives and children than in career pursuits.*

Overall, the men who find themselves happily married to women with larger incomes are family men—very involved in the daily routine of keeping a home, raising the children and maintaining harmony throughout the family.

This is no accident. These men understand the value of a stable home and a happy family and the importance of creating an environment in which all family members can thrive and grow. What's more, they work hard to be participants in the family, even to the point of sacrificing career and higher income to put more time and effort into the greater whole.

Leo, a forty-six-year-old utility worker in Indiana, accepted and then rejected the last offer of promotion he received when he and his wife, Helene, married five years ago. Their first child was born a year later and their second just sixteen months ago. "People still have the attitude that women are supposed to stay home with the kids. I'm a happy person and my wife and kids are very important to me," he said. While Leo still holds a full-time job, he has more time at home and more days off than Helene, who manages a technical division of a local corporation. "I'm the guy at home here who washes and irons the clothes, I do the cooking, I change diapers and I take the kids to the doctor when they get sick. Things that people tell me a woman should do. I want my kids to know that it's okay to clean toilets and wash floors. It's nothing to be ashamed of."

Leo, who is African-American, learned to appreciate the rigors of housework from his grandmother, who put him to work around the house to fill in the gaps while his mother, a nurse, worked full-time. "Dad was a bricklayer—and he was from the old school. He didn't do the things I do," Leo said. "But my grandmother would have me do a lot of stuff like ironing and mopping floors. Even though I grew up with five sisters, I still did some of the cooking and lots of other things around the house. I picked up the habit way back then."

Helene is keenly aware that her husband may have given up a higher income in favor of spending more time with her and their children—but she expressed no regrets about his decision. "The nice thing about his job is that he's home two to three days a week," she said. "He loves being a dad and he takes the kids out to have fun on his days off. This is a great time for him to be home and the kids have a great relationship with him. I also have a great relationship with our kids, but I love the fact that they get to spend so much time with their Daddy."

How did Helene get so lucky, you might ask? This isn't about luck so much as investment—a personal investment on Leo's part to find the best way to be true to his own need to spend more time with his family.

This family is exceptional, but no exception among the ranks of wives who make more and the men they marry. More than 25 percent of the men with whom I spoke had made a deliberate choice to give up a steady or larger paycheck to spend more time with their families or to become principal caregivers to their children.

4. Men satisfied with wives who earn more are accustomed to seeing women as leaders.

I expected many of these men—most of whom are in the twenty-eight to fifty age range—to come from families in which their mothers embraced the feminist movement and held part-time or full-time jobs outside of the home, acting as role models for the do-everything women of the 1990s and 2000s. I had theorized that the husbands' understanding of women's equality in the marriage relationship came from years of observing this at home.

Instead, the vast majority of the men I interviewed began the descriptions of their childhood homes with the words, "I grew up in a *Leave It to Beaver* family." The sons of traditional families in which their fathers worked full-time while their mothers took on full homemaker responsibilities, these men described their mothers' roles as household managers, leaders and financial contributors. "My father was the bread-winner," said Andy, a sixty-year-old manufacturer's representative in Oregon. "He worked very hard, a lot of overtime and a lot of night work. My mother stayed home and watched the kids. Then when I was in eleventh grade—that was 1954—my father died. At that point my mother had to go to work to keep things going. My older brother and I had jobs and we contributed to the running of the house, but when my brother got married and left, it was just my mother and me."

When Andy and his wife, June, decided to move to another city so that June could advance her career in higher education, Andy—then fifty-four years old—suddenly found himself with fewer clients, fewer lines to represent and more time on his hands. As June's salary surpassed his, Andy was surprised at how comfortable he felt about it.

"I am not money motivated, so it really didn't bother me," he said. "I knew her salary was going to surpass mine eventually." Andy began to pitch in with the housework to save money on cleaning services. In particular, he takes care of the dusting and vacuuming and cleans up after meals. "It's just because I have more time," he noted. "I feel a little bit guilty that June breaks her neck at work. So I said I would help out."

Most of the men I interviewed described the financial aspects of their childhood homes as steeped in tradition as well—fathers who earned the money and expected to dictate how it was spent, while mothers tended to the homes and children and avoided conflicts with their husbands. Ken, a forty-one-year-old financial planner, is the husband of Claire, whose career in television news in a major market rocketed her income above Ken's substantial earnings. "Our household was pretty typical of the 1960s," he said, recalling his childhood. "For a long time, dad was the sole provider. Mom didn't work while we were very small—but later on, she worked nights in a restaurant. Dad was in the insurance business for years. I think your values are certainly formed from your upbringing and I would have to say that Dad made us toe the line. He maintained a strict and tight ship. We certainly knew the difference between right and wrong and he maintained that level of values."

When Ken considered how his childhood home might have influenced his current lifestyle as the spouse with the secondary income, however, he carefully considered his position. "While my dad has mellowed through the years, his relationship with my mother is night and day from mine and Claire's. My dad is very old school in a lot of ways. He's Italian and culturally that manifests itself as a male-dominated environment. Today, societal change requires a different outlook. Claire and I are almost required to have two incomes to maintain the lifestyle we want and you need two parties taking care of the kids and the household fifty-fifty. That wasn't the case when I grew up."

Like many of the men who spoke with me, Ken holds a deep respect for his parents and the way they structured their household. In his own home, however, he can see the need to discard the dominant role of the husband in favor of equity between spouses—a relationship that brings him benefits in increased contact with his children, in the quality of his interaction with his wife and in the more comfortable lifestyle their combined incomes provide.

Some of the husbands I interviewed, however, offered a different description of their mother's role in relation to their father's—one of negative compromise. These men observed the extra effort their mothers expended to keep the home a happy, comfortable place or to keep food on the table when fathers could not do so themselves.

"My father passed away when I was ten," said Evan, a twenty-nine-year-old, stay-at-home dad starting a new business from his Wyoming home. Evan's wife, Lucy, holds a managerial position in county government. "My brothers and sisters were older than me by three years and more, so after a while it was basically my mom and myself at home. Mom wasn't too demanding; she kind of let me grow up on my own. She also recognized that I had my own responsibilities and I started working when I was thirteen. That's when she started treating me as an adult."

Evan's mother worked as an insurance agent, supporting the household by herself while setting an example that Evan would not forget as he grew up and got married. "My mother gave us loving support and it was a role model for raising my own kids," he said. "My mom managed the home on the money she made, so the money I earned was my own. As soon as I was sixteen, I bought a car."

David, a fifty-year-old advertising account executive in Minneapolis, remembers his mother pursuing a higher education against his father's will. "Dad was a salesman," he said. "They divorced when I was about seven years old. One of the reasons they broke up was that she wanted to go back to college and he wasn't keen on that. After they divorced, she went back to school, finished her master's degree and took a job working at a university. She actually created the audio-video lab there."

Later, David and his mother went into business together, which led to his career in advertising. "I learned from her," he said. "I used to hang out with her and play with the equipment. Eventually I worked on a freelance basis. That's how I got started in the field."

While David kept in contact with his father through weekend visits during his childhood, David saw his mother as the primary role model in his life. "She was such an independent person," he said. "I had a great deal of respect for her and I loved her very much. Since then, I have always liked the company of women who are self-sufficient. Capable, I guess."

All of the men with whom I spoke who had happy relationships with wives who earn more understood from an early age the significant role women play in earning household income—so they were ready to consider the possibility that their wives' incomes might surpass their own. This early exposure to women as family leaders opened up a world of options for breaking with tradition and creating fulfilling relationships between wife, husband and children—with the wives earning the greatest share of the family income.

If you and your husband are taking on the challenge of leaving tradition behind, the chapters which follow will give you needed recommendations, guidelines and information on the way successful breadwinner wives manage money, handle household responsibilities, share the burdens of cleaning, cooking and child care and create happy, healthy, nurturing homes for each other and for their families.

CHAPTER 6

THE NEW MATH
Money Isn't Always Power
in Negotiating Household Finances

When Donna and Gene got married and moved into their new house together, Donna quickly discovered that Gene had no talent for managing household expenses.

Early in their marriage, Gene had been the principal breadwinner, rising through the ranks of a large manufacturing company. "The benefits were tremendous," he said. "Company car, bonuses, the whole nine yards. But after a while, everything changed with the company—I got shuffled around. Even while it was happening, I knew I'd reached my tolerance level for corporate life."

Meanwhile, Donna's career as a physician's assistant began to move forward as she took on additional responsibility within a busy suburban practice. At the same time, Donna found that she was pregnant—and day care expenses would make any change in their combined income prohibitive.

With Gene so unhappy in his job, when the baby was born, the time seemed right to make a drastic change in the household structure. Gene gave up the corporate world to become the primary caregiver for his newborn daughter, while Donna expanded her work responsibilities to make up for some of Gene's lost income. At the same time, Gene launched a home-based business—selling and assembling gift baskets for corporate incentives and promotions—to help close the income-outgo gap.

Gene was now home most of the time, so he agreed with Donna that he should handle the day-to-day process of managing their joint checking account and paying the household bills. However it only took Donna a couple of months to be reminded of Gene's mathematical shortcomings: He still was a disaster with a checkbook.

"I laugh now, because she kids me about it," said Gene. "If I couldn't balance the checking account, I would change banks. As a single person I had changed banks about a zillion times. Banks, ugh! I don't like to deal with them."

Donna took back the money management responsibility for the household, as much for her own peace of mind as for their financial health. However, she felt it was critically important for Gene to stay informed on their cash flow, so she instituted regular review sessions with him.

"For the most part, I do the balancing of the checkbook," Donna explained. "But we both do a lot together. We sit down a few times a month and kind of look at where our money is going. Then we try to come up with how much we can afford to spend on extra things. We constantly sit down and talk about how much we are spending and where we can cut back. This is how we work together on a budget."

Working together—it's a new concept for many married couples in dealing with their finances, but an established reality for couples for whom the wife is the principal breadwinner. Donna and Gene are typical of more than 58 percent of the couples I interviewed, who share at least one joint checking account and confer regularly before making major decisions on household expenditures.

From both a clinical perspective and in popular wisdom, we have believed that the principal breadwinner in the marriage is the one who holds the power in the relationship, making the major purchasing decisions and controlling the family checkbook. This is the basis for *resource theory*, the primary theory of household finance and power employed by sociologists studying marriage in the 1960s and 1970s and even into the early 1980s. Resource theory seemed to bear out even as wives began to bring more money into the family, with working wives of the 1970s and 1980s gaining new power at home and becoming more and more involved in family decision-making, based on their contribution to the household income.

The true power in a marriage goes well beyond which spouse earns the most money and which spouse actually manages the household finances. The true power is in the decision-making process—a process decided less by the financial resources of each spouse and more by two important factors: the *gender issues* that lie within every marriage and the comparative *competence* of one spouse over another to make these decisions.

When we add the dynamic of wife as principal breadwinner to the marital mix, we expect the gender issues to gain emphasis, bringing hidden conflicts within the marriage to the foreground. Wives who make more, especially those who support their families solely on their own incomes, are certainly in a position to take control of family spending and commandeer the household checkbook, whether or not their husbands are in favor of such arrangements. This is precisely what I expected to find in my early interviews—I assumed that these high-earning women would want absolute control over their money, perhaps even giving their husbands a specific allowance for spending money or household management as many men in traditional marriages do in their financial relations with their spouses. I thought that such breadwinner wives might keep their annual earnings a closely guarded secret, even from their own husbands. I expected to see these wives managing all the household finances and making all the big decisions, based on their superior income position and the prevalent character traits I had already discovered in these women: self-confidence, high self-esteem, high overall competence. Worse, I expected to find men who were disgruntled or even humiliated by their wives' domination of the household checkbook.

I was stunned to learn how wrong I was.

There are couples who fit this description—marriages in which the breadwinning wife manages the household finances with virtually no input from her husband. However, even in these cases, most of the husbands with whom I spoke who were part of this kind of arrangement were not discontented with the situation. In fact, they told me of their relief in not having to deal with the day-to-day concerns of household budgets.

In the vast majority of couples I interviewed, I found a far more equitable sharing of financial information, delegation of money management and joint decision-making based not on resources or on gender, but on *competence*.

Donna and Gene are an excellent example of this type of relationship. Donna is the primary breadwinner, bringing in a substantial income while her husband took on the principal caregiving role for their young daughter and launched a home-based business. In the beginning Gene seemed to have the time and inclination to handle household finances, so Donna happily delegated the responsibility to him...until that assignment resulted in bounced checks, missed payments and a hopelessly tangled checking account. Gene has the time, the knowledge of the household's day-to-day needs and the interest in how and where the family's money is spent, but he has no skill with money management. For the sake of the household health, the financial tasks must fall to Donna.

Now Donna, in these monthly discussions, shares financial information with her husband and makes certain that he knows where their money is and how much is available. She believes that both spouses need to be fully informed about the family's monetary situation, so they can share in making decisions that are important to both of them—where to take vacations, when to upgrade their furniture or buy a new home, even the optimal time to have a second child. Donna has no interest in becoming the lord of the manor, making such decisions totally on her own. Even though she holds full breadwinning responsibility for the family, she seeks a partnership with her husband, not a position as benevolent dictator.

Where is the power in this relationship? Remarkably, it is shared, even though Gene's income is negligible at this point in the marriage. This sharing takes place because *Donna has the power to choose it*—which may be the greatest single accomplishment afforded to wives when they become their families' primary breadwinners.

Are we genderless about our money?
It would be easy to assume that couples like Donna and Gene have simply discarded gender roles and outsiders' judgments to form new rules that work best for them. However, another dynamic comes into play so far as money is concerned, a more subtle but critical function of the breadwinning wife in building an egalitarian relationship with her husband.

In the never-ending quest for balance between husband and wife, breadwinning wives find common ground with their husbands in the financial management of their households. Here gender roles are not so well established as they are in areas like housework and child care, in which a clear delineation between "women's work" and men's breadwinning role was established centuries ago.

It's a favorite position of many financial planners and advisors that women fear the prospect of handling and managing their own money. Many of today's financial consultants still insist that women—*all* women—are more cautious about money than are men and are uncomfortable as the money managers in their homes. "Women have long been accustomed to avoiding financial matters, leaving that responsibility to men, the traditional breadwinners," said Anne Kohn Blau in her book, *The Sex of the Dollar*. "I have noticed an increased interest by women in learning about finance, but many of the women I have met who manage their own money admit that they do so only when forced to. Why? Because they have no male protector. They don't necessarily want the job."[1]

Colette Dowling, author of *Maxing Out: Why Women Sabotage Their Financial Security*, stated: "Our entire sense of ourselves as female has been tied to not having money, not managing it, not being financially independent...I came to see how confused we remain on the subject of what constitutes femininity, of how much independence one can achieve and still feel like a 'real' woman."[2]

The assumption that men are more comfortable with money and have always been the household financial managers, while women hide from money and yearn for a man's monetary protection, just doesn't hold up in the face of contemporary research.

Traditionally, household budget and spending allocations have been handled by one spouse or the other, but not specifically the breadwinning spouse. Carolyn Vogler and Jan Pahl, two prominent British sociologists who examined the dynamics of gender and finances within the marriage, explored this budget management question in detail. Working with data from a 1988 study, they determined that 42 percent of the 1235 couples surveyed said their finances were managed by the wife, while only 25 percent said their household budget was the husband's responsibility. Another 20 percent said the couples managed their expenditures jointly between husband and wife.[3]

Closer to home, a 1999 survey by SRI Consulting Business Intelligence revealed that men were solely responsible for financial decisions in less than 30 percent of the 3,800 United States households studied.[4] *American Demographics* reported in July 2000 that women have an equal financial say in 75 percent of all United States households.[5]

Therefore financial management has not been and is not now a predominantly male domain, even though in traditional as well as some modern marriages husbands are still expected to bring in the greater share of the household income. The perceived wisdom that the principal breadwinner in the family, traditionally the husband, is the family financial manager has been shown to be something of a cultural fantasy.

What about women's confidence in handling and managing money? In the 1995 Women Cents Study, conducted by the National Center for Women and Retirement Research, 94 percent of the women surveyed believed that women are as capable as men when it comes to understanding money and investing.[6] As if to reinforce this statement, the SRI Consulting study learned that the percentage of women who "sometimes feel stupid when asking questions about financial matters" fell from 60 percent in 1994 to 44 percent in 1998. Meanwhile, 66 percent of female-headed households—defined by the study as homes in which the wife manages the money—owned mutual funds in 1998, up from 45 percent in 1996.[7]

Not surprisingly, the Women Cents Study also discovered that women who are assertive, open to change and optimistic make smarter money choices than those who fear failure and the unknown. These positive traits aptly describe the wives who make more, a segment of the female population who are especially comfortable managing money, making major financial decisions and choosing investments for the family.

Beyond confidence to control

Do wives who supervise the household accounts manage every aspect of the family's finances? Earlier studies by Pahl and others have shown that while wives are more likely to manage household expenditures and budgets, the actual *control* of the couples' income traditionally has fallen to the man. Larger spending decisions, allocation of money to household accounts or to savings and amounts for personal discretionary spending have been controlled by the breadwinner in the family—usually the husband.[8]

When the wife is the principal breadwinner, the control over the money shifts and with it, the decision-making power. Wives who make more have the opportunity to take over the spending decisions, keep large amounts of money for themselves and allocate funds to accounts for household expenditures. However, with only a few exceptions, *they do not do this*. The wives who make more also *share* more, bringing their husbands into the decision making process of allocating funds to savings accounts, investments and major purchases.

Why are these wives so generous? Veronica Tichenor offers an explanation from her research, based in the traditional view of gender: "...Wives with more resources do not use these resources to make claims to greater power but rather the reverse. They often defer to their husbands in order to demonstrate that they are not making claims to power. Through this kind of interaction, this doing of gender, spouses preserve the husbands' power in the relationship, despite the potential power advantage of the wife's greater resources."[9]

I believe, based on my research, there is an additional dynamic at play. Once again, the central theme in my study comes to the surface: Breadwinning wives are not looking to take a superior position above their husbands, eliminating men's roles as providers or partners. The wives who make more have a unique opportunity to establish an authentic equality with their husbands, perhaps for the first time in history. Sharing the financial decision-making responsibility creates equal footing between husband and wife—made possible because the wife's contribution to the family pot is larger than her husband's.

Cash flow for husbands

I have found it especially significant that not one wife I interviewed provided her husband with a set allowance for household allocations or personal spending. Instead, even the husbands who do not work outside their homes receive an unconstrained supply of cash or credit as they require it. "I write Paul a check and when he runs out of money I write him another one," said Zoe, the doctor introduced in chapter 1. Paul is a full-time stay-at-home dad who cares for the couple's preschool-age daughter. "They're big checks. He buys the groceries and whatever else he needs. Last year he bought himself a computer and all the peripherals. When he needs more, he tells me. Generally, I don't ask questions about where it goes. He's never been irresponsible about it."

Other couples with whom I spoke described arrangements through which the wife handles all the finances and simply pays the husband's credit card and other bills as they arrive. Sandra, a corporate executive in California, has agreed with her husband, Al, to make all of his purchases with one credit card. "At the end of the month, I just pay the whole thing off," she said. "He's never out of line with what he buys, but if he needs new clothes or supplies for his woodworking, he shouldn't have to come and beg me for money. That's humiliating for both of us. This way, I just pay the bill. If we have some big purchase to make, we talk it over together."

Why don't the husbands take this "blank check" approach for granted and run up huge bills? And how can their wives relax with the knowledge that their lower-earning or non-earning husbands could be out frittering away their hard-earned dollars?

The precedent for this arrangement, oddly enough, originates in the more traditional gender roles, established well before wives began to earn substantial amounts and make major contributions to the household income. Studies by Vogler and Pahl show that the lower-earning spouse—in their study, most often the woman—tends to be more frugal and less willing to spend freely, even when she supervises the household finances. When the gender tables are turned and the husband is the lower-earning spouse, Vogler and Pahl observed that breadwinning wives tend to protect their husbands, juggling their own finances to ensure that their husbands would have adequate spending money and would not feel the pinch of deprivation.[10]

Indeed, today's breadwinning wives continue to take this protective role in their husbands' lives, making certain their husbands never feel imprisoned by their status as lower-earning or non-earning spouses. Meanwhile, their husbands adopt the lower-earning spouse's role described by Vogler and Pahl, curtailing their own spending for the good of the family. These husbands described conservative spending habits, a lack of interest in material goods and a concern that their wives should not be taxed by overwork just to pay the credit card bills.

Not one of the couples I interviewed described extravagant spending on the husband's part. Several, however, noted that the wives were fairly free with their money—sometimes driving their husbands to object strongly to their spending patterns.

"I used to think that fifty dollars was a lot of money," said Kurt, a twenty-eight-year-old husband whose wife, Monica, holds a high-level position in corporate management. "It's okay to want things and to have things and it's good to make money, but it's not my whole life." At the time of our interview, Kurt worked in a fast food restaurant while he looked for more fulfilling work, with no specific profession in mind. "I'm thinking I may like to become a social worker," he said. "So I think I will need more schooling."

Monica, however, sees money as a critical element in her happiness. "I pretty much always made more money than Kurt," she said. "Right away, I started noticing that I definitely had more power somehow. If I wanted something, I went out and bought it. Then we would work it into our plan later. If he wanted to buy something, it would pretty much have to be in the plan. I don't think he ever felt he had the power to just buy something."

Monica admitted that she enjoys buying things far more than Kurt does. "I like clothes and outdoor gear," she said. "I work hard and I feel I deserve to spend the money. So I buy what I want. Kurt sees it a little differently, however."

Indeed he does—so when Kurt felt that Monica's spending had gone beyond his tolerance, he forced the issue and insisted they get outside help together. "We go to a twelve-step program called Debtors Anonymous," he confided—a fact Monica had not shared. "We've started doing a spending plan every month. We sit down together once a week and write down everything we've spent and then we total it up so we keep track of our expenses. That way we come to an agreement about what we're going to spend."

"I've sort of stopped buying whatever I want," Monica admitted. "It feels like it's more equal, because that's what Kurt wants me to do. When we write down a spending plan, it seems to help Kurt have a better understanding of how we handle our money. He's a lot more pragmatic about expenses—he balances me out. He says we need to have savings, we need a reserve. This is all kind of new for me."

The financial health of these marriages comes with its own set of checks and balances: sharing the decision-making while one person handles the actual bills; trusting one another to control personal spending; and respecting the ebb and flow of income to establish a level of comfort for each spouse.

Joint and separate means equal

How do wives who make more and their supportive husbands split up family finances and what do their financial arrangements mean to the quality of their marriages? I found three general styles of money management in these families:

1. All joint accounts
2. All separate accounts
3. The three-account system

1. Joint accounts

The "big pot" is the favorite choice for 55 percent of the couples in my study. Both husband and wife deposit all of their earnings into a joint checking account, which is managed by one spouse or the other—depending on each spouse's interest in managing the household finances and on the spouse's competency with money and investment.

In most of these households the spouses work out their plans for spending together, making joint decisions on major purchases and sharing information on investments and retirement accounts. The wives in these marriages express a great deal of concern that both spouses be informed about the family finances, whether or not they are personally involved in managing the funds or writing the monthly checks.

"The absolute truth is that Thatcher does 98 percent of the money management," said Connie, an architect in the Baltimore area earning about $80,000 annually. Thatcher works as a construction foreman, with an income of about $50,000. "He handles checking, savings, paying bills and so on. I keep a mental picture of what is going on and ask him, 'Hey, did you mail that bill? How much money is in the checking account?' But he does all of it—that area is not my thing."

"I always joke with Connie about money," Thatcher added. "When we go to Marshall's and there's a $100 dress and it's forty percent off, I say, 'Connie, how much is the dress?' She has a master's degree and she took calculus, but in reality she has trouble adding two and two. So I took over the financial management from day one."

He paused. "I can't say I am extremely good at it. I usually bounce one check a year. It's just that I may be a little more organized and know when the bills are due. Now it's part of my job in the family."

When all accounts are jointly held, the actual money management responsibility falls to the more competent spouse, *not* the one who makes more money or the one dictated by gender tenets. Thatcher took over when Connie's disinterest became obvious, very early in their marriage. "I said, 'I am not doing it,' and he said, 'Okay,'" Connie remembered. "That was about it."

Yet Connie joined Thatcher in the creation of a monthly budget for the household, now managed by Thatcher. And when it came time for the larger decisions about retirement plans, establishing a fund for their infant son's eventual college education and other savings choices, Connie became very much involved. "We work with a financial planner on a regular basis," she said. "We both have retirement accounts and we both have other minor savings. And we have a huge piece saved up for our son. I have stocks and bonds, money I put away from a previous job. Every year, we do a little bit more."

With Thatcher in charge of paying the bills and both spouses participating in savings choices, Connie and Thatcher maintain a high comfort level with their financial situation. "Our friends comment when Connie buys a lot of clothes," Thatcher noted. "But I tell them, 'If she makes the money, it's okay for her to spend more of it than I do.' I'm not at all uncomfortable with that. I can see that the bills are getting paid; we're meeting our savings goals and there's money left over. Why shouldn't she enjoy it?"

The downside of joint accounts

With a healthy amount of money in the family and both spouses earning their own income, the joint account arrangement can be the most comfortable for both spouses. When money is tight, however, or the balance is less equitable, joint management—even with one spouse in charge—can take a turn for the worse.

"Early on I started making choices and found out that people would pay me pretty nicely," said Karen, a forty-seven-year-old executive in a high technology start-up, where weekly paychecks have yet to arrive dependably. "Once I got into that world I decided that I liked it and liked having that kind of money. If I wanted to go out to dinner or to a movie or buy a book, I didn't have to worry if I could afford it."

Two major changes in Karen's life turned this pleasure into a paradox: her marriage to Howard, a telemarketing representative earning about $25,000 annually, and her decision to move into the uncertain world of dot-coms. "When I made the move to the start-up environment, I had to start counting the pennies and wondering if I could pay the mortgage. It was a much more difficult adjustment for my husband than for me. When we got married, I guess I had this notion that this would be really good, because I know how to live on my salary and make ends meet. I thought it would be nice just having my husband's additional income, even though it wasn't much.

"The disappointment was that it didn't work that way," she continued. "Suddenly I found out two can't live as cheaply as one. Having his additional salary didn't make any difference—we bought a condominium and some furniture and the next thing we knew, the money was gone. And then we got into debt and had to pay that off."

When financial trouble rocked their marriage, Karen and Howard tried a marriage counselor. "One of the things the counselor suggested was that we pool our resources. I must say I was reluctant, but I did it," Karen said. "I understood the reasoning behind it. It was obvious to me that Howard was never going to make a lot of money and that I would. Unless we pooled our money and it became 'ours,' that uneven dynamic would just eat away at our relationship."

In a tougher twist that stretched Karen's comfort level to the limit, she gave up financial control and agreed to let Howard manage their money. "I didn't think he could do it, quite frankly," she admitted. "We had a rocky year as we tried to figure that stuff out—bouncing checks for the first time in my life and here I was in my forties. I thought I could do a better job, but on the other hand I passed the responsibility on to him, because I felt that if he didn't do it, it would gnaw at him. It all just keyed into his self-esteem issues."

Over time, Karen began using her business credit card for some of her personal spending, paying the company back for these purchases and justifying this behavior as "convenience." "I just didn't want to have a discussion with Howard about what I spent for clothes," she said. "It was hard for him to go buy himself a pair of socks. I was not going to live like that. He couldn't spend money on himself—even if he were to win the lottery tomorrow, he would find it difficult to really spend money on himself."

With the difference in spending styles, the conflict over earning potential and the struggle to maintain a comfortable lifestyle while Karen worked to build the new company, Howard finally confronted Karen about her income. "I was sitting here at my desk one day and he came into the office and said, 'So when are you going to call it quits?'" Karen remembered. "He said, 'Seriously, at what point are you going to decide it isn't working, go out and get a real job?'"

To Karen's credit, she did *not* respond by berating Howard for his lower income and his inability to support them while she worked to grow her business. "I said, 'Never, Howard. This is what I do,'" she told me. "'I run this business. I will make it and I have put things in place that I know will increase the income in the coming year. I don't want to go back—I have the right to starve if I choose and I have the ability to achieve things based on my own work.'"

Howard "stomped off," Karen reported. Faced with the frustration of trying to pay off debt and make ends meet on a limited salary— with his income substantially smaller than hers, even with the irregularity of her paychecks—Howard turned on Karen and blamed her for their predicament. Pooling their money made Howard fully aware of their lack of discretionary income and his role as money manager essentially made their current situation his personal problem to solve.

On the positive side, Howard is fully engaged in the couple's financial issues—Karen does not bear the full weight of this knowledge alone. Once ready and willing to make fairly large expenditures paid for with Karen's money, Howard no longer suggests big purchases or assumes that Karen will pay for everything. The downside risk, of course, is a shared frustration that permeates the household, as Howard stays in a low-paying job and the realities of small business growth curtail Karen's earning power.

Shared information and shared responsibility worked together to help Karen and Howard put a series of house rules in place for curbing their spending and beginning a minimal savings plan. "I know that if we are going to have any kind of retirement, I have got to jack this' business up to the next level so that we will have the money to enjoy," Karen said. "We started late to allocate our resources and it's not adequate. But at least we started."

2. Separate accounts

A whopping 39 percent of the couples I interviewed have no joint accounts at all—they each maintain a checking account and one spouse (typically the wife) pays the household bills from her account, receiving a monthly check from her husband for his "half."

Does this happen because these spouses don't feel they can trust each other with joint funds? Studies of household financial arrangements often note that couples who do not combine funds expect their marriages to fail and keep their money separate in anticipation of this.[11] Sociology researcher Carole B. Burgoyne offered another explanation: Women who earn a substantial income may decide to maintain their own accounts so that their contribution to the family remains highly visible to their husbands. While many marriage counselors recommend pooling money in joint accounts to achieve a psychological sense of "our money," these women draw a careful line between "his" and "mine," making sure that their husbands know whose contribution pays the bills.[12]

Marta, a forty-two-year-old Dallas plastic surgeon with an income more than ten times that of Jack, her freelance cartoonist husband, wouldn't dream of relinquishing a penny of her financial responsibility.

"We have separate bank accounts," she said. "All of our money is separate. Jack pays his bills and I pay mine. But I pay a lot of our joint expenses."

Marta bristled almost immediately when I began to ask about money. "In theory, we plan our investments together," she said, "But in reality I'm the only one who has any money to invest, so I make the decisions."

In her third year of marriage to Jack, she's still working against the sense that he's taking advantage of her. "We had an early expectation that everything would be equal and shared and it has been a sign of maturity for us both that we now feel that everything doesn't have to be exactly equal," she said. "I don't think either one of us feels right admitting out loud that I am supporting him, which is why I don't feel comfortable."

Jack does his best to make a contribution to their household by buying groceries and paying other household expenses, but his income from drawing single-frame cartoons for publications from *Funny Times* to *The New Yorker* is sporadic and often insubstantial. The bulk of the household expenses falls to Marta, especially because they've chosen an expensive house in a North Dallas neighborhood that is well beyond Jack's means. It's impossible for him to contribute an equal share to Marta's in paying the mortgage, furnishing their home or maintaining their active lifestyle.

"He will give me a check every month—he'll give me money to go toward the household expenses, because I am paying the whole mortgage. I didn't want to set a monthly amount, because I didn't want to be upset if he didn't come up with that much. So it's a little game I play.

"When he's making those financial contributions, I feel that things are pretty equal." She paused, then added, "As equal as they need to be."

Marta finds herself trapped between her desire to share her life with Jack and the reality of her financial arrangement with him. In her early adult life, before she finished medical school, she fell into relationships with men who outearned her—powerful personalities with whom she felt more competition than affection. Later, as her income grew, she moved on to relationships with the kinds of men who appealed to her suppressed love of art and culture. "Before Jack, I had been involved with other people who were artists and writers," she said, "and some of them just sort of lived in this fantasy world, like 'I am an artist and because of that I can't get a regular job.' So they let me support them."

When she met Jack, Marta discovered a new kind of relationship. "Jack isn't like those other men. Sometimes he's out of work for weeks at a time and when I'm in a bad mood his reasons sound like lame excuses. However, it's not permanent and I know he eventually is going to get work. He'll tell me every few days about jobs that he's going to get and things that he's trying, so I know he's not unaware. He's even told me that he knows his unemployment pushes my buttons and that he's very sorry when he's out of work." She paused, considered her words and then went on. "Maybe I think he should try a little harder."

With an income so much higher than her husband's and an underlying assumption that artists can't handle money well, Marta made the choice to take charge of all of their financial affairs and manage them alone. "Jack doesn't even know what I make," she said. "When we bought this house, I suggested that it would be nice to put both our names on the mortgage. Frankly, I was so tired of being the one who always had to be responsible for all the monetary debts, I thought it would be refreshing to share. He said, 'No, I can't, I have major credit problems.' These turned out to be bad credit card debts."

Wanting very much to have this marriage work better than her previous relationships, Marta shared her frustration with Jack. "I told him that I'd been in a number of relationships with people who basically just stopped working after a while and I felt exploited. They were taking advantage of me financially and eventually not giving me other things that are important in a relationship."

Jack tried to ease Marta's discomfort by handing over his checks to her when they arrived from magazines and publishers who bought his work. "In a way I appreciated the gesture," Marta said, "but I didn't appreciate being made the banker. He would sign over his checks to me and then would ask for spending money. I said, 'You know, this really *does* push my buttons. I have been in other relationships where people have made me play banker and put me into this mommy role.' I suggested that he just take his checks, deposit them and write me a check for an appropriate amount, leaving himself enough for spending money."

Jack did as Marta asked, but his low income and the irregularity of its arrival often left him broke after he provided her with his share of the household expenses. Marta responded by creating more rules for the use of his money. "I told Jack that there would come times when he would have a slow month and would have to ask me for money. I'd feel uncomfortable with that. So I suggested, 'How about we cut a limit? Like, just give me no more than $500 or $600 a month. That's plenty, because you're paying for the groceries. We eat at home every night and groceries are not cheap.' Then I suggested that he start banking his money, until he had—say, a thousand dollars. Then he could write me a check for the extra over the thousand and try to always keep a thousand dollars in the bank."

The unasked question here is obvious: With Marta making more than ten times Jack's income, why did she expect him to contribute to household expenses at all—let alone equally? Why not live on her very substantial paychecks and save Jack's money or use it for other things, like entertainment or special purchases?

Marta is one of the wives I interviewed who feels she is in a bind, in which financial reality conflicts with her need to be an equal partner in a relationship. If the situation were reversed, Jack might simply accept the breadwinner responsibility as an expected part of his husband role. However, Marta and wives with similar feelings often struggle with their positions of financial superiority, because they are contrary to their ultimate goal: equality with their husbands on all levels.

While many of these women told me that they could not imagine being happy with men whose incomes were higher than theirs, they have traveled to the opposite end of that spectrum and found this arrangement wanting as well. They experience a sort of reverse competition, through which they expect their husbands to strive for financial equality and carry their own weight in the household. But often by design, they have chosen men who cannot possibly match their own earning potentials.

The complexities of Marta's and Jack's conflict over household finances are closely linked to the role Marta has chosen for herself—breadwinner, banker and eventually (in her own words) surrogate mother. While she battles against accepting this role, she simultaneously embraces it, creating a network of pitfalls for her husband and making it nearly impossible for him to respond in constructive ways.

Couples like Marta and Jack face a double quandary in achieving comfort levels within their relationships. Not only does Jack display discomfort with his lower-earning position, his discomfort stems directly from Marta's own lack of satisfaction with the arrangement she has created. Distrustful and concerned that her husband could be taking advantage of her, Marta braces up her financial relationship with Jack as if shielding herself from a storm looming on the horizon.

Marta made her uneasiness even clearer in her refusal to allow me to interview Jack. "Oh, he's so shy, he would be so embarrassed if he knew I was even talking about this," she told me. "I don't even want you to ask him if he'd be willing; he'd just be mortified."

I heard this assessment of husbands from only a small number of the wives I interviewed. However, as my research progressed, I saw a pattern emerge: The wives who were the most protective, mothering and dominating in the relationship were the wives who *absolutely refused* to allow me to approach their husbands for interviews. The majority of these wives sounded like Marta, women who fought against their own resentment of their breadwinning roles, their husbands' comparative lack of earning power and the additional stress these wives bear because of their breadwinner status.

Not all these couples having this problem maintain separate finances. Conversely, not all the couples who maintained separate checking and savings accounts are this unbalanced in the way they share financial power between husband and wife. However, separate accounts can lead to secrecy, mistrust and awkwardness, as each spouse determines his or her own level of financial disclosure within the total relationship.

3. The three-account system

Some couples I interviewed choose a system of three checking accounts: a joint account from which they pay household bills and separate, no-questions-asked checking accounts for each spouse. This is particularly prevalent among two-income couples. Each spouse deposits a specified monthly amount into the joint checking account, which is managed by the spouse with the higher interest in doing so and the greater competence with financial matters.

Most of these couples also maintain separate credit card accounts for each spouse, and each is responsible for his or her own credit payments. If both spouses own cars, the monthly payments might also come from the separate checking accounts, leaving the joint account to pay the mortgage, utilities, telephone, maintenance and repair bills.

Adding another level of complexity to this kind of money management process, these couples also may maintain separate savings accounts, retirement accounts and investments. Even with separate accounts, however, saved money may be managed by just one spouse—again, the one with the higher level of competence in investing or the one with the higher motivation to do the necessary research to see the family's money grow. In many couples electing such a system, one spouse pays the monthly bills from the joint checking account while the other maintains the investment responsibility. This remarkably equitable partnership yields high results and considerable satisfaction for both partners.

"I would probably be lost if I had to pay the bills," said Jennifer, the executive director of a large, non-profit, cultural organization in Connecticut. Jennifer's income exceeds $100,000 per year, while her husband, Marc, earns about $25,000 a year building custom furniture for a select group of clients in his home workshop. "Marc handles the checking account and the household bills. But I'm the money manager and the financial planner," she continued. "Early on, Marc made fun of me, really, in terms of things I did with financial plans and management, but now he feels differently."

Jennifer's ability to see the bigger picture made her the logical spouse to manage the couple's savings. She squirreled away large sums in her own name for the two of them and their four children, even before she reached a substantial income level. "I felt for a very long time that I wanted my daughters to go to the best schools," she said. "I didn't know for sure how I was going to pay for it, so I have been scrounging money every chance I get. I took fifty dollars a paycheck and put it into a separate account. Marc used to think it was silly and that we should spend the money. But now, he's grateful."

Marc understands the day-to-day running of the household and the cash outflow that requires. His home-based business gives him more exposure to the rhythms of his children's lives and the immediate needs of the family. "It's funny," Marc admitted, "but with all the budgeting and managing Jennifer does at work and all the mutual fund business, I just don't trust her with the joint checkbook. So I pay the bills and keep track of that. It seems to work pretty well."

Between Marc's daily management of their cash flow and Jennifer's constant attention to their savings, this couple can live entirely on Jennifer's income and save all of Marc's earnings. "I feel very good about doing what we are doing," Jennifer said.

"If something is being done well, then why worry about it?" Marc concurred. "When we built our house eleven years ago and when we started talking about what we were going to do with it, Jennifer had a lot of ideas. I remember that the one thing I wanted was an automatic garage door opener. The point is, the money was there for what we wanted. Jennifer decides what she wants to do with it—handling the investments and mutual funds. It works for both of us."

Recommendations: Managing Money When the Wife Makes More

1. The more money-savvy spouse should be the money manager.

It's just common sense that the spouse who is better at handling money should be the one to keep the checkbook balanced and make sure the bills get paid. If the thought of tracking day-to-day expenditures drives you nearly to tears, your breadwinning status is no reason to saddle yourself with money management responsibilities. Judge your skills with a checkbook honestly and be prepared to relinquish the task if your partner is more capable of taking care of it. Conversely, if your partner's skill with family cash threatens to ruin your credit rating, don't try to spare the person's ego—just take over.

2. Both spouses need working knowledge of the household finances.

Even if you're not the family money manager, you need to know where your money is, where it's going and how much you have to spend. Work with your partner to build a plan and keep tabs on the plan on a monthly basis. Like Donna and Gene, share the information and make decisions together about how much to spend and save.

If the wife manages the money, she should share numbers with her husband—even if she maintains all separate accounts from his. Make certain he understands how much money you have and how much you don't have. The more he knows about available income, the more likely he will be to help you control spending when necessary— and increase your "fun money" when it's appropriate. He may become just the advocate you need for loosening the purse strings when it's time for a vacation, a special purchase or a night out.

3. Set family goals.

In any business, there are two basic ways of increasing cash flow: Spend less, make more. In a family, the same general rules apply. When the house needs painting or you'd like to move your child into a private school system, you need additional cash—and your spouse is part of that picture.

Even if the husband has no income, he plays a critical role in the family's overall financial success. Share the household challenges with him and set goals together for cutting back spending, finding new sources of income or saving more money. Make him a willing and important participant in the process—both to move you closer to your goals and to make yourself more comfortable as the breadwinner. When both spouses are involved in reaching a goal, the breadwinner spouse is no longer trying to sustain the family alone.

4. Be honest about the breadwinner's income.

Little good comes from keeping the facts of the wife's higher income a secret. Marta noted that Jack has no idea what she makes—although he is certainly aware that their affluent lifestyle comes from her paycheck and not his. Worse, Marta shelters Jack from financial decision-making, only letting him know that she feels stress about her breadwinning status. If Jack and Marta lowered their guard and had a candid discussion about money—how much comes in and how much goes out—they could work together to ease Marta's discomfort.

The less one partner knows about the other's income and financial goals, the more likely it is that the spouse earning less will react in one of two ways:

- The husband may see his wife as a constant source of discretionary cash. If he doesn't know that his wife wants to save money for a special purchase or for retirement, he may believe that the wife's money is there to spend, in unlimited supply.
- The husband may try to control the household spending based on his own income, rather than on combined funds. The wife may find herself struggling with him over purchases she's made with her own money, because he doesn't realize how much discretionary income the wife may have available.

If you are a breadwinner wife and you haven't shared the truth about your income with your husband, you need to address the reasons for this. What do you fear will come of this discussion? Will he be shocked, even though you've clearly been paying the lion's share of the household bills for an extended period of time? Will he be angry with you for earning a larger income than he does? Will he be embarrassed by his lesser earning power? Do you believe his knowledge of your income will damage your relationship?

If these are the things you fear, you are better off knowing sooner rather than later if your earning potential is threatening or humiliating to your husband. The longer you try to mask this issue, the longer you may be hiding from something critically important in your relationship.

5. Don't make the spouse earning less beg.
Asking for money is humiliating, especially for adults. Even young children have the opportunity to earn money through allowances and payment for household chores; your low-earning or non-earning spouse should not be forced to ask you for spending money. Create a way for your partner to access cash when he needs it—from your joint account, a separate personal account with an ATM card, an accessible cash reserve or a weekly or monthly check for an amount that amply covers his needs. Moreover, don't set up long lists of rules for how he spends the money. This is especially important if he is an at-home dad or is otherwise not working outside of the home—don't make him a prisoner of his situation. He will use the money for household expenditures, but he also needs money he can use for himself.

6. Live below your means.
Don't trap yourself in a situation in which your spouse cannot possibly make a significant contribution. Think carefully before you buy the biggest house on the block or live on every dollar from the breadwinner wife's paycheck. The happiest couples with whom I spoke were those who worked toward family financial independence, invested a lot of their money and took the financial burden off the higher-earning wife. The wife should give herself the option of taking time off, leaving the job or taking advantage of another opportunity if she so chooses—an exorbitant monthly "nut" of mortgage, credit card bills and maintenance payments will force the breadwinner wife to maintain her higher income and will limit life choices and satisfaction for both of you.

CHAPTER 7

BUYING, GOING, DOING
The Emotional Tax on Luxury Spending

Carrie and Vern had just returned from a vacation in the Florida Keys and her voice tightened as she described the experience. Not for the first time in their five-year marriage, Vern had neglected to bring much cash with him for the trip—so at every meal, every hotel and every attraction, he stepped back and waited for Carrie to pay the bill.

Carrie's position as a radiologist with a major Chicago hospital provides her with an income at least five times that of Vern, who manages an auto body shop. "Each time we go on vacation, I pay for the whole thing. Given the fact that I do make so much more money than he does, it seems reasonable that I pay for the airfare and hotels. However, it secretly bothers me a lot that he doesn't take the initiative to make sure he has spending money."

Vern earns a steady income and contributes to the household budget, but when it comes to luxury spending, he leaves the decisions— and the dollars—to Carrie. "I have been very careful to avoid this in my previous relationships, but I seem now to have fallen into a repeating pattern," Carrie groaned. "It's like he's a teenager and I'm the parent. Part of it is the income difference and part of it is that we're living a different lifestyle from his previous experiences. He just doesn't have the practical experience of figuring that if we're going on vacation, we will be eating in restaurants and that means X number of meals a day and X number of dollars per person and money for souvenirs, and so on. He's just not used to considering things like that."

As much as this repeated phenomenon bothered Carrie, she could not bring herself to confront Vern head-on about it. "He is very sensitive and I don't want to make him feel badly," she said. "But some day, I will find the right time to gently suggest that it would make me feel better if he would plan ahead. If I didn't get traveler's checks for both of us, he'd have no money at all. That would be a big problem."

Carrie and Vern have entered what I call the "Assumption Zone."

For couples in which the wife makes more, the logistics of getting the household bills paid pose little challenge when compared to the conflicts that arise over discretionary spending. A breadwinning wife can be perfectly comfortable writing the big checks for mortgage, groceries, utilities and any number of additional expenses, but she may bristle when she has to pay for dinner out with friends or plane tickets to the Caribbean. When it comes to spending money for her husband's luxuries, she may face a series of unexpected negative emotions: anger, resentment and a strong sense that she's being taken for granted.

This is the Assumption Zone, in which the husband no longer appears to notice or appreciate his wife's constant cash output for expenditures outside of the household budget.

When couples enter the Assumption Zone, the wife finds herself forever pulling out cash or credit card to pay for dinner, small purchases, gifts, vacations or anything else that goes beyond the monthly amount her husband contributes to the household bills. In the Assumption Zone, the husband has ceased to acknowledge his wife's above-and-beyond contribution and seems oblivious to the fact that there are opportunities for him to contribute as well. Some wives report that their husbands even forget to bring their wallets or carry cash when they travel or go out to dinner.

How did these couples get into the Assumption Zone?

In chapter 5, we discussed the similarities between husbands who are comfortable with their wives significantly outearning them. Generally, these are men who do not define their personal successes according to the size of their paychecks—to many of them, money is simply a tool, not a goal. These men understand that pleasant lifestyles are purchased with money, but the wherewithal of actual dollars and cents payments are not foremost in their minds.

This is not to say that these men are fools who don't understand that the piper must be paid at the end of the tune. They understand the need for payment—and they know that their breadwinning wives will cover the tabs.

How do they know this? *Because the breadwinner wives do it.* Every time the check comes, even if the wives wait to see if their husbands will contribute, they eventually are first to go for their wallets. If it upsets the wives, chances are they keep this to themselves, for fear of beginning discussions that inevitably lead to fights about money. The wives are not eager to tell their husbands, whose incomes are significantly lower than theirs, that it's time the husbands started picking up the check at dinner once in a while. The wives may have watched the weekly spending money dwindle alarmingly between paychecks while they pay all the entertainment or other ancillary costs for both partners—and then cringed when their husbands purchased something new for themselves with the money they're *not* spending on nights out and vacations.

It is the countless dinners wives pay for in full, the gifts that are not reciprocated or the vacations filled with resentment that cause breadwinning wives and their husbands to clash. After all, in the dating phase, even in the ultra-modern 1990s and 2000s, most of the wives enjoyed their husbands-to-be picking up the tab for treats, special occasions, evenings out and gifts. In their marriages, however, the lion's share of the money comes from the wives—and many of these husbands simply can't afford to do the things that their wives can do with their greater income.

So what's a woman to do? Stay home and never go out to dinner unless her husband can pay? Plan a weekend at a nearby park instead of a week in Paris? Never give her husband that set of golf clubs or the expensive watch he's had his eye on, because he can't possibly give her a gift of equal value? Sounds like dry, dull lives for women who work hard for their money and deserve to enjoy it.

On the contrary, the social and recreational lives of wives who make more should indeed fulfill their dreams of fun, whatever the size of their family budgets. Breadwinner wives need to examine and adjust both their own *and* their husbands' perceptions of spending, so that they share the benefits of their breadwinning status as generously as they share the rest of their lives with their husbands.

"Making more" doesn't always mean high incomes

Not all breadwinning wives are high earning women with management jobs. In fact, the Bureau of Labor Statistics' Current Population Survey states that in 1998, nearly 37 percent of all women who outearned their husbands made less than $25,000 annually.[1] With the nation's poverty guidelines for that year set at $16,450 for a family of four,[2] these women carry a considerable load in supporting a husband and children at this income level.

Vacations, expensive gifts or frequent nights out can strip the household budget, making these luxuries impossible to afford even in the best of circumstances. For breadwinning wives who are in the nation's lower earning brackets, the realities of daily life severely limit the family's discretionary spending. If this is the case, the wife who supports her family knows that spending the household money on a vacation, gifts or a restaurant meal may be out of the question.

It's understandable that a wife who is supporting her family either involuntarily or due to unfortunate circumstance can feel anger and deprivation as weeks, months or years pass without an improvement in the family's income status.

These wives may find that the very definition of luxury purchases changes when money is tight. In my days as a beginning journalist in the early 1980s, when I earned $200 a week (taking home about $130) at a small, upstate New York magazine, "luxury spending" meant having enough extra cash to replace over-laundered underwear or to buy a new lipstick. With adversity comes an appreciation of simpler things, because the larger extravagances are unobtainable.

However, almost all couples face days when the wives must make decisions about spending money outside of the household budgets on items or occasions that are important to them, even though their husbands cannot possibly afford them. How do such wives reconcile their needs for occasional luxuries with the realities of their husbands' low-earning or non-earning statuses? What contributions should these wives expect from their husbands and how should they make the decision to spend their own money?

Let's look at three common areas of discretionary spending: vacations, gifts to one another and dining out.

Vacation Aggravation
"Should we take a vacation that my husband can't afford?"

I talked with wives who simply didn't plan vacations, because their husbands couldn't pick up the tabs. Worse, I talked with wives who took their husbands on the expensive vacations they both craved, then spent the entire trip feeling resentful, because their husbands could not split the cost with them.

By definition, all breadwinning wives are married to men who make less money than they do. Many of them have made this choice deliberately, marrying a man whose company they enjoy regardless of his income, with whom they share common goals, outlooks and interests. Still others actively place their husbands in the non-income position, supporting him financially while he takes care of the children, recovers from an illness or starts a new business.

Why, then, are these wives sometimes stunned when it comes time for vacation and their husbands can't pay? Why would they suddenly expect their husbands to come across with money they cannot or do not earn?

In the quest for equal footing with their husbands, breadwinner wives often turn back to them to match newfound equality with commitments of time, effort...or cash. In later chapters, we'll discuss how this manifests itself in areas such as housework and child care, two areas in which men had never been expected to shoulder equal shares of the burden before now.

When it comes to luxury purchases like vacations, some breadwinner wives look to recapture the romance of their pre-married states, when men knew they were supposed to pay and often did. These wives want their vacations to be special treats, gifts that come without concerns about cost.

The fact is that vacations cost money—money the husbands of breadwinner wives simply may not have. So it's up to the breadwinning wives to get comfortable with whatever their husbands can bring to the discretionary spending pot and enjoy the benefits of combined resources, however unbalanced.

Here are some questions breadwinner wives should ask themselves when considering vacation options.

Do I want to take this vacation with my husband? Your higher earning status may give you the opportunity to choose, plan and enjoy a vacation with the man you married. What a wonderful position for you! You and your husband can afford to take this vacation, because you work hard and earn a good income.

Do you want to take a great vacation with your best friend—and is that best friend your husband? Are you excited about the idea of sharing a week or longer doing things you enjoy together, just the two of you, or with your children? If so, keep this thought foremost in your mind as you plan your trip. This is one of the rewards of your position as breadwinner. It's not important who *pays* for the vacation; what's important is that you can *have* the vacation.

Imagine that the tables are turned and you are the lower-earning spouse while your husband makes the larger income. When it came time to plan a family vacation, do you believe that your husband would feel resentful or taken advantage of if he were expected to pay for the entire trip? Chances are he would accept this as part of his breadwinning role. Now you are the breadwinner; this is part of your role as well. Take your husband and family on vacation and enjoy the opportunity to do so.

What would make this vacation feel more equitable for both of us? If you're picking up the entire tab for your trip, what will make you feel that your husband was an appreciative and equal participant? Talk about this with him in advance and agree on a contribution from him that matches his ability and income.

Perhaps he could take the children for a day (not the whole week—he deserves a vacation, too) while you shop or enjoy a tour on your own. You could agree that he buy breakfast every morning or dinner every night, while you pay for transportation, hotels and other meals. Maybe he's in charge of the driving, which can be a source of considerable stress on a long vacation.

Whatever his contribution, talk it over objectively before you go and gain his commitment. A clear understanding of your needs will make it much easier for your husband to comply.

How much does it bother you to spend your money on a vacation and why? Is there another major expenditure lurking in the background—a house purchase, college tuition, a car or some much-needed repairs? Your discomfort with spending money on a vacation may be linked to the need to spend money elsewhere, rather than to your husband's lack of discretionary funds.

No matter what kind of vacation you take, you won't enjoy it if you spend the time worrying about making ends meet when you get home. Your concerns about taking on debt or maintaining financial stability can torment you—and turn you against your husband as you zero in on his smaller contribution to the household as the source of all your problems.

Be honest with yourself and with your family about your ability to go on the vacation you want. If you'd love to spend two weeks in Cape May, but really need to have the house painted, so be it. *All* families must make choices about how and when to spend money on luxury items like vacations. Guide this decision within your family by sharing financial information with your husband and making it clear when it is an either-or choice or when the family needs to save money to cover expenses and must forgo a vacation.

By the same token, if you *can* afford both the big expenditure and the vacation, but you are still uncomfortable, search in earnest for the source of this discomfort. Perhaps you take an ultra conservative approach to all spending or perhaps you are unaccustomed to indulging yourself when it costs money. Our own attitudes about money can color our judgment when it comes to bridging the gap between necessities and luxuries—your unwillingness to take this leap may come from influences that embedded themselves long before you met your husband.

Of course, your unwilling attitude may come directly from your husband. Your reluctance to plan and pay for a vacation may reflect a larger issue. Many wives who make more are in the Assumption Zone, experiencing the disquieting sense that their husbands have come to expect them to pay for everything. In many cases, the men no longer offer to pay—they even wander away when it's time to check out at the hotel or pay the bill at a restaurant.

If you have entered the Assumption Zone and your husband has the means to contribute to the cost of your vacation, it's up to you to break the cycle. Begin by planning your vacation together with your husband, choosing a destination, your means of transportation, the activities and attractions you will enjoy and your accommodations.

Add up the projected costs and discuss them with your husband. Say to him, "I can pay for this portion of this trip, up to this amount. What can you contribute?" Do not ask him if he'd *like* to contribute to the vacation; make it clear from the beginning that he is *expected* to pay for some portion.

Be realistic in your expectations about his financial responsibility. Remember that your husband may also be in the Assumption Zone. If so, he is likely to balk at your question at first, startled out of his assumption that you will pay for the entire trip. He has become unaccustomed to spending money on trips, dinners out and other entertainment, so he will need to adjust the way he views such expenditures.

Do not expect him to pay half, unless your incomes are closely comparable. However, get his commitment to pay for specific activities or to contribute a set amount toward the total package. Tell him when you need to make deposits, pay for the trip or pay off the credit card you've used to reserve in advance. Be pleasant but firm in setting a deadline for his share.

A vacation should be a happy occasion, not a battleground. Treat this negotiation between you as a business transaction, not as a statement on the quality and strength of your relationship. The more you share with your husband about your family finances and your eventual use of discretionary income, the easier it will be to engage his assistance in paying for the things that make marriage fun.

Here are some questions breadwinner wives and their husbands should ask together when planning a vacation.

Can we save for this together? Legends abound about couples who drop their change into jars every night and then take anniversary cruises purchased by their quarters and dimes. There's no question that saving together for a special trip or purchase creates dual ownership—both financially and emotionally. Agree on a destination well in advance, determine the cost of the trip and then set a savings goal for the family. Establish a simple, accessible method of saving, so that you and your husband can make deposits quickly when cash is available. When you reach your goal, schedule the trip. Everyone can contribute—even older children, if they will be joining you—and everyone can enjoy the accomplishment of "earning" the trip, removing the onus of paying for the entire trip yourself.

Can we buy in advance? Deciding in advance how much will be spent and then heeding credit card receipts or the cashing of travelers' checks can help you and your spouse stay constantly aware of the money you're spending while on vacation. Purchasing a package in advance that includes everything—travel, accommodations, food, even gratuities—also imposes predestined limits. Cruises and specialty group tours offer these packages, as do resorts like Disney World and Club Med. Your vacation is paid for well before you go, so you're not reminded at every meal or tourist attraction of the bills you're accumulating—and you can control additional on-site spending as your comfort level dictates.

Packages range in price from economical to luxurious; you may still spend a pretty penny when you choose the package that matches your vacation fantasies. However, you'll spend it weeks or months before you actually take off—and you'll be more certain to actually take the trip, since it's already paid for, instead of canceling to meet looming work commitments or giving in to your general discomfort about spending more than you can afford.

Giving Without Receiving

"I can give my husband extravagant gifts, but he can't possibly reciprocate. Should I do it anyway? What should I expect from him?"

A Timex or a Rolex? Wearever or Calphalon? A Sears cordless drill or a Delta Unisaw table saw? Wives face such choices every time a birthday, anniversary or December holiday approaches, as they consider their options in giving their husbands their hearts' desires.

Breadwinner wives have their own money and they have the opportunity to surprise and delight their husbands with higher-cost

gifts—items the men often cannot buy for themselves. But such gift giving can be fraught with new perils, as the wives realize that their gifts
are unlikely to be reciprocated without considerable struggle on their
husbands' parts.

Many of the husbands of breadwinning wives are men to whom
money and prestige are neither important nor motivating, so they are
not likely to be impressed by expensive gifts of jewelry, timepieces or
clothing. However, nearly everyone longs for a particular item he or she
might enjoy for recreation, hobby or work: the top-of-the-line power
tool, the ultimate single-lens-reflex camera, the fastest computer, the
professional-grade golf clubs or the finest chef's edition guaranteed-for-
life cookware.

Breadwinner wives sometimes are in positions to buy their husbands' dream gifts, but they hesitate. Probably he will never be able to
buy her the gift of her dreams, whatever it may be. Will he be embarrassed if she goes ahead and makes the expensive purchase for him?
Worse, will the breadwinner wife resent the fact that he is unlikely to
do the same for her?

Even in the twenty-first century, women are led to believe that
men should be the great romantic gift-givers while the women should
be the delighted recipients. Tradition dictates that when a man proposes marriage, he is expected to present his fiancée with a fabulously
expensive engagement ring. Sumptuous television commercials for diamonds make reference to the "two months' salary rule," while encouraging men to "tell her you'd marry her all over again" with costly
anniversary jewelry. High-end car commercials show us a wife's delight
when her husband presents her with her very own Lexus. Flowers,
chocolates, even lingerie are all meant as romantic, sometimes costly
demonstrations of a husband or boyfriend's love for the woman in his
life.

Syndicated *Washington Post* columnist Michelle Singletary took
on this issue in a February 2001 article on Valentine's Day spending.
She quoted a survey recently completed by the International Mass
Retail Association (IMRA), which discovered that men, on average,
would spend $122 on gifts for their wives or significant others for the
approaching Valentine's Day, while women expected to spend approximately $50. "The survey of about 1,000 consumers showed that men
buy fancier cards and spend more because women's expectations are
higher," Singletary observed.[3]

Well...not exactly, said Edie Clark, IMRA spokeswoman, in a
personal interview. "Valentine's Day appears to be a holiday on which

men want to make a difference," she said. "I don't know that it's so much about women's expectations. It's more that men choose this day to make a statement. This is the day men 'fess up and say that yes, they are romantic."

Sometimes, even the lowest-earning men want to demonstrate their love to their wives with major gifts—and they may go to considerable lengths to do this. "Men think more about keepsakes than women may," Clark noted. "So they may lean toward a piece of jewelry or something the woman will keep for a long time."

One year, on my birthday, I was the delighted recipient of a Movado watch I'd admired in jewelry stores for several years. Over the course of months, Nic had put money aside to make the purchase and did so—and now, nine years later, I still wear the watch every day. Did I expect this gift? Certainly not—which made it all the more precious when it appeared.

The critical question, then, is not about what breadwinning wives deserve from their husbands, but what these wives *expect*.

Most of the wives I interviewed were already in the breadwinning position on their wedding days and many others could see themselves taking over that responsibility in the space of a few months or a few years after the wedding. These women knew from the beginning that they would outearn their husbands, perhaps for the entire duration of their marriages.

When we marry men who will always make less money than we do, are we looking for high-priced gifts from them? Do we expect them to use their earnings to buy presents for us—or do we want to see those dollars put toward household expenses and discretionary purchases we can both enjoy together?

Not a single wife I interviewed spoke of receiving high-ticket gifts from her husband. In fact, not a single breadwinning wife expressed an expectation that her husband would come up with diamonds, furs or any other luxury gift for them. However, many *single* women with high incomes brought up this issue as we discussed my research findings—women who are used to spending their money on luxury items for themselves.

If you are a single woman reading this book to see if you would be happy in the breadwinning role, I say this: If jewelry and other expensive gifts from your husband are critical to your happiness, *do not* marry a man who makes less than you do. Not only are you unlikely to receive such gifts, you will condemn yourself to a life of resentment, because your husband does not have the means to please you.

The other side of this coin, of course, is that as breadwinning wives, many of us do indeed have the means to please our husbands with expensive gifts. Should we do so? Do we break some steadfast rules of the universe when we spend two, three or ten times as much on gifts as our husbands will spend on us?

Before you click a Web site's "check out" button or scan your debit card at a department store for that high-priced gift, there are some important questions you should ask yourself. Answering them honestly may help clarify your feelings.

What is your motive? Are you buying this gift because you know your husband will love it and you can't wait to see the look on his face when he opens it? Then do it, by all means. But if you have any other motivation besides this, think again before spending the money. Like so many of the emotional aspects of marriage, gifts can come with all kinds of additional baggage.

Sometimes we give in hopes of dropping a colossal, expensive hint to our husbands that they should appreciate us more, or should attempt to match the value and quality of the gift with a reciprocal purchase. Breadwinning wives whose husbands earn substantially less than they do need to discard this strategy altogether. These husbands are in no position to make such purchases. More important, if these husbands actually spent their money on such extravagances instead of contributing to the household, most breadwinning wives would feel more discomfort than delight. As I said to my husband when we decided to marry, "If you've got two months' salary to spend, don't you dare buy a diamond. Save it for the down payment on a house."

Some breadwinner wives may buy expensive gifts for reasons that taint the pleasure of receiving the gifts. "If you're giving me a gift because you want to point out to me that you make more money than I do, or because you want me to go out and make more, then just tell me," one husband noted. "Don't waste your money trying to make me feel inadequate or unworthy."

How will your husband feel about the gift? Even if your motives are absolutely pure, you can run the risk of emphasizing the income gap between yourself and your husband if your gift is particularly extravagant or if it comes at an inappropriate time.

Pay attention to the dynamic between you and your husband when you consider a large gift. If this is a time when your husband is struggling with his lower income position, a big surprise gift from you may only make him feel worse. Furthermore, a large gift given as an apology after an argument or as a thinly veiled bribe in exchange for some behavior you want from him—more participation in housework, for example—can do you both more harm than good.

Think carefully about the gift you're giving and the timing of its presentation. You know the signs of tension in your own marriage—if you see them, you may want to consider a lower-level gift for the time being.

In addition, hold off on giving your husband a big gift on a holiday like Christmas, Hanukkah or Valentine's Day, when he will have a gift for you as well. Don't dwarf his gift to you with a more lavish present for him. Do your best to match your gift to the level of spending he can afford for you, so that you can both enjoy giving and receiving on equal footing.

Must it be a surprise? Your husband's birthday is coming up and you've seen him admiring an $800 pair of binoculars in the optics catalog. However you're worried that such a gift from you might trigger unexpected conflicts within your relationship.

Why not ask him before you order? Even if the binoculars are not a total surprise on his birthday morning, he will appreciate them equally as much when he's using them in the field to examine a rare bird. Spare yourself days or weeks of worry and the potential for conflict where none should exist and check with your husband before making that extravagant purchase. A simple, "Honey, I see you looking at those Leica 8x42s in the catalog. Would you like them for your birthday?" will eliminate the ambiguities, while showing him that you're observing what interests him and you're thinking of doing something nice for him.

If he is adamant about not wanting you to spend this money now, *don't do it.* Choose a less expensive gift with which you can both feel comfortable.

Picking up the Tab for Evenings Out

"When we go out to dinner with another couple or a group, which of us should pay?"

Nights out with friends, family or business associates can bring an entirely different and unique anxiety to a breadwinning-wife couple. When the check comes, who reaches for it—husband or wife? How obvious should it be to others that the one holding the cash is you and not your husband?

The real question here, of course, is not about which of you pays the check. As soon as people outside of your relationship enter the picture, that picture changes—you see yourselves through the eyes of others who may not share your progressive views about the household structure.

At the same time, you may be firmly entrenched in the Assumption Zone. Whether it's dinner at a favorite restaurant, tickets to the theater or a concert, a night out clubbing or a hot dog at the ballpark, breadwinning wives can find themselves stuck in a rut, shelling out the nickels, dimes and dollars that taint their good times. Always the ones who provide the treats for their families, these wives begin to feel as if there are no treats in store for them unless they pay for their own.

How can breadwinning wives break this pattern and begin to share this responsibility with their husbands? And what about those nights out with others, when the matter of paying the check has the potential to become a political issue?

Here are some questions couples should ask themselves as they approach their entertainment choices.

What is your husband's source of cash? If your husband has steady employment and a regular paycheck, you're not being unreasonable in expecting him to pick up the check once in a while. But if your husband's work is seasonal, sporadic or still in the embryonic stages of a start-up business, he simply may not have the cash on hand to spend on entertainment.

If you are your husband's primary source of spending money, because he's an at-home dad or he's between jobs, the question is moot. He has no money of his own; it's up to you to pay if you're planning a night out.

It seems like an obvious point, but I talked with wives whose income exceeded their husbands' tenfold, and wives whose husbands did not work outside the home—and they were still annoyed when these men didn't come across with money for movie tickets or dinner with friends. Have realistic expectations of your husband's available disposable dollars. If he truly can't afford to pay and you want to go out, use your own money.

Who are your dinner companions and how important are their opinions? The chances are good that your closest friends know of your situation and would hardly take notice of which spouse contributes to the dinner check. It's those outside your inner circle whose opinions could turn a pleasant evening into a political morass.

Research tells us that more than 40 percent of wives are in charge of household finances, while 75 percent say they have an equal voice in the way the household budget is spent.[4] So it's not an immediate statement about your breadwinning status if you are the one holding the cash or pulling out the credit card at the end of the evening—all this tells the casual observer is that it's your turn to pay or that you handle the family finances. Remember this before you jump to the nervous conclusion that your husband's friends will think he's a wimp if you pay for dinner.

However, if you're dining with your Uncle Sherman, who lives by Buck's Logic and already believes that your husband is a freeloader who should get himself a better job and support his wife like a proper man, the appearance of your credit card at the end of the meal is only going to fan the flames of indignation.

When it will cause embarrassment or conflict if you pick up the check or if you feel your financial situation is nobody else's business that evening, a little pre-planning can help you avoid unpleasantness.

- If your husband has no income of his own, get a credit card in his name for these occasions and other times when he needs ready cash. This gives you the option of saying, "Honey, could you take care of the check while I go to the ladies' room?" You will still pay the bill later when the credit card statement arrives, but you will avoid unnecessary discomfort at the dinner table.
- Give your husband cash or a credit card before you leave the house. He can pay the bill, so it's not an issue.
- If your husband can pay, decide in advance which of you will pay for dinner. Determine a spending limit if necessary, so that the final bill will be within your husband's budget as well as yours.

Is this the night you need to make a statement? Even with one in three married women in America outearning their husbands, most breadwinning wives remain snugly in the closet about their higher income status. Whom you tell and why is entirely up to you—but be prepared.

We all have our reasons for sharing details or acting in revealing manners about our marriages and our household structures with other people. Sometimes it's friendly commiseration with acquaintances, sometimes the information is important, sometimes we may be working to build new friendships and it's our turn for self-disclosure. Whatever the reason or the occasion, sharing such information or actions may not always produce the reaction we expect.

Before you assume the role of bill payer at the end of the evening, think about what reaction you're inviting. Are you prepared to engage in a discussion of the women's movement since 1963 and how women have left no room for men in the job market? Are you ready for the raised eyebrows in your husband's direction, silently implying that he's less of a man than he should be? Do you want to find yourself making excuses for your own success and your husband's lifestyle choice?

There are plenty of individuals who will find your situation intriguing, progressive, even daring. But there are plenty of others who will shake their heads and tsk-tsk at you, labeling you a castrating witch and your husband a loser. It's entirely up to you if this is the night you plan to duke it out with an acquaintance. Make the decision ahead of time, but arrange with your husband to have him pay if you'd rather avoid other people's misplaced judgment and advice.

Make no mistake! I am absolutely *not* advocating the "closet" position for breadwinning wives. In my heart, I would like to see us all take every opportunity to proclaim our success and show the world that our nontraditional marital configuration is not only viable, but natural and fulfilling for wife and husband alike. I would love to take every naysayer in the country to task, educating him or her on the merits of wives' breadwinning status, the importance of equal partnership in marriage and the struggles women have endured for generations to arrive at this advantageous position. I relish those moments when I can speak my mind on the tyranny of the 1950s household structure and the strengths that are possible when both husband and wife can choose what's best for the family as a whole over what society dictates as "correct."

However, not every meeting is a battlefield and not every dinner engagement requires this disruption. We all number among our acquaintances many members of the unenlightened, the unaware, the inconsiderate and the old-fashioned. In the simple interest of polite behavior, I recommend that you choose your battles and choose the people to whom you allow a glimpse of personal financial information about your marriage.

If you make the decision to pay for the evening yourself, don't take the bait if you become the target for barbs from wisecracking relatives or thoughtless acquaintances. When you swallow hard and pretend you didn't hear whatever jab your so-called friends hurled at you, you have the satisfaction of knowing that you made your point, which is that in the grand scheme of things, it doesn't matter which spouse pays. At the same time, you chose not to turn this evening into an inappropriate assessment session on your marital lifestyle. You've treated your breadwinning status as if it were commonplace and nothing to make a fuss over—as it should be, whether or not our society has come to understand and accept such a phenomenon as a viable alternative within the marriage structure. The harder we all work to normalize our place as breadwinning wives, the closer we come to true normality...and true acceptance within all of our social circles.

Recommendations: Recreational Spending

1. Be realistic. If your husband has no income or his earnings are a tiny fraction of your own, you are in charge of discretionary spending—because the family money is yours. Vacations, major purchases or big evenings out all will be bought with your dollars, so it's up to you to decide if you are comfortable spending that money.

If you resent the fact that your husband cannot contribute, there may be other factors at play. Take a hard look at your monetary situation, your relationship and your husband's other contributions to the household to find what's getting under your skin and solve that problem. Take this approach instead of depriving yourself of a purchase or vacation you would enjoy, simply because he can't pay for it.

2. Examine your motivations. Gifts should be given with love and joy, not with ulterior motives. Give a gift only when it gives you pleasure to do so and when your husband will enjoy receiving it—not because you want to prove a point, make a statement or persuade him to take some action.

3. Plan together. Whatever the large expenditure or the luxury purchase, set spending limits and plan your cash outlays with your husband. Make certain he understands how much money there is to spend—and what this spending impacts throughout the family budget. Make choices based on this shared understanding and then find ways for both of you to contribute to the goal: if not in money, then in time or activities that make the vacation or special night out fun for both of you.

4. Delight, without surprises. You'd like to buy your husband a pricey gift, but you're not certain he will appreciate the expenditure. Ask him before you do it! You'll eliminate your own anxiety while ensuring that your thoughtful gift won't strike an unexpected nerve.

5. Establish a comfort level. Decide in advance if you would be more comfortable if your husband paid the bill for dinner or if you would prefer to do so yourself. Then take the steps suggested earlier to supply your non-earning husband with cash or credit card if he is going to pay. In nearly every cultural pocket in American society, it's still considered impolite to talk openly about your own and others' personal income, so it's unlikely that you will be engaged in this conversation unless you provoke the discussion yourself—perhaps by pulling out your wallet at the end of the evening. Your home economic situation is your business; it's up to you whether you want to share it with others.

6. Break out of the Assumption Zone. If your husband can pay but never does and it rankles you every time you go to a movie or dine out, break the cycle. If he suggests dinner out, tell him you're short on cash and would like to split the tab with him. If you're going to a ball game, tell him you'll buy the snacks if he'll buy the tickets. Whenever possible, find ways to ease your husband back into the habit of participating by asking him directly to pay for some share of the fun. Over time, he will understand that you should not be the sole contributor to financing family leisure activities—and that you enjoy treats from him as much as he enjoys them from you.

CHAPTER 8

HOUSEWORK:
THE GREAT DIVIDE
Husbands and Wives
See Chores Through Different Eyes

I ambushed my husband, Nic, on the hallowed battleground of the kitchen to go to war over the subject of household chores one frozen Sunday evening in February.

The previous week's frenetic race at the advertising agency left me with flagging energy as I rushed to keep pace with incoming projects. With the economy booming that year, the agency enjoyed a period of "rich person's trouble," as my ex-boss used to say—the mixed blessing and curse of increased business coupled with ultra-low unemployment and tough hiring competition. My staff and I were well compensated, but desperately overworked. I'd put in seventy grueling hours of project work and supervision of my six-member staff over the previous six days, coming home every night to a stack of dirty dishes in the sink and a growing pile of laundry in the bedroom.

As luck would have it, that Friday, winter weather curtailed Nic's activities, so he spent a great deal of time around the house while I worked like a maniac at my office. Significantly, it had not occurred to him even once to take care of the chores accumulating around him. Or, to be fair, if it had occurred to him, he had not acted on the thought.

If this particular weekend had been unusual, I might have taken it in stride—but since I had become a supervisor and received the expanded responsibilities of managing other staff, this weekend was like every weekend. I had adopted what Arlie Hochschild called *The Second Shift* in her groundbreaking 1989 book of that name: the additional full

work day of housekeeping and child care many wives face when they
return home from their full-time day jobs.[1]

On Saturday morning my treadmill just continued to run, as I
rushed to finish errands I couldn't get to during the week—grocery shopping, dry cleaner, ATM machine—and attacked the week's worth of
dishes, picked up after my husband and began the first of seven loads of
bulky, cold-weather laundry. The word "attacked" here is no accident—
with every dish and every trip up and down the basement stairs I got
angrier. Why on earth should I have to spend my one free weekend day
cleaning, when Nic was home and not working every day? In our topsy-
turvy, nontraditional economic relationship, why was I still holding onto
this housewife role, especially when I was also the principal breadwinner?

Sunday evening arrived with more laundry and more cleaning
scheduled, when all I wanted to do was sit down with a cup of tea and
a good book.

Which, of course, was exactly what my husband was planning
as he stood over the teapot.

I was exhausted, crabby and dreading the following morning's
launch of another breakneck workweek. I turned to Nic. "It seems like
all I do on the weekends is dishes and laundry," I said to him. "It's just
never-ending."

Nic thought a moment, clearly pondering the situation to find a
helpful solution. "How about if you threw in a load of laundry every
night after work, so it wouldn't all pile up on the weekend?" he suggested

Honest to God, he thought he was helping me. Instead, he
threw gasoline on smoldering coals. And I exploded.

"Look, you're home all day every day and you never think for
one minute about doing a load of laundry or washing your own dishes?
It never even occurs to you? You think that's the right way to have a marriage? You think that's a partnership?" I yelled.

I continued yelling for a long time. In fact, the ensuing argument
lasted three days and was the first of many over the following several
months. I actually stayed home from work one morning to battle this
problem out with Nic, a morning neither my husband nor my long-suf-
fering staff are likely to forget. Later that same day, acting on a misplaced, subconscious need to take control of my home life, I actually
ordered two account executives to clear the conference table of coffee
cups and lunch dishes before they accompanied a client into the art
directors' studio to see the layouts of his new brochure.

In those confrontations between Nic and me, twelve years of
pent-up anger came tumbling out of me. I said things I should never say

to another person, much less to my husband. I had waited for more than a decade to even begin to take control of an unbalanced situation and I did it in hurtful ways that took a long time to heal. However, I learned a great deal from my own anger and from my husband's responses.

The most important insight I gained from the experience was this: It wasn't simply that I wanted Nic to do the dishes every day (although as a result of this confrontation, he now does all the dishes *and* the laundry). I had a far more important and urgent demand: I wanted the respect and consideration his participation in household tasks would demonstrate. Like so many breadwinning wives, I wanted my husband to show me that he appreciated my contribution to the marriage and that he understood the responsibility my higher income status carried with it.

At the end of the day, I desperately needed to know that Nic saw us as equal partners, sharing in all things—including household management. As long as he felt he deserved to relax more than I did or that his work was more important than mine, our so-called equal partnership was meaningless.

Years later, as I talked with breadwinning-wife couples across the country about their own balance of household responsibilities, I was stunned to hear so many of the same needs and attitudes from them. Even in the twenty-first century, as we explore possibilities in marriages that were impossible a decade ago, as we see one in every three married women outearning their husbands, the majority of wives continue to perform the greater share of housework and child care. Many of them receive little gratitude, participation, respect or even acknowledgement for this effort from their husbands.

Is the fifty-fifty sharing of household responsibilities in marriage a myth? My survey says...not anymore. I discovered couples who do indeed share fairly equally in management of the home. Yet many of the wives I interviewed repeated the same scenario Nic and I encountered, a litany of disturbing patterns they could not seem to break.

Volumes have been written on the housework conundrum, especially since women moved into the job market and two-income households became commonplace. The new balance required has not usually been attained. When the wife makes more, however, the dynamic changes. A husband's sharing of household responsibilities can be the ultimate acknowledgement of the wife's contribution to the overall well-being of the home...or the husband's lack of participation in chores can be the outward demonstration of conflict, misunderstanding and communication breakdown throughout the marriage.

Slowly, the tables turn

When sociologists started to explore the division of household labor in marriage, it's not surprising that their early theories were about money, not about gender.

The traditional family structure led logically to the development of *dependency theory*. Simply put, wives took care of household chores in exchange for their husbands' financial support. Even in households in which wives worked, they generally earned less than their husbands, so their completion of the cleaning, cooking and other household tasks repaid their "debt" to the men who supported them.[2]

If this theory were true, then today's breadwinning wives could expect their husbands to take over all the housework responsibilities automatically, as a natural extension of their lower-earning role. Indeed, about 30 percent of the breadwinning wives I interviewed have seen dependency theory in action: These wives say that *their husbands are the primary housekeepers* in their families. Another 18 percent say that their husbands share the housework burden with them.

However, 46.5 percent of wives tell us that their lower-earning husbands feel no obligation to help out—21.5 percent say that their husbands do not participate in housework at all, while another 25 percent have hired professional cleaning services to take up the slack in their homes.

Significantly, the men see it differently. Fifty-one percent of the husbands I interviewed feel that they are the *primary* housekeepers, while another 11 percent feel they share the chores equally with their wives. Only 13.5 percent of the men say that they do no housework at all, while another 22 percent note that they enjoy a professional cleaning service paid for by their wives.

We can begin to see that while dependency theory plays a role, there is more at work here than a sense of duty—or lack thereof—on the part of the lower-earning spouse.

Once again, we turn to gender behavior for answers. As we discussed in chapter 1, husbands and wives are likely to "do gender," which is to behave in traditional masculine or feminine fashions, so that the spouses maintain a semblance of their male or female roles within the relationship. When wives make more than their husbands, the gender roles lose their sharp focus—so both spouses may grasp at whatever gender-specific activities they can to reassure themselves and others that they are "real" men and women.

Housework is one area in which gender roles are sharply defined, both by tradition and by society. Even the most liberal thinkers know that our society quickly recognizes cooking and cleaning as "women's work." No matter where a husband stands on the feminist perspective, his instinctive reaction to housework is filtered through decades of media messages, television, movies, family expectations, personal role models and peer judgments that tell him his wife should cook and clean *because* she is the woman.

What, then, is the man's role? Julie Brines, a sociologist at the University of Washington at Seattle and the author of a groundbreaking study on the division of housework in breadwinning-wife couples, poses the question. "What, in terms of positive content, do people regard as 'men's work?' The answer surfaces routinely in a variety of contexts: 'men's work' remains associated with primary providership for the family."[3] Men are supposed to bring home the bacon, while the women fry it up in a pan.

In a household in which the wife takes on the breadwinning role, men are often left to find a new way to assert their masculinity. "The [gender] display perspective suggests that such arrangements throw an uncustomary wrench into the dynamics of symbolic interaction between wife and husband," Brines notes. "Neither partner, on these grounds, engages in behavior that exhibits or affirms their 'essential nature' as men and women."[4]

Brines worked to untangle the theoretical knot around division of labor at home, by analyzing data gathered in 1985 for the Panel Study of Income Dynamics conducted by the Institute for Social Research at the University of Michigan. Working from an original sample of nearly 5,000 United States families, Brines discovered that the wider the income gap between breadwinning wife and dependent husband, the less housework the husband is likely to do.

"This dynamic is particularly evident among (though not limited to) married men in low-income households," Brines observes. "Men currently dependent on their wives as a consequence of prolonged joblessness are also prone to disavow household work."[5]

Thus, many breadwinning wives find it virtually impossible to relinquish their traditional role as sole housekeeper, even when they work long hours and outearn their husbands many times over. While Brines didn't address specifically the wives' side of this story, we can extrapolate from her research that breadwinning wives who insist on carrying all the housework responsibilities at home are also clinging to their traditional gender roles, proving their value as women while playing the traditionally masculine role of primary income provider.

Hochschild's breakthrough research, detailed in *The Second Shift*, also sheds some light on breadwinning wives' difficulty in splitting housework responsibilities with their husbands. She put forth the concept of "balancing," through which husbands and wives readjust the power in their relationships when men sense their power trickling away. "According to this principle, if men lose power over women in one way, they make up for it in another way—by avoiding the second shift, for example. In this way, they can maintain dominance over women. How much responsibility these men assumed at home was thus related to the deeper issue of male power... Women who 'balanced' felt 'too powerful.' Sensing when their husbands got 'touchy,' sensing the fragility of their husbands' 'male ego,' not wanting them to get discouraged or depressed, such women restored their men's lost power by waiting on them at home."[6]

So are we locked into these gender roles? Are wives who make more money doomed to a second shift of endless toil, because their husbands' participation in housework will somehow damage their masculinity?

My research indicates otherwise. *The key to men's willing participation in household chores is in their willingness to be the lower-earning spouses.*

"When people ask what I do, I generally tell them I'm the primary parent, the primary cook, the house maintenance person and I write on a part-time basis," said Doug, who gave up his position as editor of a national trade magazine ten years earlier. At that time, Doug and his wife, Polly, decided they wanted a parent in the house when their elementary school-aged children arrived home every afternoon, instead of sending their son and daughter to a wraparound after-school program from 3:00 to 6:00 daily. Polly's medical practice easily supports the entire family in their suburban Indiana home.

"What do I do on any given day?" Doug began. "I get up around 6:00 A.M. and read until I have to take the kids to school at 7:30. Then I come home and work in the office after cleaning up the house to meet even my minimal standards. I work until noontime and then come back for a short time in the afternoon. That's interspersed with doing household errands or grocery shopping. Then I get supper started and there's usually somewhere the kids need to be after school—sports practice or lessons or another commitment, so I take them and pick them up. It's a full day."

Doug and Polly met while they were graduate students. As Polly began the long years of medical school and residency, Doug's writing and editing positions made him the principal breadwinner. "For eleven years I was the primary wage earner in the family," he explained. "Then for the last fourteen years, Polly has made the lion's share of the money.

It was my choice to leave full-time work, because I could see the value in staying home and taking care of children. Every family has to have someone doing this stuff, because it's intrinsic to the well-being of the family. And I'd worked hard for a lot of years by then. I was ready for a sabbatical."

Such an outlook on his position as at-home father and house-keeper did not come naturally to Doug. "There were four children in my family and my father didn't do anything around the house," he said. "That was the model I grew up with. So when I approached Polly with the idea of my staying home for a while, she said, 'You are not competent to stay home. If you want to do this, you have to know what you are doing.' So I began to take on more responsibility at home, because I wanted this and she was very up front and honest about what she expected of me."

Polly admits that she was delighted when Doug approached her with the concept of becoming an at-home husband. "When we were both working, our dates were at the supermarket on Saturday nights," she said. "We figured there had to be a better way. He said, 'Look, either you quit or I quit.' He thought the kind of rat race he saw in the 1950s when men went away to work in the city and came home exhausted was just so much craziness. Men were working themselves to death, to an early grave. I had no argument. I didn't want him to aspire to that life."

As wholeheartedly as she agreed with his decision, however, Polly proceeded with caution, making absolutely certain that Doug understood her expectations. "The secret is that we women have to stop being the default function," she said. "You can kind of beg or cajole your husband to get him to do more housework, but what really worked for us is that I just stopped doing it all. Then he gradually assumed that if it was going to get done, he was going to do it. Then he saw the value in it."

Indeed he did—Doug now takes care of every aspect of house-keeping except laundry, which Polly actually enjoys doing on her own. He shops for clothing and school supplies with the children, handles the lawn care and snow removal, makes dinner every evening and shares the clean-up afterward with Polly. "Despite making as much money as she has relative to what most people have, Polly teaches by example that the simplest things in life are really the most fundamental things," Doug said. "Looking for more knowledge and experiencing the comfort of a close relationship with another person—that's what is important in life. We are not in this life to make a certain amount of money or retire at a certain level of status. We're here to enjoy our relationships with other people."

Doug is a classic example of the central issue: When husbands choose to *enjoy* the personal flexibility they find in marriage to a bread-winning wife, they are far more likely to accept at least partial responsibility for cooking, cleaning and other household tasks.

Stay-at-home dads. Full-time householsbands. Entrepreneurs starting up new businesses from home. Men who gave up the corporate life to pursue alternative careers. *All* of the husbands I surveyed who report these circumstances also participate in keeping the house clean, getting food on the table and making sure there are clean clothes for the children.

And in a stunning display of gender neutrality, *all* of the stay-at-home dads I interviewed have embraced the full role reversal in their marriages, maintaining primary responsibility for all the chores in their homes.

Husbands as housework leaders, not just helpers

It's a trend that has gained momentum since the mid-1970s: As more and more wives take on full-time jobs outside of the home, more and more husbands are willing to help with cooking, cleaning, laundry and more.

Men spend more time doing household chores now than they did twenty years ago, reports the Family and Work Institute's 1997 National Study of the Changing Workforce. At the same time, women spend less time on housework than they did in the 1970s—a direct indication that men are making a significant effort to pick up the slack. While women still spend more time on housework overall than do their husbands, the gap between husbands' and wives' participation has narrowed by as much as an hour a day.[7]

Gallup polls taken forty-eight years apart tell us that married men in general are considerably more involved in "helping" with housework than they were just after World War II. In 1949, 62 percent of married people said that the husband in the household helped with housework, 40 percent said he helped with cooking and 31 percent indicated he helped with dishes. Decades later, in 1997, these numbers all increased dramatically: 85 percent said husbands helped with housework, 73 percent said he pitched in on cooking and 57 percent agreed that husbands helped with the dishes.[8]

However, the Gallup poll made the implicit assumption that wives are still in charge of housework tasks. Gallup phrased the question to wives, "Does your husband help with the housework in the home?" underscoring the assumption that the wife is still the primary housekeeper.

When wives make more, that assumption gets knocked out of the box. Let's look closely at the findings I discussed earlier.

A remarkable 51 percent of the men I interviewed consider themselves the *primary* family housekeeper. Not only do they participate in dusting, vacuuming and picking up after the family, these men feel that they are actually *in charge* of these activities—if they don't do them, the chores don't get done.

But here's the catch: Only 30 percent of the wives I interviewed agreed that their husbands are the primary housekeepers. Those who disagreed with their husbands' assessment generally felt that both husband and wife are involved in housework responsibilities, although the wife continues to be the primary housekeeper.

Chart A: Who Cleans?

	Husband's response	Wife's response
Husband does all housecleaning	51%	30%
Husband shares in housecleaning with wife	11%	18%
Wife does all housecleaning	13.5%	21.5%
Professional housecleaning service	22%	25%
Other (older children do chores)	2%	3%
Don't know	.5%	2.5%

When wives make more, we see an additional statistic not measured by previous studies. One in four breadwinning wives hires out the regular housecleaning chores to professional cleaning services. While only one breadwinning wife I interviewed had a full-time housekeeper and one considered her resident mother-in-law to be the primary cook and house cleaner, many others are using their discretionary funds to eliminate the conflict of who cleans in their homes.

Chart A shows us that in breadwinning-wife households, the husbands believe that they not only help with housework, half of them see themselves as taking it over altogether. Sixty-two percent of husbands say they either take the lead in housework or consider themselves active and equal participants.

However, only 48 percent of wives agree that their husbands are this involved in housework responsibilities. Of the men who see themselves as the primary house cleaners, about a third of the wives in these marriages disagree—and most of these wives see themselves as active, if not primary, in keeping the house clean.

Where does the discrepancy come from? Essentially, my interviews with these couples showed two specific problems:

1. Men are willing to participate in cleaning the house, but wives are less willing to accept their husbands' completed housework as adequate.
2. Husbands and wives have different definitions of housework and specific chores. What a husband may consider unnecessary may be of utmost importance to the wife, and vice versa.

When I examined the responses of individual couples who assessed the husband's participation differently, I found that while the husbands felt they did the majority of the housework, their wives usually responded that they shared the housework equally. Husbands commented that their wives "like to tidy up" or "She's always looking for things I didn't do." Wives noted, "He'll run the vacuum and dust, but he never gets the bathroom clean enough, so I go over it when he's done" or "He has no idea how many other things need doing that he doesn't do."

Indeed, in some cases the balance seemed real, most often in households in which the wife's income was only slightly higher than her husband's. Here the spirit of partnership prevailed and the couple had achieved an equitable—if complex—split between the two of them to resolve the potential overload problems.

"Edwin kind of gravitated toward doing laundry and some of the cleaning," said Molly, a forty-two-year-old county communications director whose husband experienced a layoff from his corporate job the previous year. When we talked, Edwin, who was also forty-two, had just begun a new career in teaching. "But I have to be honest—I had to lower my expectations a little," Molly continued. "If you are not going to do it all yourself, you can't count on it being done the way you would do it. Sometimes I just leave the house the way it is and when it bothers him, he cleans it. Then if things are really bugging me at work, I am less productive at home. So Edwin takes up the slack."

The more Molly and Edwin each described their division of household labor, the more it appeared that they have truly achieved the fifty-fifty split so coveted by breadwinning-wife couples. "I cook most of the time and he does most of the cleaning up after meals," Molly said. "For lawn work, he mows and I weed. Whoever gets to the thing that needs cleaning first, cleans it. Sooner or later, we're both involved in everything."

"We don't have a set-down plan," agreed Edwin, "we just go with whoever has the energy to start the job. Sometimes it goes in cycles—I do meals for a week or two, then she cooks for several weeks after that. Sometimes I get frustrated when things are getting dirty, so I vacuum. I take care of the truck and the car. It just all works out."

Molly made it clear that she would rather accept Edwin's lower standards for cleanliness than accept the full responsibility for cooking and cleaning. With three children, several dogs and cats and a large piece of property in Iowa to contend with, the last thing Molly wanted was to shoulder the upkeep burden alone.

From Edwin's point of view, cooking and cleaning are his ways of repaying Molly for her contribution to the household as breadwinner—just as she once did for him. "I was in my last job for four years and I had about a hundred people working for me," he said. "That required a lot of time on my part. Molly always supported me in my professional pursuits, even though she was building her career at the same time. I guess the least I can do is support Molly in hers."

Molly and Edwin have an enviable arrangement. Their expectations of each other's participation in household chores stay fairly low, with each pitching in when time permits. Molly struggled at first with the dirty corners, crumbs on the dining room table and occasional dishes in the sink that signaled her husband's less stringent requirements for cleanliness—but she learned to avert her eyes and relax with a less-than-perfect environment, whisking through every so often to tidy things to her own specifications.

Edwin, meanwhile, bears no gender expectations of Molly when it comes to housework. He respects her financial contribution, understands the opportunities it makes possible for him during this job transition and is grateful that his layoff didn't force the family to sell their property or compromise their lifestyle.

If only all breadwinning-wife couples were so levelheaded and tolerant about housework! In most relationships, the scales quickly tilt until one spouse's share of the household responsibilities weighs considerably more than the other's portion—and in many cases, the heavier side belongs to the husband.

Russ, a thirty-three-year-old former middle manager for a Massachusetts publishing firm, left his job a year and a half before our interview to become a full-time at-home dad for his newborn daughter. His wife, Clarice, owns and manages an agency that places temporary help in office settings.

"I've been doing the majority of the housework," Russ told me with a sigh. "Cleaning, cooking, laundry, dishes. I try to get Clarice to pick up after herself and things like that. I don't have much luck, though."

The more specifically I asked about chores, the more Russ's home workload mounted: He did all the gardening, bought his daughter's clothing, handled the grocery shopping and acted as primary parent for the baby as well. "Clarice just doesn't help," he said. "This wasn't what we agreed to. This wasn't what I expected."

Clarice spoke as if entirely oblivious to Russ's plight. However, the condition of the home she described spoke volumes about his general discontent. "One of the things that we agreed upon when Russ left his job was that the house was last," Clarice said. "We have a busy life with lots of things going on and I'm learning to condition myself to feel that it is okay if the housework is not taken care of. The bathroom isn't perfectly clean this week or the laundry piles up for the weekend. When we do get to the housework, we do it as a team. I say, 'Okay, this is really bad, we have got to dust. We have got to organize a half-day when we can concentrate on getting the house in order.'"

From Russ's vantage point, however, Clarice is a non-participant at home. "My understanding when we started this was that she was going to help," he said. "I am still looking for that fifty-fifty thing. But it seems that wasn't her understanding. She doesn't expect to have to do anything. I can't stand a dirty house, so I will do it. But sometimes, I let it get pretty messy, just to see what she will do."

The pattern for this behavior began to emerge early in their five-year marriage, Russ said. "I have always done a lot of the housework including the laundry and cooking, even while I was working. So staying at home wasn't that big a transition. The big difference is that now that I'm home, Clarice expects a lot more detailed cleaning—and a lot more regularity. I don't like doing it. So it hasn't worked out too well. I guess none of this has ever been resolved."

Clarice was more circumspect. "Men, I think, traditionally don't look at their home like we women were raised to look at the home," she observed. "There is a lot of difference in how women clean and what is important today. Is it more important to play with the baby and have fun because the sun is shining or is it more important to have the laundry done? That's been the major point of contention in this transition— my expectations versus his expectations and not really verbalizing all our expectations before Russ left his job."

Both Russ and Clarice were quick to verbalize their expectations to *me*, but they clearly had not undertaken the challenge of working out their differences with one another. Russ went on to express frustrations about Clarice's handling of money, her lack of involvement with raising their daughter and more—while Clarice continued to describe her decisions to reassess priorities and let most household responsibilities go while she built her business and enjoyed her child.

What role reversal hell is this? Russ sounded like the housewives described in *The Feminine Mystique*, trapped and unhappy in an unrewarding situation and unappreciated by the breadwinning spouse. He has learned to set traps for his wife in desperate attempts to get her attention, hoping that she will focus and help him resolve his growing discontentment. Clarice, meanwhile, spoke like the businesswoman she is, fully expecting her husband to adapt to his situation and sincerely believing that she is an equal participant in creating a happy home for the family.

Yet Clarice is not entirely unaware of the reality of Russ's existence. "My father said it perfectly when we were home for the holidays," Clarice said, "He said to me, 'Clarice, you have turned into the man that you never wanted to marry.' He was *so* dead on. I thought, *Oh, wait a minute. I need to change some things.*"

Clarice paused to consider, as if deciding right then what she would change first. "Russ complains that we don't spend enough time together. I always seem to put the wife part of me on the back burner. That's something I know I've got to work on."

Are we really reversing roles?
To explore the question of household role reversal further, let's look beyond the basic dusting and vacuuming to specific household chores: cooking, laundry and dishes.

Chart B: Who Cooks?

	Husband's response	Wife's response
Husband does all cooking	43%	46%
Husband shares cooking with wife	30%	18%
Wife does all cooking	16%	23%
Eat most meals out	0%	5%
Other (children involved)	6%	3%
Don't know	5%	5%

A whopping 73 percent of all husbands say they share the responsibility for putting meals on the table on a daily or nightly basis, with 43 percent acting as primary chefs for their wives and children. Remarkably, even more wives—46 percent—identified their husbands as the chief cooks. While 30 percent of husbands believe they share equally in the cooking, only 18 percent of wives agreed with them. The women who disagreed believe that they themselves do the majority of the cooking.

Husbands' high participation in cooking probably comes from several factors. Over the years and with the onset of cable television, cooking has become less stigmatized as a woman's task—thanks in part to Jacques Pepin, Emeril Lagasse, *The Iron Chef* and a host of other famous male chefs and popular cooking shows. Today it's trendy, perhaps even manly, for men to cook at home. Additionally, as husbands face the reality of their higher-earning wives' long working hours, they take on cooking as a basic necessity. After all, we don't need dirty laundry cleaned everyday to sustain life, but we absolutely need to eat.

Many couples reported that they split responsibility for cooking by actual days: Monday, Wednesday, Friday and Sunday were the wife's nights, while the husband put dinner on the table on the other three evenings. However, many of these wives observed that on their husbands' nights to cook, they would often order take-out or defrost leftovers rather than prepare fresh meals—so the wives felt that they themselves did most of the actual cooking.

Chart C: Who Does the Laundry?

	Husband's response	Wife's response
Husband does all laundry	40%	27%
Husband shares laundry with wife	27%	24%
Wife does all laundry	20%	34%
Professional	2%	3%
Other (children involved)	3%	4%
Don't know	8%	8%

Chart D: Who Does the Dishes?

	Husband's response	Wife's response
Husband does all dishes	43%	28%
Husband shares dishes with wife	22%	28%
Wife does all dishes	14%	25%
Professional	0%	0%
Other (children involved)	5%	3%
Don't know	16%	16%

Slightly fewer husbands professed a commitment to laundry and dishes, although husbands' participation remains high. Across the board, wives and husbands continue to disagree significantly over the level of support husbands provide—for example, while 40 percent of husbands believe they do all the family laundry, only 27 percent of wives agree with them. Here more wives believe themselves to bear the primary responsibility.

Once again, interviews indicate that these differing points of view stem from the definition of each task. For example, many men felt that doing the laundry meant actually washing and drying the clothing, while folding and putting garments away might be tasks left to their wives—although these men would call themselves the primary agents in the completion of laundry, without acknowledging the final steps as part of the process. The same discrepancy appeared in the area of doing the dinner dishes: While husbands wash the dishes, wives reported that they considered putting the dishes away, wiping down the kitchen counters and scrubbing the sink to be part of the dish-doing task—parts their husbands often did not complete.

"When the dishes are done at the end of the evening, I want to see a vista in the kitchen," Carol, a former breadwinning wife, told me at a dinner party. "I want a total view of the shining counters, the clean sink, everything clear and sparkling. Try to tell *that* to your husband."

Even though husbands' participation in household chores is quite high in these relationships, many wives told stories of discord, resentment, constant frustration and anger with their husbands over their less than perfect contribution. In response, many husbands expressed their own bewilderment, criticized their wives' "perfection-ist" behavior or described baffling arguments that seemed utterly inappropriate, given the men's willingness to help throughout the house.

How can wives who make more learn to accept their husbands' participation in household chores with smiles instead of bitter words? And how can husbands learn to see the bigger picture through their wives' eyes? We'll discuss these and more conflict-ridden housework habits—and how to break them—in chapter 9.

MAKING HOUSEWORK A PARTNERSHIP

Gaining Husbands' Real Participation in Home Tasks

"**B**ruce runs the home, right down to what we have for dinner—the whole nine yards," said Julianna, the owner of a commercial printing firm in New Jersey. Bruce, her husband, left his family's dry cleaning business three years earlier to stay home full-time with their three children, one of whom is developmentally challenged. They have an older child in school and a third child in diapers, born since Bruce became an at-home dad. "I run my business and he runs the house," Julianna added. "It's great."

Within seconds, however, her face darkened as she stabbed at a salad with her fork and when she continued her voice was hesitant. "I think that I don't feel good about this, so I almost hate to say it to you," she said quietly, "but I tend to tell him what to do sometimes and it bugs me and I know it bugs him."

As Julianna chewed a piece of lettuce for a moment, she squinted her eyes, puzzling over her own disclosure. We were in one of the area's most trendy restaurants, a place filled with businesspeople in expensive suits, talking in low tones about pressing financial and logistical matters. Julianna had carefully chosen the location for our interview, as if to emphasize the point she was about to make. "One of the difficulties I think Bruce and I have, at least from my perspective, is that we both live in two different worlds for the majority of the day," she said. "I'm living in a really fast-paced environment, really stressful, a lot of demands. There are days when, by three o'clock in the afternoon, I have so much in my head I can't control what comes out of my mouth. So when I come home sometimes at night, the children are hanging out playing on the computer or Bruce is doing something with our middle daughter, Susan, who is physically challenged and the other two are into something, and the kids' rooms are a mess, the house looks like a bomb went off and I've been at the office running all day from problem to problem...."

She threw up her hands, toppling a silver pepper mill. "I get so frustrated! I think about all the things I got accomplished in the day, when he accomplished nothing."

Then, embarrassed by her outburst, Julianna put both hands in her lap. "I know I'm not being fair," she said. "Of course Bruce has accomplished something. He's home all day with our daughter, who needs a lot of extra care. He's so terrific with her! She's doing great and I know it's because he's there with her all the time."

She picked at her salad, choosing her vegetables as carefully as she chose her words. "I have a hard time with her therapy," she explained slowly, not looking at me. "It's so tough for me to see her struggle. Bruce is much better than me at getting Susan to do things that are difficult for her." Julianna's resolve returned as she stabbed a slice of tomato. "But to make that possible, for me to support us all while he is home with her, that means I have to give my all to the business, which means working late. And he makes that possible, because he likes being home and he's better at being domestic than I am. I just see what a wonderful guy Bruce is. He's like the rock in our family."

A former business manager and a college graduate, Bruce certainly had no trouble finding his way around household chores once he started spending his days at home. He laughed when I asked him about housework in an interview a few days after my lunch with Julianna. "Jules has her moments with me," he said. "Some days I'm busy with the kids and I just don't get around to the dishes. She comes home and there they are in the sink. I figure, what's the big deal? But to her, it's a big deal, all right."

Julianna's assessment of Bruce's daily accomplishments had little to do with his own opinion of his full days. "I spend all the time I can with the kids," he said. "Frankly, taking care of Susan, the middle one, is a full-time job in itself. She needs a lot of care the other kids either don't need now or won't need eventually. I spend the whole day with her and with the baby and I love being here with them—but let's face it, it can wear me out.

"Some days I say to myself, who cares about what gets picked up and what doesn't? It will all still be there tomorrow and I might have more time then. But Julianna wants me to work on *her* timetable and do what *she* wants to see done. I hear myself say to her, 'You're not a boss here! This is *our* home.' I just wish she'd relax and enjoy it more."

Julianna is not unsympathetic to Bruce's position. "I think his biggest challenge is that he gets so tired of picking up after everybody. At the same time, I'm more of a perfectionist. I don't like a lot of clutter around. So I guess his idea of the house being tidy and mine are probably pretty different.

"What I really want is for the house to be clean when I get home—the rest of the day doesn't matter, just when I get home. It's like pulling teeth to get a husband to understand why it's important to me that things be done," Julianna groaned. "Procrastination drives me crazy. I have a sense of urgency on some things that I have to do. Bruce is on the opposite end. I just feel that sometimes when I come home, the two worlds are colliding."

On the surface, we might guess that Julianna has the perfect set-up: a husband who is happy to spend his days at home with the children, cooks and cleans, handles the daily care of a child with special needs and who expects no participation in housework from his wife. "I just want her to enjoy the kids and spend her free time with them," he told me. "She works hard and she gets so little time with them. They love being with her. Me, I get them all day. That's great. I want to share that with her."

However, Julianna can't bring herself to relax and enjoy her marital partnership. She can't accept that in relinquishing control of the household, she has given up the right to supervise its level of cleanliness, the speed with which chores are completed and the amount of untidiness she is willing to tolerate. Now the house operates according to Bruce's rules—and these rules make her crazy, even though she fully understands the additional challenges her husband faces while caring for their daughter.

Somehow Julianna believed that her househusband would behave the same way her mother did when her father was on his way home from work. "About four o'clock every day, my mother would go into hyper-drive, because my dad was coming home," she explained. "By 5:30, in that hour and a half, everybody—including all five kids— would get their rooms cleaned, the table set, the house picked up, everybody had their chores. That was how it was in a really traditional family."

How strange to compare one's modern husband with the life of a traditional mother and wife in the 1960s! Yet her mother provided the only reference Julianna could use to set her own expectations. Julianna believed a household should be run efficiently, with respect for the breadwinner—who doesn't want to see mounds of laundry, clouds of dust or piles of dishes upon arriving home.

"What do I really want when I get home? A drink and the television," she said. "I spend fifteen or twenty minutes in our hot tub, which relaxes me a lot. But I really understand how these men used to sit in their underwear with the remote control all evening. Let's face it, work is tough. You're drained at the end of the day. You just don't want your home to create any new challenges, because the whole day is about problems and challenges. You want to come home to peace, not aggravation. Is that so much to ask?"

The new homestead

Julianna appears downright ungrateful as she describes her reaction to Bruce's lackadaisical attitude about housework. Indeed, my research indicated she is an especially fortunate breadwinner wife to have a husband who wants only to please her and to be a good father to his children. Yet Julianna doesn't understand that what she wants at home isn't going to happen—not because Bruce can't do it, but because her constant complaints cause him to continue on the same, unwavering course.

Julianna wants to set deadlines for the completion of chores. Bruce doesn't believe in timetables and wants to put time with his children first. Julianna comes home and is instantly angry at Bruce for not cleaning up. Bruce understands Julianna's frustration, but has no intention of changing his attitude or his cleaning schedule.

Where will this eventually lead? Perhaps over time, Julianna will learn to relax with a higher level of clutter, so that she can enjoy her time at home with her children and put her differences with Bruce to rest. However, the far more likely scenario is that Julianna will re-adopt doing chores she has long since relinquished to Bruce, so that she can see them done to her satisfaction. Like so many breadwinning wives, Julianna measures her own worth against *both* her job performance and the spotlessness of her home and grades herself harshly as a housekeeper—even though that responsibility is no longer officially hers.

It's certainly not biology that still makes women the primary housekeepers. What perpetuates our position as chief cleaners, cooks, laundresses and shoppers is that we consider these responsibilities our own, regardless of our own belief in or rejection of the traditional wife's role. As wives and as women, we see what needs to be done and we tacitly accept that we will be the ones to do it—even if our marriages are ones in which these tasks are considered to be the husband's.

Why do wives who make more have such difficulty discarding this connection to a traditional past? My survey indicates that these wives react to housework in a number of ways unique to their breadwinning status:

1. **Some overcompensate and try to do it all.**
2. **Some expect the job done right—or they'll do it themselves.**
3. **Some want respect for their contributions to the household.**
4. **Some straddle a fine line between their roles of wife and mother.**

As if their higher incomes make them less feminine or less "wifely," many wives who make more "do gender" by turning housework into their domains or by refusing to give their husbands credit for their participation. Some furiously clean and cook to maintain exaggerated levels of perfection—ones their husbands could not hope to attain with their own comparatively more casual contributions to household maintenance. Other husbands who offer to help are cheerily rebuffed by wives who tell them, "By the time I show you what to do, I might as well do it myself."

Some of these wives, as if they are trying to make up for the potential embarrassment they have brought their husbands by outearning them, barely permit their husbands to take out the trash, much less perform larger duties like meal preparation or laundry. In response, their husbands quickly learn to leave *all* the housework for their wives...and the cycle of action versus inaction, resentment and anger continues.

Let's take a look at some couples whose behavior demonstrates the patterns breadwinning wives find so difficult to break.

1. Some wives who make more overcompensate, trying to do it all.
David and Lisa lived together on and off for five years before they finally married. David's exploration of his talent as a studio artist did not translate well to the profit-making world—so he found jobs that took no special skill and was paid accordingly. Lisa, meanwhile, worked three jobs—including her main position as a systems analyst—to support the house she'd purchased in her own name two years before she and David married, while he was working out of town as a sculptor's intern. Lisa's income ranged from $35,000 to $45,000 annually, depending on the volume of outside work she accepted. David averaged about $20,000.

When he returned from his yearlong internship, David moved in with Lisa...but saw no real reason to contribute to the mortgage or upkeep of the house.

"She was paying for it and maintaining it herself before I lived in it," David noted. "So I thought she didn't need help."

When they got married five months later, David and Lisa agreed that if they were to start a family, it was time for David to find a more lucrative career direction. He enrolled in a local university and began a master's degree in engineering, supplementing the family income with a low-paying retail position. Their first child arrived a year after they married and David began to see a change in Lisa's overall demeanor.

"Lisa has a hard time asking for help," David said. "She feels things need to be taken care of. I, on the other hand, don't feel that a lot needs to be taken care of around the house, so I didn't know that she needed help. I was blissfully unaware of whatever was stressing her out. For a while, she was experiencing great amounts of stress trying to do everything and not asking for help."

This continued for more than a year after their first son was born. When David could no longer attribute Lisa's drawn appearance and constant irritation to the tribulations of handling a newborn, he finally asked her if she needed his assistance.

Lisa responded: "It never occurred to me to ask him. In my mind, I am responsible for everything and I haven't allowed him to be responsible for things. So I can't really fault him for being irresponsible when I haven't asked him to give."

On the surface, this all feels comfortably resolved between them—Lisa is learning to ask, while David is learning to give. The reality, however, is not so neat and tidy, either figuratively or literally.

"I have a lower threshold for mess than Lisa does, so I get frustrated by my environment," David observed. "And as a result, I get frustrated with Lisa for not being as aware as I am. It comes time for housecleaning when we're having company—and then I'll do all the vacuuming while she does all the picking up." But until company comes, David is unlikely to become involved in household tasks, even though the condition of the house grates on his nerves.

He speaks of many chores as if there are absolute rules for them—rules that only *he* follows in his own home. "Laundry, for instance," he said. "I do that. Which means it doesn't necessarily get done. I'll take it downstairs, wash and fold it, but I won't put it away. And if it turns out that it lies in a heap on the floor and I have to wash it again, then so be it. I will not put someone else's clothes away."

Cleaning up after meals, David said, is "a sore subject. I feel that if you eat by yourself, you should clean the dishes, clear the table, not leave them in the sink. I really despise moving someone else's mess. So I try very hard to lead by example. I have been very vocal about my wishes, too."

When asked about dishes and laundry, Lisa simply replies, "We all clean up after meals. I usually get to the dishes before David does. Laundry—he does that, I guess."

David is perpetually unhappy about the way the house is maintained—but when his wife didn't ask for his help, he never thought to pitch in, even though she works more than sixty hours a week and carries the full responsibility for the care of their child. Now, even when she has finally asked for assistance, he is more likely to dictate his instructions than to make a meaningful contribution.

The fact is, David made the choice to change careers, but until he completes his degree and gets an appropriate job, he remains in the subordinate income position. His non-participation in housework reads as part of a classic passive-aggressive power struggle, between a wife who makes more and a husband who is uncomfortable with this.

For the most part, Lisa has resigned herself to accepting David's attitude about housework, taking whatever concessions she can get from him while continuing to maintain the greater share of responsibility. What's more, she has even accepted the responsibility for his lack of participation: "I only asked him to get involved recently," she explained, quickly excusing his behavior. "He says sometimes he feels like I don't need him. And that I'm the kind of person who tries hard to not need anybody. So we are still working on those things."

David and Lisa have created a complex web of responsibility, expectation and excuse that makes it difficult for Lisa to pass tasks to her husband, even though he knows she needs his help. As she says, "I am responsible for everything."

In the end, Lisa struggles to keep up with housework, child care and her burgeoning career.

Can there be a permanent remedy to David and Lisa's dilemma?

There could be. However, what has not occurred here is a frank discussion of household responsibility versus actual circumstances. Lisa, truly cowed by the idea of asking for help, believes she will relinquish some of her own power as household manager, mother and breadwinner if she admits that she can't do it all. What she does not realize is that she has already done this. David holds the majority of the power in the relationship, turning Lisa's own need to be in charge to his advantage. As long as she feels totally responsible for house and home, David has no particular responsibility. He is free to pursue his art, work low-paying jobs, continue his education and enjoy his existence, while Lisa works harder and harder to maintain their lifestyle.

At work, Lisa is not afraid to say what she feels when she finds herself in an unjust situation. At home, she fears loss of womanly control or even loss of love, if she confesses her discomfort. What does it mean about her own ability to function as a wife and as a woman if she admits that she can't do it all?

My answer to Lisa: *No one can do it all alone.* No married woman should have to try—especially a breadwinning wife.

Wives who make more must make choices in their lives, the same kinds of choices men made in the 1950s, when most wives stayed home with the children and kept house. At that time, men made the choice not to be homemakers—and no one blinked at this, because women had no expectation of household responsibilities from them.

Total household management fell to women, even as they began to climb corporate ladders, complete high-level degrees and filter into boardrooms, surgical theatres, courtrooms and CEO's offices across the country. Now, as wives who make more, we must begin to insist that our husbands assume some of the responsibility we have carried *de facto* for the last fifty years.

Solution: The List/Enlist Method

Thus, Lisa has the right to ask, even demand, that David participate in the running of the household. She has the right to further reject the stereotype that she has already rejected as a breadwinning wife. However, she has to take that terrifying first step and talk frankly with her husband about her concerns.

David noted that he has "been very vocal about his wishes" in regard to dirty dishes and he stridently drew the line in the sand about putting away laundry. What if Lisa followed his example and made her own wishes known? Not by wheedling, cajoling, kidding or sweet-talking her husband into listening—but by approaching him as an adult and an equal and telling him what she needs?

We are not talking about an argument, but rather a level-headed discussion in which Lisa *lists* the points in the home with which she needs the most assistance and *enlists* David's help in alleviating her stress.

Lisa should set aside private time with David for this discussion and choose a neutral setting, where they won't be interrupted by children's needs or other activities. She should choose a time and situation in which she is not emotionally rattled—in other words, *not* in a moment when she is already angry or frustrated with a task left undone or a new mess discovered. In essence, this is a household business meeting, requiring planning and logical discussion rather than outbursts and anger. David should know the agenda in advance, so that he does not feel as though he's about to be ambushed with a litany of his faults.

In preparing for this discussion, Lisa should make a list of the top three household tasks that create the greatest stress for her. While there may be a hundred tasks that could go on this list, she should choose only her top three for this meeting—a manageable number that keeps the conversation from becoming a speech about David's shortcomings.

The actual conversation might be as follows:

Lisa: David, it's especially hard for me when I get home from work and have to start dinner every night. I want the children to eat on a regular schedule, so that we can get them to bed on time and get some quality time for ourselves. But I can't do it alone. What can we do together to make this easier?

Note here that Lisa has *stated the problem* and shown David the *benefit to himself* (to both of them) if he will help her. She has also specified that the solution will involve both of them *together*—she will not be satisfied with a solution that causes more work for her while letting David off the hook, nor is she looking to him to do all the work. Lisa *lists* the problem, then *enlists* David's assistance.

While David doesn't respond well to emotionality and criticism, he can help Lisa find concrete solutions to well-defined problems. When Lisa presents a problem in rational terms—not at a time of high emotional stress—David can help look for a way to solve it. This is territory in which both David and Lisa can be comfortable while determining and implementing a real solution.

Lisa should also be ready with her own suggestions on how to solve the problem, to help get the discussion moving in a direction she will find acceptable.

Lisa: I was thinking that, since you get home first, I could leave you a menu and the recipes in the morning, so you could get dinner started. Or maybe we can split this up so that three nights a week I make dinner and three nights a week you make it.

At this point, David has something to which he can respond. He might offer his own preferences for solving the problem, or he might agree to one of Lisa's suggestions and embellish it with his own ideas. David may also choose to suggest things Lisa can do herself, once again removing himself from the responsibility of action. (Remember my own husband's suggestion that I do a load of laundry every night, instead of saving it all up for the weekend.) Lisa *must reject* suggestions which create more work for her, even though this may cause short-term friction in the discussion. The goal is to engage her husband in household management and gain his commitment to act, not to increase her own workload.

It is very easy for wives to acquiesce in discussions such as this. Women naturally work toward consensus, looking for ways to make those around us satisfied and happy. Unfortunately, it also comes naturally to many women, particularly those who outearn their husbands and continue to run the household, to sacrifice their own comfort to make others more comfortable. It's not that our husbands deliberately use this against us—but they do enjoy our impulse to please them.

However, wives who make more often have negotiation and facilitation skills they use at work, but not in their own marriages. The List/Enlist exercise can help wives set a new precedent for expressing their needs, relinquishing some household responsibility and working toward a more equally balanced relationship.

Using the List/Enlist method, David and Lisa can both be involved in changing the way they handle household responsibilities. They can work together as partners to improve their life together, breaking the cycle of self-blame, accusation and frustration that now impairs their relationship.

2. Some wives who make more want the job done right—or they'll do it themselves.
Stacey believes she will never be dominated by a man, but Clyde, her husband, never lifts a finger around the house.

Clyde has been working for years to set up a non-profit agency to create sports leagues for city schoolchildren. The organization generates virtually no income, even as it provides excellent after-school activities that keep at-risk children off the streets. Clyde is lucky if he brings home a paycheck every several weeks—and none of these paychecks are more than a few hundred dollars.

Stacey is a teacher and high school counselor in a high-income suburb, with a moderate but steady income. On top of her daily work load of lesson plans, papers to grade, conferences with parents and after-school activities, she performs just about all of the household management tasks. In addition, Stacey and Clyde have two teenage children.

Stacey described the home in which she grew up and her father's dominant role as breadwinner. "My parents were very much old-fashioned," she said. "My father was the breadwinner and my mother took care of the house and kids. There were four kids in the house. My mom worked in the school cafeteria—she hadn't finished high school. My father went to night school and I remember his graduation from a local university. It took him a long time to get that degree."

This experience shaped Stacey as she grew up. "One thing I learned and decided was that I would never be in my mother's position—that is, completely dominated by a man. By earning enough money to support myself, I satisfy my own subconscious need to be in charge of the relationship," Stacey said emotionally.

But how "in charge" is Stacey at home? She listed the tasks she handles on her own or with minimal help from her children: cleaning, cooking, laundry, cleaning up after meals, lawn care, gardening, child care. "There are times when I get annoyed at my husband's lack of participation," she said. "Usually, what I do is let it stew for a few weeks. Then I express my feelings rather vehemently. Then Clyde will pitch in, but it only lasts a few days. Then we fall back into the old pattern."

The pattern, Stacey noted, involves her simply picking up wherever she left off. "I'll clean up whatever Clyde didn't," she said. "Or if I don't like the way he did something, I'll redo it myself. Pretty soon he's not doing anything at all again. Then the whole argument starts again."

Stacey added, "Clyde is often out at events and meetings, networking to build the volunteer and funding base for his non-profit organization. His work is important. He needs to make contacts. So he is involved a lot outside of the house. I'm the one who's here, so I see what needs to be done and I just do it."

Clyde, on the other hand, feels he makes a worthwhile contribution to household tasks...on occasion. "I try to help. We split up the laundry and we try to divvy up lawn care. But she likes the riding mower and she doesn't mind doing that—she says it gets her out in the fresh air." He realizes that his minor participation is not what Stacey would prefer, however. "She comes after me sometimes, out of the blue," he said. "Like, 'Why don't you do more?' So I try to get the kids to do more."

He paused. "Now that we're listing all this stuff off at once, Stacey's life sounds pretty miserable."

Stacey and Clyde demonstrate a classic pattern between couples of all income types—the wife does most of the work and gets fed up, turning to the husband in anger for assistance. However, Clyde knows that if he ducks the responsibility long enough, Stacey will become exasperated and do it herself.

As soon as she picks up the dust cloth or starts the vacuum cleaner, Clyde knows he's won the battle again. His housework responsibility has ended, until the next argument.

The worst part of this cycle is that Clyde knows exactly what he's doing and knows that it angers his wife. Assuaging her anger is just not enough of an incentive to make Clyde perform tasks he doesn't enjoy. Instead, he tries to engage the children's participation, couching this as an example of good parenting—while his children learn to do as Dad says, not as he does.

Solution: Delegate and drop it.

Stacey has children in their teens, who are old enough to learn to clean up after themselves and prepare simple meals. Her husband has long been conditioned to wait until Stacey throws up her hands and starts cleaning again. Now it's time to break that conditioning, and retrain Clyde to have no expectations and to shift for himself.

It sounds drastic, but it's remarkably freeing to simply put down the dustcloth, close the door to the laundry room and walk away, never to return again. The transition will be sticky, uncomfortable, inconvenient and even hard to tolerate. But a transition *will* take place.

Total resignation from all cooking and cleaning is more than I would recommend to any breadwinner wife whose husband abrogates his responsibility—especially one with young children who depend completely on Mom and Dad for all of their needs. But as long as Stacey reinforces Clyde's staunch refusal to do household chores by doing them herself, the longer she will do these chores without his participation. Stacey needs to respond definitively, provocatively and absolutely to make change in her house.

Like Lisa in the previous example, Stacey should choose two or three tasks that cause her the greatest amount of stress. In a neutral setting and with clear-headed, objective statements, she should make it known to Clyde that these tasks are now his responsibility. To seal the deal, she must gain his spoken commitment to handle these jobs and she must follow the discussion by showing him how to do the tasks with which he may be unfamiliar. If he's never done laundry, Stacey needs to teach him to use the washer and dryer. If he's never run the dishwasher, Stacey will need to show him how to put the detergent in and turn it on.

Then, no matter how long it takes before Clyde begins or how poorly he does the tasks required, Stacey must refrain from doing them.

There will be consequences to this—whatever the task is, it may sit undone for several days or longer. Laundry will pile up (it may be wise to buy some extra underwear before delegating the laundry to Clyde). Dishes may get stacked in the sink for days at a time. But soon, Clyde will have no choice but to do the job Stacey and he agreed he would handle.

Older children can also take on household tasks, whether or not they receive an allowance or other reward based on their participation. Once again, a frank and decisive discussion will need to take place between Stacey, Clyde and their children. Working mothers today are commonplace, so it should come as no surprise to a husband or teenagers that the burdens of supporting the home and managing the household are too much for one woman to bear—even their superhuman wife or mother. Stacey must be clear that she is not *asking* for their assistance; she is giving up the responsibility for specific tasks so that she can be more effective in supporting them and so the family can save for the children's college education. She must be specific in outlining her expectations for each task and each child's responsibilities and she must train the children to complete these tasks effectively.

Stacey noted that she considers Clyde's work "important" in his quest to create a viable non-profit organization that serves inner city youth. Indeed, this work is important—but in a household in which the wife carries the breadwinning responsibility, her work is clearly equally important, if not more so, to her own family. Stacey must acknowledge that what she does, as well as her contribution to the home, should not come second to Clyde's noble pursuits. She carries the greater household responsibility as chief wage earner and she has the right—even the responsibility—to make sure she can continue to do this, especially when there are others in the house who can share in more household tasks.

3. Wives who make more want respect and gratitude for their contribution to the household.

"I've come to realize that one of the biggest differences between men and women is that the man *decides* what he is willing to do," said Doris, a fifty-year-old business owner in Vermont, married to Steve, a forty-eight-year-old construction worker who recently changed careers to become a computer animation artist. "There are some men who say, 'I don't mind cleaning,' but if they don't like to cook, they don't cook. In most of the relationships I know, the men choose first. Every husband says he is willing to help, but he picks what he's willing to do."

Doris found some solace in the housework battle with Steve, her husband, by letting him make these choices. "I love to cook and I really hate to clean, but since Steve likes to cook and he won't clean, I am better off letting him cook. If I let him do what he's willing to do, at least he does something and I don't have to do it all."

Steve, however, responds to his wife's pleas and occasional tirades about housework in a different way. "We fight. Most couples do," he observed. "Doris came in one day and said, 'You have to do something about helping with the dishes. There are too many dishes. You have to do something.' The next day I bought and installed a dishwasher. When she really bugged me about doing housework, I hired someone to come in once a week to clean the house."

On the limited income from Doris's start-up retail business and Steve's entry-level animation position, these expenses might seem extravagant. However, Steve sees them as necessary peacemaking tools. He responds to conflict by looking for the fastest, most efficient resolution—in this case, preferably one that eliminates work for both spouses. Meanwhile, he contributes to the household in other ways. "I do the lawn mowing, I built an addition on our house and I still maintain the darn thing," he said. "I did the electricity and I do some plumbing. And I grow most of our food—which can be a full-time job in itself."

Indeed, Steve maintains a massive vegetable garden and completes all the canning and preserving for the winter months from his own harvest. Doris readily acknowledges Steve's contributions on this and other levels. "Yesterday, I said, 'Oh, the toilet is leaking,' and by the end of the day there was a new toilet there," she said. "My mother once said to me, 'Steve will never make a lot of money, but he certainly gets things done around your house.'"

Do all these extra tasks Steve performs dissolve Doris's anger about housework? Some days, yes...but some days, she said, she wants to explode. "If I cook, I have to do the dishes afterwards. If he cooks, I still have to do the dishes. It would be nice if we could split things down the middle instead of him saying, 'I don't do that.' When I'm in a bad mood, I just go around and scream like hell. When I'm in a good mood, I say, 'It could be worse, he could not do the cooking and the gardening.' I guess in the perfect world, someone should be able to take over when somebody else doesn't want to do a certain task. This just isn't a perfect world."

Is Doris ungrateful? Is Steve insensitive? Essentially, what we're observing is a classic difference between husband and wife, which becomes even more pronounced when the wife makes the higher income. Doris supports the family, pays the mortgage and all household expenses, buys the groceries and her children's clothing and pays for vacations and other expenses—so she feels she has the right to ask her husband to do the tasks she wants done around the house. Steve, however, feels he makes a significant contribution as the family handyman, construction expert and farmer and should not be required to add things he doesn't enjoy to his to-do list.

The fact is, they are both right. Doris struggles to appreciate Steve's contribution, because *it's not the contribution she wants*. Her priorities differ from Steve's—she wants to come home to a clean house, not to piles of unwashed laundry and dirty dishes. Steve sees these basic household necessities as unimportant—he wants to handle the larger picture, building an addition on the house and filling the cupboards with a year's worth of fruits and vegetables. Despite his accomplishments, Doris's anger grows.

How can Steve and Doris reconcile their situation?

First and foremost, they need to acknowledge one another's contribution to the household. Doris chafes when Steve unveils the results of his major projects, because he becomes a hero in the eyes of their children, their neighbors, even Doris's parents. Steve delivers very visible, tangible results, for which he gets a great deal of praise and applause. "Dad's great," the kids say to Mom...and Mom fumes, forcing a smile until the children are out of earshot.

When she has the opportunity, Doris lets her anger spill over. "I say, 'Well, you did all these great things, but you couldn't do them without my supporting you financially.' I pay for the car insurance, the dentist, the mortgage, food and clothes. I tell Steve that I'm sick of his telling everyone what he did, while I do all this other stuff that everyone just expects."

Doris feels that her family takes her contribution for granted—it has always been there, it will always be there and her income provides for the unglamorous necessities of life. While Steve tackles large challenges, Doris is left with the mundane chores of dishes, laundry and housecleaning. While Steve enjoys his projects as much as he enjoys his work, Doris simply hates housework—but because Steve's contributions to family life are so large, she feels like a nagging crone when she insists he share in smaller tasks.

Doris is looking not so much for help with housework, but for *appreciation*. If Steve would pitch in with the ever-present, repetitive tasks of keeping the house in order, Doris would take this as a demonstration of his respect for her and for her larger financial contribution to the family. When she asks for help, Steve's response is usually to find a long-term solution to the problem: buy a dishwasher, hire a cleaning service. He has eliminated some of the work, but he has not demonstrated that he appreciates his wife and is willing to help her in areas that are significant to her.

In buying a machine to do the job Doris hates, Steve has said to her, "Your efforts are easily replaced by an object that can do this job." He has *not* said to her, "I know how hard you work and I want to make your life a little easier at home," even if that's what his purchase was intended to say.

We need to remember that classic, age-old quote used in almost every husband-and-wife situation comedy: The wife asks, "Do you love me?" and the husband replies, "Are you kidding? I'm here, aren't I?"

Steve believes that his major projects around the house are expression enough of his appreciation for his wife. Doris, however, wants and needs Steve to express this appreciation on her terms. Doris is asking for the wrong things. She expresses her need in terms of dirty dishes and dusty floors, but she really wants recognition and acknowledgement of her efforts.

Solution: Ask for what you need.
Doris needs to explain to Steve that it's not the dishes, it's the *attitude*— his refusal to pitch in and help with housework is a slap in the face to Doris's feelings of self-worth as the principal breadwinner. She needs to know, in words and deeds, that he respects her and cares about her well-being. She needs his gratitude for what she does at home as well as at work. She needs to see him take some of the load off her daily grind of endless housework.

To both Steve and Doris, my advice is this: *Say "Thank you."* Steve should take a few moments every day to thank Doris for doing the dishes, clearing the table, making a meal, dusting the living room. Thank her for the clean socks in the drawer and the clean sink in the bathroom. And thank her in front of the children, so that they understand that these daily acts have value. It takes almost no effort to do this, yet husbands and wives forget many common courtesies quickly after they marry.

At the same time, Doris needs to thank Steve as well—for his many contributions of time and effort that clearly save the family money, even if they don't save Doris from the daily rigors of housework. Every big project Steve takes on is another attempt on his part to demonstrate that he contributes as much as she does to the well-being of his family—in fact, he overcompensates with countless acts of "doing gender," tilling the land, using power tools to raise walls and installing electrical conduit. Doris needs to acknowledge Steve's significant efforts, rather than chastising him for circumnavigating the tasks he sees as female-specific.

A little appreciation makes a difference to the wife who is stuck with the menial, dull, unending household tasks and to the husband who works daily to prove his worth as a man. If Doris and Steve can meet in the middle on these points, they can overcome the tension in their home.

4. Some wives who make more straddle a fine line between being wife and mother to their husbands.

For women whose incomes significantly exceed their husbands', the role of wife may feel at times more like the role of parent. This is especially true of couples in which the husband's income is suddenly and involuntarily eliminated, throwing the wife into the breadwinner role overnight.

Julie Brines' study of 1985 data provided evidence that the greater the difference between the husband's and wife's income, the less the husband participates in household chores.[1] In my research, the real-life examples of this phenomenon came from households in which the husband found himself without an income because of sudden disability, job layoff or other unforeseen circumstances. Often, out of humiliation, frustration, depression or simple necessity, the husband allows his wife to truly manage the entire relationship—handle all the financial decisions, pay all the bills, choose vacation destinations and make the lifestyle choices of home location, family car and so on.

It's no surprise that wives who are so entirely dominant in all aspects of the marriage also find themselves in charge of housework.

Stephanie and Chuck, who are forty-one and forty-eight, enjoyed fairly equal earnings in the first years of their marriage—she as an engineer for the local health department, he as a facilities manager at a nearby university. They found little conflict in their relationship until the day Chuck was crossing the street at an intersection and fell prey to a drunken driver running a red light.

"He broke his neck and lower back," Stephanie said. "Chuck was out of commission for a good year and a half, nearly two years. He didn't work at all for about a year."

Stephanie did her best to be optimistic about the situation, reminding her husband that miraculously he was not paralyzed and would not be permanently bedridden. "But he just kept getting deeper into this black hole," she said. "He was miserable to live with. People would call up and say, 'How is Chuck, but more important, how are you?' I was like a superwoman—running to day care, doing work, going grocery shopping, caring for our baby son."

Even as Chuck began to heal and regained some mobility, Stephanie continued to carry the full load of household responsibility. "He was well enough to participate, to do some things that didn't require a lot of physical effort," she said. "But he just wouldn't. It went on for months and months. I told people, 'I have two children. One is eight months old and one is forty years old.'"

Finally, thinking that this would be her fate for as long as she and Chuck were married, Stephanie turned to an attorney who she saw on Valentine's Day. "I said, 'What do I need a husband for? I'm self-sufficient, I'm making the money and he is just a slug.' I told the attorney I couldn't stand it anymore."

Before the attorney advised Stephanie about divorce, however, he recommended a marriage counselor. "So I told Chuck," Stephanie said. "I found out that he felt the same way—that he couldn't go on like that, either. We went to counseling and found out that he was severely depressed. They put him on Prozac. It was all very stressful, but now we are back to normal."

While Chuck is partially disabled and will never return to his previous work, he earns a living and participates in household chores to the best of his abilities. "He does the cooking, which is nice," Stephanie said. "I've also found that after this crisis, my priorities kind of changed. I would rather spend time with my husband and son than clean. The house will be here; if I dust, I dust. If not, it can wait until I get to it."

Many other couples echoed Stephanie's and Chuck's experience, confronting similar emotional barriers to the husband's participation in household tasks. Jessica, a forty-five-year-old high-technology project manager, found herself with larger problems than she expected after marrying Andy, a financial planner. When they met in college, the couple had assumed that Andy would be the principal breadwinner with his strong financial background. But his early "career" as a drug dealer caught up with him as soon as he began applying for positions.

"He had a criminal record," said Jessica. "I'm not stupid; I knew about it. But he'd been through rehabilitation and had cleaned up his act years before, so I thought it was behind us. Not so, it turned out. The jobs he wanted actually involved a background check. He couldn't get work in his chosen field."

The only work he could find was in blue-collar construction jobs, not at all what Andy had planned for his life. "We moved around a lot, to see if a change in community would make a difference," Jessica explained. "Finally, we realized he couldn't work at all in his chosen profession. That had a negative effect on our relationship."

With Andy home a great deal while Jessica was working, there was ample opportunity for Andy's bitterness about his situation to manifest. Housework became a battleground. "I'd suggest projects for him to do around the house," Jessica said. "He'd wait all day until I got home to start anything—things like cleaning the house, doing the yard, working on our boat. He wanted me to see him working and to see how much he resented having to do these things. He was like a sulky teenager and I was the scolding mother. That was incredibly stressful for me. We had some big arguments."

Andy found himself faced with a major crisis of self-esteem, one he took out on the wife he had planned to support. After conquering a drug habit, surviving prison and turning his life around, he found that he'd made another impossible life choice for himself by pursuing a career in which employers were unwilling to take the risk of licensing or hiring him. In anger and deep depression, he lashed out at his wife— the woman who now humiliated him further, however unintentionally, by earning a good living when he could not.

Finally, Andy and Jessica resolved to work together to bring about positive change in Andy's career. "Right now Andy's in graduate school in chemistry," Jessica said. "We know now that a lot of what he was going through was symptomatic of depression—but at the time, he denied that altogether. Now, he has been willing to admit that the whole thing was pretty devastating to him."

With Andy in school, Jessica noted, he is more likely to help out around the house. "He does most of the cooking," she said. "He enjoys that. But when we're in someone else's house or if someone comes over, he goes into that typical-male thing. He doesn't participate and he tells me what to do."

Depression, lowered self-esteem and the grief of unemployment can debilitate and emotionally paralyze anyone—but for husbands who had planned to support their wives, the loss of income and accompanying subordination can be devastating. For wives, the loss is just as great as husbands recede into themselves, pull back from their loved ones and leave all the responsibilities to their wives.

In such situations, husbands and wives need to work together to be certain they are resolving the right conflict. A husband's unwillingness to do housework, no matter how belligerent, may be an outward manifestation of his sense of damaged masculinity. This man didn't choose to be the supportive husband of a breadwinning wife. He had the position thrust upon him and he is not likely to learn to relax and enjoy it. Even if the breadwinning wife is happy to hold that position in the marriage, the relationship could soon be on the rocks if the husband is miserable.

I urge conflicted couples like Jessica and Andy to seek advice from mental health professionals, physicians or clergy who can help them resolve their differences and find ways to repair the damage—with a change in the husband's career, retraining, a search for new opportunities or even diagnosis and treatment if depression or another emotional disorder is indicated.

Good news and bad news

The winds of change have whistled through our homes as well as through our workplaces and affected both men and women. Even as women secure positions of greater authority and higher remuneration than ever before, more men are willing to participate in housework or even take over the entire responsibility so that their wives can increase their earning potential.

That is the good news. The bad news is that most wives still feel that they are the primary housekeepers or that they need to supervise their husbands' work and follow the men's efforts with clean-up rounds of their own. Still other wives find that their breadwinning status has bought them nothing at all at home, as they fulfill themselves in the wife/mother role, in which they perform a full second shift of home care after their full day at the office.

Recent studies indicate that men are more willing to share the housework burden than ever before and many already pitch in and carry a fair share. It's up to us as wives who make more, then, to encourage this behavior and lower our own stress levels as we learn to invite and accept our husbands' participation in the kitchen, in the laundry room, and throughout the house.

Recommendations: Moving Toward a Fifty-fifty Housework Split
1. Ask for what you want.
Wheedling, hinting, cajoling and suggesting are all fine for accomplishing some things—but they can be handicaps in getting your husband to participate in household chores. Make a clear statement about your expectations and about the task you'd like him to perform and why you'd like it done. Engage your husband in finding solutions to the most nagging housework problems—and then choose the solutions that give him a role in keeping house and home running smoothly.

2. Don't make housework a punishment.

You're not likely to fool your husband Tom Sawyer-style into thinking that loading the dishwasher is the most fun he'll have today, but don't make the chore seem worse than it is by assigning it in anger. Sit down with your husband and discuss the inequity in your household workload calmly and come to an arrangement together.

> *Wrong:* "I'm not washing another dish! It's up to you from now on and if it doesn't get done, that's just the way it is!"
>
> *Better:* "You vacuum and I'll dust. Then we'll get it all done more quickly."

3. Have patience.

You may wait for hours or even days for your husband to complete the chore you want done. The dirty dishes in the sink or the lint on the living room carpet may not faze your husband in the least—so if you want his participation in housework, you may need to put the brakes on your impulse to tongue-lash him for his slower response or, worse, do the task yourself.

Try providing a concrete, sensible reason that the task should be completed on your timetable instead of his. I found this worked with the problem of the day's dishes in the sink before I'd begun to prepare dinner. Nic scoffed at my insistence that the breakfast and lunch dishes must be done *before* dinner, telling me, "But we're just going to get a bunch more of them dirty, so why not wait until after dinner and do them all at once?" I explained that the pile of dishes in the sink blocked my access to water and to the garbage disposal, impeding my progress in preparing dinner. Now, when it's time to cook, I face a clean sink.

4. Resist the urge to criticize the job.

We are so certain of our own abilities as household managers and so convinced that our husbands—or children, or cleaning services—can't do the job as well as we do. Yet when we constantly undermine our husbands' confidence or insult their intelligence by criticizing their performances of menial housekeeping tasks, we can bet that our husbands will give us ample opportunities to prove our superior skill! Criticizing your husband will never improve his cleaning performance. No one wants to be the subject of continuous scrutiny, faultfinding and exasperated exclamations. If you've convinced your husband to do chores—or if he's volunteered—he will develop his own style and his own level of competence. Give him the space and the encouragement he needs to make these tasks his own.

5. Make real deadlines.

You would love to come home to a spotless house every day, but your husband sees no reason to rush through cleaning just because five o'clock is approaching. To him, your deadlines seem arbitrary. Together you should define a real time frame for a certain level of cleanliness in your home—tangible events or needs for which specific household tasks must be completed. The laundry must be done by Thursday this week, because your daughter needs her leotards for dance class. Company is expected for dinner on Wednesday, so the first floor needs dusting and vacuuming. The baby is learning to crawl, so you'll need to keep the floors especially clean and put away all potentially dangerous items. Share your reasoning with your husband—and then praise him for the chores on his list that get completed on the new timetable you have set together.

6. Make choices.

Is it more important to sort the week's newspapers for recycling or to play with the baby on a beautiful day? Give yourself and your husband the option of neglecting the less critical household tasks in favor of your quality of life. If you can live with a little extra dust on a Saturday so that you can enjoy a walk in the woods together or if the dishes can wait until morning while you plan a romantic evening, then do it. Housework will always be there; opportunities to spend time with the people you love become scarce as your life fills up with chores and obligations. Take time to relax. The dirt will wait for you.

7. Hire help.

If you're in a position to do so, find and hire a cleaning service to take the weekly maintenance tasks off your hands. There's nothing like the satisfaction of coming home to a lemon-scented, highly polished home at the end of the day—especially when you know that you didn't have to clean it yourself! Cleaning services charge either by the hour or by the square footage of your home; most will provide an estimate and will stick to a weekly rate, with extra fees for occasional tasks like cleaning the oven. They often bring their own cleaning equipment and products, building that cost into their fees. You will need to straighten up the house a bit before the service arrives, washing dishes, clearing tables, the floor and other flat surfaces so the cleaners can dust, mop and vacuum—but this provides the once a week deadline your family needs in picking up and putting away their belongings.

8. Lower your standards.

There's one sure way to get over the anguish of a less-than-spotless home: Stop thinking about it. It's possible to live with an extra layer of dust or with a scuffed kitchen floor without feeling like a failed wife, mother and housekeeper. Many wives told me that they had simply decided that the perfectly clean home had lost its importance in their lives. No longer did they strive for the title of Perfect Homemaker— instead, they concentrated on their children's contentment, their intimate moments with their husbands and their ability to maintain their positions as family breadwinners. Consider a reassignment of your priorities, moving daily housework to a lower level on the list. You're not giving cleaning up altogether, you're just letting it wait its turn while you concentrate on things that make a difference in your family's overall quality of life.

9. Say "Thank you."

It's so simple and so effective, yet we almost never remember to show gratitude for the things our husbands do around the house. The main reason we neglect to thank them is that most of our husbands rarely thank *us*—they have come to take our completion of housekeeping tasks for granted.

When your husband completes the task he's chosen, resist the urge to blurt out, "Well, it's about time you got around to doing that!" Instead, say, "Hey, thank you for taking care of that. That was really important to me." Tell your husband he did a good job and tell him again the next time he does it as well. You want him to continue to participate in housework, so make sure he knows how much you appreciate his contribution. A little appreciation goes a long way toward encouraging positive behavior and participation in household tasks.

Then, tell him to thank you for your contribution, too. Don't wait for him to figure out that you could use a little gratitude—he probably won't. Ask for the recognition you need and over time it will come more spontaneously.

CHAPTER 10

GUILTLESS CHILD-RAISING FOR BREADWINNER MOMS

How to Handle Outside Perceptions and Inside Realities

Sonia is the thirty-five-year-old vice-president of research and development for a large industrial corporation in California. Always a career-focused woman with a strong preference for science over sentiment, she never imagined how the birth of her first child, Jacob, would change the way she felt about working.

"I thought, when I got pregnant, that I would be out eight weeks and go right back to work and put my baby in day care," she said. "But then the maternal instinct hit me really hard. So I went back to work part time."

At the time Jacob was born, Sonia held a position of less responsibility at the company than the one she holds today. She was already the family breadwinner, however, and she'd been tapped for more and more influential assignments at work. Because of the department's considerable dependence on Sonia's skills, her supervisor was reluctant at first to consider Sonia's request for flextime, but he finally acquiesced to a short-term, part-time schedule that would help Sonia keep her place in the corporate line of ascension, while she shared in providing primary care for her new son.

The flextime arrangement was only part of the equation for Sonia and her family, however. Sonia and her husband, Donald, crafted a family work plan that allowed her to go to the laboratory in the mornings, from eight until noon, while he stayed home with Jacob. Sonia returned home at lunchtime and Donald left for a one-to-nine shift as an insurance claims adjuster, a position that paid him about $42,000 annually.

When Jacob turned two, his parents felt that he would benefit from time spent with other children during the day. They began what turned into a grueling search for appropriate day care, with the hope of finding a facility that also would offer preschool as Jacob grew older. It took months to find a facility that met Sonia's and Donald's standards for excellent references and stimulating activity. Not until Sonia was comfortable with Jacob's care situation did she return to full-time work—and upon her return, she became eligible for the high-paying position she holds now, at a salary that tops $125,000 annually.

Almost immediately after they put Jacob into the day care facility, the situation took a bad turn. "I had a tremendous run-in with the day care person," Sonia said. "A potty training issue, of all things." Over a period of weeks, Sonia sensed disapproval, even hostility, from day care workers who seemed to resent her commanding demeanor and her corporate position of authority. "It was very frustrating to deal with these people—they didn't understand the concept of corporate America for a woman," Sonia said. "They didn't understand that I had fourteen men reporting to me, so I was used to presenting myself in a forthright way. They thought I was trying to intimidate them. They couldn't understand that when I said what I felt, it wasn't meant to be intimidating—it was the way I did business."

Sonia began to fear that the day care staffers' negative attitudes toward her would influence their care of her son, so she and Donald moved young Jacob to a different center. "This one was unbelievably bad," Sonia groaned. "They actually let my son get into bad situations without stopping them. They called me at work during the day and said, 'You have to come and pick Jacob up, he has bitten another child.' He'd never done anything like that before. It was obviously the wrong place for him."

Sonia and Donald's next choice was a big step up in cost and quality: a Montessori school close to home, so Donald could pick up and drop off Jacob easily every day. Donald also could be there quickly when their child's illness or other events required his attention. "It was one of the agreements we made when I went back to work," Sonia said. "If I took this higher level job with so much supervisory responsibility, Donald would take care of the transportation for our children. He did that for a long time."

As summer approached, another conflict loomed—one that would be even tougher to resolve. The high standards of the Montessori situation were wonderful for Jacob, but Montessori operated as a school—with winter and spring breaks and summers off. "I didn't mind paying more, because we were getting our money's worth," Sonia said. "Nevertheless that meant we were suddenly traveling in an affluent group, beyond our normal means. Most of the mothers who sent their children there also had nannies at home who cared for the children when the school was closed for holidays and for the summer. Those other mothers were all set, but I had to find alternate care for my son."

With weeks of winter, spring and summer recess spreading before them, Sonia and Donald made the painful choice to move three-year-old Jacob yet again, to another high-quality private day care and preschool closer to Sonia's place of business—which meant that Sonia took over the responsibility for transporting Jacob. This meant more adjustments to her work schedule—adjustments that make her supervisors question her commitment to the company.

Sonia's voice took on a hard edge. "I wasn't supposed to have to deal with the picking up and dropping off. That was Donald's and my deal. But suddenly, going to a school so far away was an inconvenience for Donald. What about the inconvenience to me? I was the one with the early morning meetings and the responsibilities that went past dinner. Many days I worried about how this was affecting my job.

"We are coming to the realization that family life is not cut out for working moms, especially mothers who are also breadwinners," she observed. "The most frustrating thing to me is summer vacations for school-aged kids. Every working mother in America with a child in school has to deal with this problem. This is hitting us really hard—as Jacob reaches school age. We'll have to put our son in private school just to deal with this situation, and we had made a point of buying a home in an area with a great school district, even though the taxes and property values are much higher. I can handle transporting during the school year—I can work three-quarters of the day or go in at 6:00 A.M. and get off at two or three, to be there when Jake gets home. But what am I supposed to do during the summer?"

Meanwhile, Sonia is pregnant with their second child. "We plan to have three," she said, "and with the third one, Donald is just going to stay home and be with them. He is very supportive of my career and he really enjoys being around children. So that may be a solution for us.

"My peers and my boss know that my husband will be staying home soon," she added, "partly because they tend to worry about my longevity with the company and my ability to keep up with everybody else, because I am managing both the house and the job. My boss has two children and his wife stays home. My peers are all men and all of their wives stay home. That's what the business world understands."

Mother, not monster

Of all the arguments we hear from the media, opinion leaders, politicians and social commentators for and against wives as principal breadwinners, the discussions of motherhood are the most insidious.

Since the arrival of *The Feminine Mystique* in 1963, men and women have lined up on either side of the working motherhood issue. When we compare the commentary of the 1960s to the opinions we see and hear in the media today, we find that we have not come nearly so far as we would like to believe. In essence, working mothers argue— sometimes desperately—that their children are not harmed or influenced by their early years in day care, while full-time mothers and a plethora of critics argue that children are not only harmed when their mothers work, they could even be in mortal danger.

Much has been written about the 180-degree turn the American public took against Deborah Eappen, the working mother whose child died of head injuries attributed to shaken baby syndrome in 1997 in the arms of Louise Woodward, the family's au pair. Some public critics went so far as to turn Mrs. Eappen into the villain for placing her child in harm's way, as if her position as a full-time medical professional had made her uncaring and oblivious to her own child's well-being. Suddenly, the entire subject of working mothers was thrown into sharp relief. How could we possibly know what happened to our children during the day if we blithely left them in the hands of strangers? Media coverage focused on working mothers as disinterested in their children—as if a profession, by its very existence, would erase a mother's love and concern for her child.

We've seen an even greater conflict in the public's response to the potentially groundbreaking Hector vs. Young child custody case, currently in its fourth year in the courts. Alice Hector, a high-powered corporate lawyer, has battled her husband, stay-at-home dad Robert Young, for custody of their two daughters. While Hector won custody in the initial case, Young won the first appeal...and Hector won the second. As of this writing, a third appeal by Young is on the court records, waiting for a decision.

Both parents feel qualified to provide a stable and sound home. Hector clears $300,000 annually, while Young, an architect by training, has no income and assumed at-home father status in part because of his lack of employment. At the time of their decision, the three appellate judges who awarded custody to Young noted, "It is clear from the record that it is the architect father who is available to the children after school, takes the children to the doctor and dentist appointments and actively participates in the children's school and after-school activities."[1]

Apparently, the public agreed with the court of appeals: When *Dateline NBC* aired the story on August 24, 1999, viewers voted four-to-one in favor of giving custody to the father. "It's a lawsuit that strikes terror in the hearts of some professional women who work long hours, make big money and fear in the event of a divorce they could lose their children as a result," wrote Harriet Johnson Brackey of Knight Ridder news service in a January 2000 recap of the custody battle.[2]

Must it be work *or* family?

Breadwinner wives who outearn their husbands struggle to balance the conflicting strains on their self-image as professional woman and as mothers. On the one hand, statistics tell us that corporations are more willing than ever before to promote women to top positions and that the wage gap is finally narrowing between men's and women's earnings for the same work. We are told that women at the top can be more humanistic, strategic and caring managers than the men who traditionally held these positions before them. Women, according to some views, are the newly discovered valuable resource in corporate ranks, both in bricks-and-mortar companies and throughout the new Internet economy. In her book, *Why the Best Man for the Job is a Woman*, Esther Wachs Book observes, "A growing number of female chief executive officers and presidents have replaced men or excelled over rivals in male-dominated industries because they possess the qualities of leadership that top firms are seeking today. These women are not only driven individuals who are skilled at marketing and sales, but they wield considerable financial skills and have a talent for managing people in a fast-paced economy bent on non-stop innovation."[3]

On the other hand, women who succeed in their careers hear ugly words used to describe them: words like *selfish* and *greedy*. Voices from the other side of the issue tell them that their efforts to bring needed income into their homes can only be motivated by a desire for materialistic acquisition. They hear that the satisfactions of intellectual achievement, career success and recognition of their abilities should never be enough to take them away from their children, even for a few hours a day. In the eyes of many publicly vocal critics, "real" mothers are still cast in the "angel in the house" image of the Victorian era—the pure, selfless creature who puts her children before her identity, her intellect and any inappropriate desires beyond motherhood she may harbor.

How are ambitious women to react? We are encouraged to succeed, yet we are chastised for doing so. We are beckoned into the workforce, yet we are pressured to return home. As a *New York Times Magazine*
special issue proclaimed on April 5, 1998, "Mothers Can't Win."[4]

Adding further complexity to the argument about the motivations of working mothers, Arlie Hochschild provided yet another point
of view in her most recent book, *The Time Bind*. She suggests that parents work, in part, to *escape* the pressures and anxieties of home life—in
particular, the strains of caring for children at home. Hochschild argues
that mothers who work often pile on overtime hours and weekend work
projects because they provide an excuse to stay out of the house and
away from family stress. "In this new model of family and work life,"
Hochschild wrote, "a tired parent flees a world of unresolved quarrels
and unwashed laundry for the reliable orderliness, harmony and managed cheer of work. The emotional magnets beneath home and workplace are in the process of being reversed....Some people find in work a
respite from the emotional tangles at home. Others virtually marry
their work, investing it with an emotional significance once reserved for
family, while hesitating to trust loved ones at home."[5]

No doubt there are working mothers who experience some of
these problems—but they did not surface in my research. Not one of the
couples I interviewed described anything like the situations *The Time
Bind* suggests. What I constantly heard from my respondents were
laments that time escapes *them*: the split shifts they chose to help them
provide at-home care to their children keep their families from enjoying
time together; fathers willingly give up hours on the job—or even the
entire job—to assist in child raising; mothers discourage or cut back on
overtime so they can spend more time with their children.

I talked to caring, loving mothers to whom children are of paramount importance, even though these mothers are successful in their
careers and bring home the family's larger paycheck.

Some critics, including Dr. Laura Schlessinger in her latest
book, *Parenthood by Proxy*, go so far as to suggest that women with high
professional goals should not have children at all.[6] Indeed, 19 percent of
the breadwinning-wife couples I interviewed are childless—and as the
average age of this sample is thirty-two, they are likely to be childless by
choice. But even childlessness raises suspicion and anger among our
peers. As a childless breadwinning wife, I have been the target of ugly
accusations: I'm told that I am not only greedy and selfish, but heartless
and unfeeling as well. When I made the choice to be childless in my
early twenties, I actually saw friendships dissolve as other women I

knew became young mothers and assumed I could not and would not understand their love for their children. My subsequent professional success only served as further evidence that greed mattered more to me than my God-given duty to raise a family.

Even our modern society—in which working wives and mothers are a staple of our existence—praises us for our success in busting through the glass ceiling and achieving equal footing with our male colleagues...and simultaneously accuses women who work of trading in their family values for selfishness, material goods and the cold corporate environment.

Right or wrong, good or bad, the fact is that 69 percent of all mothers *do* work outside the home in twenty-first century America,[7] and a significant percentage of these working mothers are wives who make more than their husbands. While many articles and books encourage the concept of "sequencing"—staying home while children are small and returning to the workforce gradually as children enter school—many working mothers do not choose to do this. Working women with ambitious professional aims know that in most major companies, taking a few years off for child care can mean that they will be passed up for promotions and high-level corporate positions.

There's another, even more important reason, according to my respondents, that some breadwinning wives do not interrupt their careers to become at-home mothers: They know that such a move would make them utterly miserable. Of the dozens of breadwinning wives I interviewed, only two wished they could be home full-time with their children. Many others commented that stay-at-home motherhood simply was not for them.

My point is not to argue the merits or faults of day care, full-time parenting or working motherhood, but to provide some insights for breadwinning wives into the issue of working motherhood as it affects their own lives, the lives of their husbands, their children and their outside caregivers. We also will look carefully at the role of husbands in the child caregiving relationship—and how this role changes significantly when the wife brings home the larger paycheck.

Working women are still good mothers

Is it possible that children are actually harmed by growing up in day care instead of in the constant care of their own mothers? Are breadwinning mothers endangering their children's development by placing them in the care of someone outside of the home, even if these mothers strive to find the highest quality child care situation available?

As I spoke to breadwinning wives and mothers across America, I heard this fear voiced over and over. Most families at all income levels now require two incomes to maintain their standard of living, so most of these wives could not afford to support their husbands as full-time child caregivers—and many of their husbands would never consider such an arrangement. The greatest fear these working mothers share is that their professional successes are actively damaging their children. If research could prove otherwise, it would make all the difference for these mothers' potential peace of mind.

Indeed, that research exists.

Two highly respected landmark studies, completed in the last two years, provide evidence that working motherhood does no damage to children in day care or with alternative caregivers. Both point to the overall relationship with the parents—fathers as well as mothers—as making the greatest difference in the children's well-being as they grow up.

The National Institute for Child Health and Human Development (NICHD) recently released the preliminary results of its longitudinal study of early child care. Begun in 1991, the study is the most comprehensive of its kind to date, designed to determine how variations in child care are related to children's development. The NICHD Study of Early Child Care strives to answer questions about the relationship between the child care experience and the child's developmental outcome.[8]

The NICHD study has followed more than 1,300 children and their families in ten locations across the United States, with variations in background, economic status, race and family structure. The children studied were placed in a wide variety of parent-chosen day care situations: fathers, other relatives, in-home caregivers, child care home providers and center-based care. This is the first study to follow children from birth to age seven; most studies to date examine children's development in child care situations in their first three years of life.

The most striking finding of the study to date is this: The characteristics of the family itself—especially the relationship between the mother and child—are stronger predictors of children's development and behavior than the child care situation. In other words, the family environment—including family income and mother-child interaction—is far more strongly linked to a child's development than is child care.

One of the leading researchers in *attachment theory*, or the development of a child's trust in his or her parents, is Jay Belsky, Ph.D., of Pennsylvania State University. Belsky is a key leader in the NICHD study as well. The findings released by NICHD to date disprove highly publicized earlier research Belsky conducted in the 1980s, through which he determined that children placed in day care at a young age did not develop secure attachments to their mothers.

Belsky appears to fully accept the more recent study results and their evidence that the parents, not the child care situation, have the greatest impact on child development. "If God gave you the choice between putting a child in a well-functioning, well-resourced family but lots of crummy child care or into a poorly functioning, poorly resourced family and lots of good child care, there's no choice," Belsky told the *Monitor on Psychology* when the NICHD study results were released. "You'd have to choose the former. With all the debate about child care, I think we lost sight of that reality. Any effect child care has, it has in the background of the overwhelming effect of the family."[9]

This study tells us that a loving, caring relationship with mother and father sustains positive effects even when children spend most of their waking hours in the care of people outside of the family. While the study finds links between variables in the child care situation—quality, number of hours in care, child-to-adult ratios, group sizes and teacher training—and the child's development, the size of the correlation is much smaller than expected. Most important, the strongest correlation exists between the child's development and the security of his or her relationship with the parents.

As I write this, National Public Radio is reporting yet another study that suggests that toddlers who receive more than thirty hours of non-parent care each week are more aggressive and have more behavioral problems than children at home with their parents. Buried in this story is the fact that only 17 percent of the 1,364 children tested were found to have this aggressive tendency, which means that 83 percent do not exhibit behavioral problems, a far more significant statistic.[10] Yet the story's lead tells us only that children in day care develop behavioral problems.

As working women and caring mothers, we must be vigilant in gathering the facts about the influences of day care on our children. The news media presents only capsule versions of detailed, involved studies that reveal far more than we hear on the nightly news. We must be careful to take news reporting with a grain of salt as we find the right mix of out-of-home care and nurturing, loving home life for our children.

Can working women be loving mothers?

According to many reports, children can thrive in good day care provided by other people, so long as the relationship with their parents is strong, secure and nurturing. Recent studies also tell us that working mothers can be warm and loving with their children—and that their children thrive because of the love they receive from their working parents.

The Families and Work Institute, one of the leading sources of information on the roles of women as wives, mothers and working people, provides some insights in the National Study of the Changing Workforce, conducted in 1977 and again in 1997. Ellen Galinsky, cofounder and president of this institute and a leader in this study, reports in her book, *Ask the Children*, that the number of people who feel that employed mothers can have just as good a relationship with their children as at-home mothers climbed in twenty years, from 58 percent in 1977 to 67 percent in 1997. "I attribute this largely to the gradual social and cultural change as women have moved into the workforce in larger and larger numbers, and as families have become more dependent on their income," she said.[11]

The Families and Work Institute didn't stop with this survey of working parents. Galinsky led a groundbreaking 1997-98 study in which she and her research team did something no research had done before: They asked the children for their opinions. They surveyed 1,023 children ages eight through eighteen, and 605 employed parents. They also conducted focus groups with 171 individuals—parents and children—from sixty-nine families.

The study explores children's perceptions of modern work and family life. Galinsky's findings shatter many of the truisms, assumptions and common wisdom associated with working mothers and their relationships with their children—debunking some ingrained ideas including quality time versus quantity time, children's understanding of money, the insights they have about their parents' lives and the cues they pick up from their parents that influence their own behavior.

The young respondents were enthusiastic about their mothers, giving them high marks for love and attention. In fact, 88 percent of the children surveyed gave their mothers an A or a B for making them feel important and loved, while 75 percent awarded A or B grades to their mothers for being someone they could go to when they were upset. They were also enthusiastic about their mothers' availability in areas like spending time talking, encouraging them to learn, attending important events in their children's lives and appreciating their children for who they are. (Scores were similar, but slightly lower on all questions for fathers' performance in these areas.)[12]

In addition, 87 percent of children surveyed in the seventh through twelfth grades gave their mothers an A or a B for raising them with good values. Galinsky quoted one eleven-year-old boy's view of his mother: "My mother is hard working. I ain't going to be lazy working. She tries to get that out of me 'cause I am lazy now, but I'm going to try to be better at that, work harder at that. You know she tries to perfect herself. She's persistent. You know that's a good quality."[13]

Most important, Galinsky's study shows that maternal employment is not linked to children's assessment of their parents. "In not a single analysis is the mother's employment status related to the way a child sees his or her mother or father," she wrote. "Neither is her working part-time or full-time....A mother who is employed can be there for her child or not, just as mothers who are not employed can be. It is who the mother is as a person and the relationship she establishes with her child that are the important factors."[14]

What does this mean for breadwinning wives?

For wives who make more, it comes as a great relief to know that some of the recent studies not only provide guides for what is needed in good day care, but these studies tell us that we are not endangering the healthy development of our children simply by placing them in quality care while we are at work, as long as we provide the warmth, security and nurturing environment at home that they need to thrive.

Breadwinning wives' greatest obstacle to feeling secure in their roles is their own perceptions of themselves as mothers—working mothers who not only contribute to the family's income, but also sustain it. With such a strong focus on career and professionalism, how can we feel that we are making an equal contribution to the health, well-being and development of our children—ignoring the messages we hear from doubters in our neighborhoods, in our families and in the media?

Many of the couples I interviewed have accomplished successful parenting, using their solid instincts, open lines of communication between husband and wife and a great deal of trial and error. The couples who report the most success in finding a child-raising balance have broken the codes of gender division, sharing in child care with great joy. They know that there is more to child-raising than intermittent contact with their children—they create environments filled with warmth and love for their children, while battling furiously to achieve a balance between work, home and family.

How do they do it?

They create rituals.

These parents create special times they share with their children on a regular basis. We're not talking about that hackneyed concept of "quality time," in which parents were expected to structure artificial activities to prove that they were giving their children their undivided attention. Instead, these rituals are simple parts of everyday life, opportunities for parent and child to connect—on the child's terms, in the course of his or her daily activities. Rituals can be as simple as sharing cookies and milk in the evening, reading a story together every day or taking a walk to the corner for ice cream.

They treat events in their children's lives as important appointments.

Despite the demands of business life, some breadwinning wives write their children's sports matches, concerts, recitals and other special events into their calendars and leave work to be there, without apology or excuse. This is a condition they have established with their employers and they stick to it—demonstrating that they can be effective employees and still maintain a commitment to their homes and families.

They share in the discipline of their children as well as in the good times.

In the 1950s and 1960s, an oft quoted refrain of full-time mothers was, "Just wait until your father gets home!" The breadwinning wives I interviewed are not interested in turning into mean, punishing mothers at the end of the day, even if their husbands are full-time fathers and hold the primary child care responsibility. As my client, Janice, noted in the introduction to this book, these mothers recognize and acknowledge the urge to throw themselves into an easy chair at day's end, but instead trade this inclination for time with their children—to help with homework, finish projects, read books or simply supervise bedtime. Despite their roles as family breadwinners, they share the unpopular decision-making or disciplining with their husbands, so neither parent becomes the perpetual "bad guy."

They share parenting with their husbands—the children's fathers—from the beginning.

The breadwinning wives who are happiest share child care responsibilities with their husbands. While there are no good measures in place for determining "equal" participation in child care between a husband and wife, the important thing is not a fifty-fifty split; the critical factor in the couple's satisfaction is in whether each parent understands his or her role in the relationship and each spouse's expectation of the other's involvement.

This is not to say that the breadwinning wives I interviewed have everything figured out about child care. On the contrary, many of these wives and their husbands registered conflicting views on the needs of their children, the appropriate way to deal with each child, the husbands' or wives' lack of participation in child care or the quality of the care provided. So much change in the American family has taken place recently—with wives as breadwinners happening only in the last decade—that we are far from shaking out the conflicting needs and roles that have emerged in the process.

Let's take a look at some of the work these families have done in establishing balance in their homes and see what information they give us about how parents adapt to the changing roles of mother and father when Mom brings in the greater income.

Fitting into a child's life

Grace, a forty-five-year-old Midwestern county representative and mother of six-year-old George, dishes up stacks of peanut butter and strawberry jam sandwiches, carrot sticks, cookies and juice boxes for all of George's friends on weekends. This started out as a quick, convenient way for Pete and Grace to be certain that George got lunch, whether or not his friends departed promptly at noon. Eventually, their gregarious son's social circle grew...so on some weekends, there might be seven or eight children standing with hands extended, ready for their lunch treat.

Grace and Pete were already in their late thirties when they married, waiting until the troubles that hounded Pete's plumbing business had settled down. Pete became the unfortunate victim of untrustworthy employees and embezzlement, leaving the business bankrupt and Pete facing long years in courtrooms and accountants' offices. Now he runs a similar but smaller business from home, often working long hours and taking out-of-town jobs that offer him high profit for independent work.

When Pete's first business failed, Grace's income quickly rose to exceed his as she combined her partnership in an accounting firm with her elected county position. In the four years before they married, Grace's $60,000 annual salary made her the primary breadwinner, a position she is likely to maintain throughout their marriage. Pete's business brings him a salary of about $30,000 each year.

Despite their packed schedules and the turmoil they'd faced in re-establishing Pete in business, once they married they wanted children—and wanted them fast, given that their forties were just around the corner. George was born less than two years after their wedding.

Perhaps it was their relative maturity or the fact that they wanted a child so much after years of waiting—or maybe it was the simple necessity of their work/family situation. Whatever the impetus, Grace and Pete almost immediately created a seamless routine in which they truly share in the care and upbringing of their son, often letting other household responsibilities slide to give them more time with George. Grace comments that the living room usually looks "as if a Playskool bomb went off in it." At any time of the day, breakfast cereal bowls languish on the kitchen table, the milk still pooling in the bottom. Behind the house, the skeletal progress of a first-floor addition stands waiting for too-busy hands to return.

However George, a smiling, talkative, strapping six-year-old already more than four feet tall, delights in sharing his home and parents with many friends. Grace fairly glows as she watches him.

"We have a real rhythm going," she said as she spread peanut butter on bread. "On weekends, I'm the primary child care provider. During the week, it's Pete. Pete likes to be really active with George—he enjoys walking him to school every morning, even when he's going to have a busy day. That's their private time. When there's a minor illness, Pete's the one who takes George to the pediatrician or stays home with him. He's been available during the formative years to do these things."

Grace addressed each of the neighborhood children by name as she wiped their grubby hands with moist towelettes before they reached for their sandwiches. Suddenly, she cocked her head and gave the next child in line a curious look. She caught Pete's eye from his perch across the room, where he chatted with a curly-haired, blond child he clearly knew well. Pete looked up, questioningly.

Who is this one? Grace mouthed at him.

Pete glanced at the boy standing in front of Grace and returned a shrug, hands raised with palms up.

Grace knelt and looked the child in the eye. "Hi, I'm Grace. What's your name?"

The young boy reacted as if caught with one hand in the cookie jar, ducking his head and dragging one foot around the other. "William," he said shyly.

"William, where do you live?"

William gestured in the general direction of the next street over.

"Do you know your telephone number?"

He nodded, slowly reciting it. Grace handed him a carrot stick and left the kitchen counter to grab a phone. Quickly and cheerily, she dialed up William's house and introduced herself to his mother. "I thought you might be new in the neighborhood, so I just wanted you to know that William is here with all the other kids," she said. "I didn't want you to worry. Is it okay for him to eat PB&J?"

Surrounded by young faces and happy chatter, Grace was absolutely in her element. This weekend ritual is part of the way she shares George's life on his terms, accepting her husband's closeness and availability to her son during the week and making George her primary focus on weekends.

"We want the kids in the house," she said. "We want George to feel that he can bring his friends here anytime and that they're our friends, too. Yes, the living room is a mess. So what? Our son is happy."

The remarkable balance Pete and Grace have created in child rearing is no accident, rather it is the result of considered discussion, weighing of the alternatives and a mutual commitment to making a safe, happy, peaceful home for themselves and their son. "We made the decision early on that if we had a child, I would still need to work full time," said Grace. "Pete's new business was only nine months old when George was born. So I had to accept that I would work outside the home, Pete would work from home and we would try to achieve a balance. I enjoy working and I have been successful in my field. But my leisure time with Pete and George—that's what I hold most important."

Pete and Grace use the flexibility available to them in Pete's work schedule to fill the daytime gaps, during which Grace is usually tied up with clients, meetings and professional responsibilities. Each has found a meaningful way to connect with George beyond the day-to-day treadmill of work, school, outside activities and appointments, carving out special times they share with him regularly, no matter what their schedules demand.

"I still go into George's school and volunteer," said Grace. "I try to do it every other week for about an hour—I help kids read in George's classroom. I'm finding I do it more this year. But I had to sacrifice something—so that 'something' was housework. Neither of us does any real cleaning. We tried to hire someone to do it, but you have to be able to put things away and pick up before they come. We just couldn't do it, so it became a waste of money. Now I just don't think it's that important any more."

What did Grace and Pete do to create this happy environment? Each parent developed a special *ritual* with George—for Grace, it's filling the living room and kitchen with George's friends every Saturday, making her the favorite Mom on the block; for Pete, it's quiet time with his son during the morning walk to school. Not only do these rituals provide predictability and routine for the whole family, they also give George time to connect with his busy parents to talk, laugh, play and enjoy being their child.

George is not the only one who benefits from these rituals. As a breadwinning wife and working mother, Grace finds herself faced with overtime and long work hours on a regular basis. In her most stressful moments at work, she knows she has her special time with her son to look forward to—and she holds this absolutely sacred, taking no meetings or calls on Saturdays. Her weekend ritual with George is certainly not the only time she spends with him, but it has become her most predictable, dependable and cherished time.

There is more to this story than the idyllic scene in the kitchen, of course. Pete's out-of-town jobs sometimes leave Grace with full care of George for a week or longer, so she has learned to ask friends and relatives for help—an act that Grace performs with great difficulty. "I don't know what I'd do without my friends who are always willing to pick up George from school and bring him home with their own kids for the afternoon," she said. "It took me a long time to learn to ask for help, but what choice do I have? You have to depend on others and then you return the favor when you can."

Family versus work: Which is more important depends on who's asking.

One of the most critical changes that must take place throughout the business world is the acknowledgement of parents' need for time with their children, even during the course of the business day. Too often we hear stories of mothers and fathers who are "stuck at the office" and miss a child's Little League playoffs, dance recital, vocal concert or track meet. The effect on the child may be transitory (although Galinsky tells us that children do measure their parents according to their ability to be "there for them"[15]), but the parents never forget letting their children down.

As wives who make more, we often hold positions of responsibility and authority in the workplace—so when a woman of high rank in an organization places important events in her children's lives on her calendar and treats them as sacred, others may have the opportunity to follow suit. When a breadwinning wife is also a manager, she has the opportunity to set guidelines within her own organization and to provide more balance between work and family to her staff.

Needless to say, many places of business have not caught up with the encouraging trend in creating this work/family balance. I spent many years at an advertising agency that did not condone time allowances for its employees. The corporate culture encouraged long hours of overtime, weekend work, morning meetings at 6:30 and had an actual spoken rule that family came second to clients. One December, I was called away from my own birthday party on a Sunday afternoon to deal with some new emergency the agency's owner felt took precedence.

In my early days as a manager there, I hired a copywriter, Christine, who had teenage children. I asked her to come in an hour early one day to attend a meeting with an early-riser client. As the meeting ended, she asked me, "Since I came in for this, can I take comp time and leave an hour early today to see my son's tennis match?"

Sadly, I didn't hear her request as that of a loving parent. What I heard were the words "comp time," a condition that was strictly forbidden by the agency's employee handbook. Christine did not know that this was a management hot button, nor did I understand that she had already promised her son that she would attend the game. I was busy being a model manager, following the company rules to the letter.

I told her that she could not take an hour of comp time, because the agency did not permit hour-for-hour time trade-offs. As she was a fairly new employee, she called her son and told him she would not be at the game. And she spread the word of my cold-hearted edict to everyone else on the staff.

I learned my lesson—I had to be a human being first and an agency manager second. I saw the look on her face when I denied her this time with her son and I never forgot it. Christine moved on shortly thereafter to a more family-friendly employer but I paid far more attention to the needs of my staff for flextime, early departures and family emergencies after that—fighting for these rights with the agency management, who truly did not see the value. I realized, without the words at the time, that I was guilty of "blaming the culture," an act noted by James A. Levine and Todd L. Pittinsky in their book, *Working Fathers: New Strategies for Balancing Work and Family*.[16] It was in my power to make change; I only had to take the first step.

When I look back on the initial incident, I wish that Christine had simply said, "I am leaving at four o'clock today to attend my son's tennis match," without asking permission or apologizing for time away from work. She gave me the opportunity to deny her the time, which I did. This is the condition into which so many working women and working mothers are forced by their employers—they look for permission or make up excuses to miss work and be with their children, instead of demanding this time as their right and privilege as mothers.

For fathers, this can be an even worse situation, as we will see later in this chapter.

Breadwinning wives and mothers have unique opportunities to set new examples within the organizations that employ them. It's time to *stop asking for permission* to be with your children at their important events or special days—or worse, when they are ill or otherwise in need of your attention. Write the important children's events on your calendar and treat them as unchangeable appointments. A vast number of working women at every level of every organization are mothers as well as workers and are entitled to honor their commitments to their children just as they honor their commitments to the job.

Of course, the business world is a far from perfect place. Too many employers identify a female employee with a strong commitment to children and home as a woman on "the mommy track." Requests for flextime, early departures or late arrivals, shifted schedules or telecommuting situations can all work against women—and men, for that matter. Some employers will see this as disregard for the company's rules rather than the need for more flexible ones. This can be true even when the working people who request such changes are model employees, delivering excellent work and never missing deadlines. I well remember the words of the agency's female (!) president to me when a top account executive announced her pregnancy: "Well, we might as well clean out her desk. She'll get a baby in her arms and she'll be done with us."

Breadwinning wives must succeed at work, sometimes at any cost, because they bring in the family's main income. However, this drive for success is not without stressors. A 1995 Whirlpool Foundation study titled *Women: The New Providers* notes that 92 percent of working women worry somewhat or worry a great deal that their families do not spend enough time together.[17] I found fainter echoes of this in my own survey of wives who make more: only 25 percent said that if they could change one thing about their current situation, it would be to have more time together as a family. Yet every working mother I interviewed expressed a strong desire to be there for her children and to be certain that the children had the quality care they deserved.

If we want to change the way business is done by creating more family time in each day, we need to lobby for this from our employers at every level. For those of us who are employers, we need to demonstrate this family commitment ourselves and make it possible for our employees to balance work and family. This is the new reality of working in the twenty-first century—all workers, male and female, have families who need and deserve their attention. It is truly up to us, as individual employees, to move the world of work in this rewarding new direction.

It's all about choices

For wives who make more, the conflict between work and motherhood can be especially strong. While wives who supplement their husbands' larger paychecks may be in more of a position to make choices between staying home, cutting back hours or placing children in day care, wives who make more often have no choices at all. As primary or even exclusive breadwinners, these women cannot give up employment altogether and expect to maintain the lifestyle which their families feel is important. In making the choice to pursue successful careers, they have limited their choices in other areas of their lives.

This is particularly poignant when breadwinner wives experience maternal changes of heart upon the arrival of their first child.

Audrey, a managing partner of a law firm in Minnesota, had never intended to give up her work time to be home with her newborn son. When she became pregnant two years after marrying Dick, a successful attorney in his own right, she quickly sought and found a full-time, live-in nanny to care for the child.

"We have everything," she told me in low tones, so that her nanny would not hear. "We have a house by the water, because Dick loves to sail. We have a boat. We have two Lexus sedans. We travel, we dine out several times a week and we can buy whatever we want. It's a great life—we have a lot of fun. But now, I have a son—and all I want to do is be home with him. Everything is different. I cry when I have to leave for work in the morning."

Choice would not seem to be an issue for Audrey and Dick, on the surface. Audrey's annual income exceeds $250,000 annually, while Dick's "supplemental" income usually reaches $90,000. A couple can live in comfort on either of these two figures—and if Audrey cut her income by half, they could still maintain significant portions of their lifestyle.

Yet Audrey has built up a terrific resentment of her husband's lesser earning power. "He doesn't make enough to support this house and everything else," she said. "Sometimes it just makes me furious. I would like to cut back on my hours and make changes to my work schedule. I'm the boss—I can do whatever I need to. But what happens to this house? How much will we give up?"

Audrey hires out just about every household responsibility—she has a cleaning service that dispenses with the housework; an accountant handles the family finances; a lawn and garden service keeps the yard in check. Dick enjoys cooking and prepares most of the meals they eat at home. From the outside, this is a life anyone would envy—except that at the core of this idyllic existence, Audrey is miserable. Worse, she sees her husband as the source of her unhappiness.

"I've told him, 'We're going to have to cut back, maybe even sell the house,'" she said. "He's not pleased with that at all. He's always wanted to live by the water and now he has this sort of country club life. The thing is, if I decide to take time off or give up the managing partner position to go part-time, we can't stay here. It's just too expensive."

Every couple would like the opportunity to enjoy the luxuries their money can buy, but an extravagant lifestyle can become the most elegant prison we can imagine. Audrey and Dick spent years with nothing but fun and comfort as their highest priorities. When Audrey found something she valued more—time with her infant son—circumstances denied her that pleasure.

I offer no moral judgments on this. When breadwinning wives assess their earning potential, their life goals and their desire for a work-family balance, they need to take into account that priorities may change—and that there may be reasons to decrease salaries, make drastic changes in their lives or give up a high level of earning potential. I urge wives who make more to give themselves the flexibility to choose their next move, whether it's up or down the earning scale. Spending right up to your means—or beyond—can turn work-family balance into an unobtainable goal.

Recommendations: How to Be a Happy Breadwinning Mother
1. Be honest with yourself about your needs as a professional and as a parent.
Not every mother belongs at home with her children and not every professional woman (in fact, remarkably few) puts her work before her family. The happiest couples I interviewed have taken hard looks at their lives as parents and made the changes that best accommodate their combined desires for family lives and professional successes. If it's a change in lifestyle to allow you to shorten your work hours and take a smaller salary or if you need to find a better day care situation that will allow you to spend more time at work, sit down with your husband and seek solutions together. Find the right balance that will keep you from looking back with remorse as your children grow up or as job opportunities go to others.

2. Create rituals and special times with your children.

Ellen Galinsky's study tells us that children most remember and value their ordinary time with parents—not structured "quality time," but pleasant activities that take place on a predictable basis. Find ways to spend time with your children in mundane activities as well as on special occasions. Routine, ritual and tradition create stability for your children, while giving you a dependable time with them on a regular basis to share and cherish.

3. Take advantage of work-family balance opportunities.

Explore time flexibility programs that are offered or should be offered by employers; if you are the employer, create flexibility as part of your corporate culture. If your employer refuses to offer you programs for this balance or if the company gives with one hand while indicating that your acceptance could hinder your success with the other, consider finding a new employer. In the long run, you are unlikely to regret spending less time at work, but you will absolutely regret missed opportunities to be with your children.

4. Explore the stay-at-home dad approach.

It's not for everyone, but now that more than two million fathers in the United States are primary caregivers for their children, it's certainly not such an unusual phenomenon. Take a hard look at the costs of day care or split shifts versus the loss of your husband's income. If it's feasible, explore the possibilities with your husband. You may find that he's been waiting for the opportunity to immerse himself in fatherhood, perhaps as part of a larger change in his life—a shift in career, a chance to practice his art or music, a few years to build an at-home business. Have a solid discussion about this to test his interest. He may be reluctant to bring it up himself, for fear of appearing to take advantage of your higher income or seeming like "less of a man." When you give him the opening, he may be ready to take it. We'll explore this option more thoroughly in chapter 11.

5. Learn to ask for help.

You married for many reasons; one of the most important may be that you planned to raise children with your husband. If the children are here, you still may be behaving like a single parent, taking on the sole responsibility for child care as if your husband isn't an equal partner. Discuss with him what you need. Refer to the List/Enlist Approach in chapter 9 for ways to have a dispassionate, honest, businesslike discussion with your husband about the tasks and responsibilities that need attention. Asking for help does not make you appear weaker—it lets you both perform even more efficiently and effectively.

6. Give yourselves the flexibility to make choices.
It's tempting to enjoy every dollar of whatever discretionary income you have—but the larger your mortgage and the higher your credit card debt, the less flexibility you have to make changes in your life when the need arises. Use a portion of your discretionary income to build a nest egg for change, a reserve that could allow you a year off when your child is born or a more flexible schedule at a lower salary for an extended period while you participate more fully in child-raising.

7. Make time to communicate with your husband, your partner in parenting.
Schedule time every day or as often as you can, even if it's just a few minutes, to discuss your child's life with your husband. This is your time to share information, gather facts, figure out the next day's transportation and other issues and make sure that both of you are working toward the same goals. It's also the time to review the work load and make adjustments as necessary. Turn this into a special ritual of your own: a quiet cup of tea after the children are in bed, fifteen minutes when you get home from work before plunging into the next task or a late dinner or snack before turning in. By touching base on a regular basis, you will avoid many of the conflicts that arise when wives and husbands save up their concerns like so many trading cards, until they let the whole deck fly one day in a flurry of frustration. Your children deserve a great deal of your time, but you and your husband deserve time as well—to keep your marriage strong and your parenting plans on track.

CHAPTER 11

THE DADDY TRACK
Having it All—New Roles for the Wife-Husband Partnership

"My six-year-old is in kindergarten," said Martin, a thirty-five-year-old assistant pastor of a Southern country parish. He sits on the porch of his white farmhouse, the only structure on a sprawling, velvet-green, two-acre lot in the midst of Virginia's rolling hills. "She goes a full day every other day. But my three-year-old, she's home with me all day, every day. She's my buddy." Said three-year-old squealed and scampered across the lawn at that moment, hot on the heels of a cotton-tailed rabbit that nimbly out-ran her.

Formerly a planning meeting facilitator and consultant to non-profit boards of directors, Martin willingly made the switch to at-home fatherhood. Sylvia, thirty-two and the owner of a collection agency, made the choice to keep building her newly formed business after a year home with her first baby. "We looked at Martin staying home as an option right from the beginning," she said by phone from her bustling office. "We decided that whoever had the better paying job should work and the other would stay home. Once the business was up and running, the reality was that I made more money."

She hesitated. "It wasn't much more—just a little more—but everything was laying out so nicely for Martin to change careers at the same time, that we saw it as God's will pointing us in the right direction."

Martin's transition to religious leadership gave him the opportunity to work from his own home, bring people into the house for meetings and schedule his most absorbing activities for evenings and weekends, when Sylvia could take over with the children. "It's the perfect arrangement," he said. "But what's really great is my relationships with the kids. I used to come home from work and our first daughter would run right by me to Mom. Now she runs to me first. I can understand the girls' thoughts and feelings so much more now that I'm with them every day."

In the small manufacturing-based town Martin and Sylvia call home, Martin blends in much more than he expected he would. Other fathers—men who work split or rotating shifts or who work nights at the town's only large factory—are often visible with their children during the day. "When I take the kids to gymnastics, I see other fathers there," Martin observed. "They just think I work a swing shift. If this were a metropolitan or more suburban area, I might stick out a lot more."

Not everyone was so quick to accept Martin's scaled-back professional life and his preference for raising children over making money, however. "My stepfather is from the old school," he told me. "He's eighty-five years old and he believes that the man should be working and supporting his family. So from him I got the whole 'Mr. Mom' thing—about how I couldn't possibly have any self-respect if I was home doing women's work. But Sylvia said to him, 'You call him Mr. Mom! Then does that make me Mrs. Dad? You're just being unfair.' It made him stop and think, at least."

Sylvia, on the other hand, admitted that the "Mrs. Dad" moniker hit closer to home than she would like. "We did go through a time when I became the husband," she said. "You know, I came home at night tired and I would just want to sit there. So there was a role reversal, you bet. We bickered a lot, until we came to a better understanding of our responsibilities.

"Now, our partnership is going great. Martin takes care of the girls all day and I can do more crafts and projects with them in the evenings. Before, I'd be with the kids, but I'd be thinking about washing the floor. Now I can have fun with the girls and be part of their daily learning and growing."

When pressed about her involvement in daily child care, Sylvia considered carefully. "I was home with the first one for a year. When I stayed home, I spent my time cleaning and puttering around and never did anything for myself. Now, Martin does such a good job that when I come home, I do my part with the girls and then there's more time for my own stuff."

The good job Martin does goes well beyond his child care responsibilities. He cleans the house except for the bathrooms—"I told her I wouldn't do bathrooms," he informed me—cooks the evening meal, handles all the laundry and tends to the expansive lawn and garden. Never one to call a mechanic or hire a contractor, Martin performs the home repairs and teaches himself what he needs to know about carpentry, plumbing and electricity to keep the house in working order. Sylvia does the washing up after dinner and prepares the Sunday meal while Martin leads parish activities.

"We sound like the great American family in reverse," Sylvia noted, "but the truth is, I have to make a mental effort to play with the kids every evening. I'm really tired, so it's very easy to just sit there and read the paper. I have to make the extra effort to get down and play with them. Every night I take off one hat and put on the other one. I have to remind myself to switch roles."

Martin and Sylvia have found something many couples only dream about—a balance of family life, fulfilling work and a quality lifestyle, in which each of them has the opportunity to pursue interests and build careers. At the same time, they work together to provide a loving home for their children, shunning day care facilities to raise their children in their own house, under the parents' supervision.

It's not a perfect situation—Sylvia works long hours and has to kick herself out of the easy chair and onto the living room floor to share time with her daughters—but it's closer than many couples ever get to combining work and family in a way that benefits everyone.

How did they do it? By working together and examining all sides of their relationship with one another, with their children and with their professions. Martin and Sylvia were completely honest with one another and with themselves about what they really wanted from their lives. They formulated a plan and moved forward with it—and now, because they shared the same goals, they have it all.

But isn't that supposed to be impossible?

Remember the concept of "having it all?" This phrase rang through the 1970s and early 1980s and quickly became an indictment of the working wife and mother. Hand in hand with the accusation that we were selfish and greedy came the assumption that working wives and mothers wanted something unattainable—*all* of the rewards of life, be they in the boardroom, the playroom, the kitchen or the bedroom. We wanted to be successful professionals *and* good mothers, two goals that appeared to clash resoundingly in the actual execution.

I was surprised as I went about my survey at the number of women who said to me, "You can't have it all—it's just not possible." Yet these are the women who have indeed reached this impossible dream. They are successful at work, they are raising children, they have happy marriages and some of them have accumulated a fair amount of material wealth.

How can it be true that women can't have it all? The concept in itself seems to assume that women who work somehow expect to become superior human beings, juggling career, housework, child care and all other aspects of life independently and with no help from anyone. What the traditional theory of "having it all" does *not* consider is that these women are not alone. *They are married.* They have husbands who can and should share in household responsibilities, especially in the care and upbringing of their children.

Many researchers point out that the father's involvement is equally important to each child's healthy development. For example, research completed by the Children, Youth and Family Consortium at the University of Minnesota tells us that fathers' active engagement in the lives of their children enhances children's chances for academic success, a healthy gender identity and clear values and moral development, which, ultimately, lead to greater success in both family and work. "Although it's easy to imagine the importance of a father in the life of a growing son, daughters also benefit enormously from a close, loving relationship with their father," noted Martha Farrell Erickson, Ph.D., the Consortium's director.[1]

This is especially important for wives who make more. Often, these wives and mothers turn to their husbands to provide primary care for their young children, either as equal partners in the parenting relationship or as at-home fathers. Many husbands of breadwinning wives are very involved in raising their children, both as a matter of necessity and by choice. The opportunity to form close bonds with their children, especially when Mom is not there for large parts of the day or evening, gives these fathers a new perspective on parenting and on sharing their children's lives.

One of the most surprising aspects of my research was in the extraordinarily low number of breadwinning wives I encountered who described inequities in their husband's role in child care. The women I interviewed reported that their husbands are, for the most part, active and enthusiastic participants in their children's lives—bending their schedules to accommodate daily morning and evening care, sharing in family outings on weekends, pitching in on tasks from breakfast to bedtime and generally carrying an equal or greater load of the child raising responsibility.

This is a drastically different scenario than the national average. According to the 1997 National Study of the Changing Workforce, conducted by the Families and Work Institute, fathers spend an average of 2.3 hours per workday caring for and doing things with their children, an increase of 30 minutes per workday since 1977. In contrast, mothers spend nearly one hour more than fathers (3.2 versus 2.3 hours) with their children on workdays.[2]

We can attribute the child care equity in female-breadwinner marriages to several factors. In chapter 5, we discussed the similarities between husbands who are happy in marriages in which their wives are the principal breadwinners. One of the most striking similarities is that these men place family and home above their desire to make money—so it is only natural to find that such husbands are eager to participate in their children's lives. In addition, these husbands have more opportunity than most breadwinning fathers do to make time for their children, specifically because they are *not* the breadwinners. Their wives' higher income position gives these men the option of being a daily part of their children's lives.

Fathers' participation in child care is certainly not an automatic condition of marriages in which the wives are the breadwinners, however. In my research, I found that the husbands who were the most comfortable with their wives' breadwinning role were most likely to be more involved in child care. Those who expressed ambivalence, discomfort or even unhappiness with the arrangement were more likely to find child care emasculating and stay out of it altogether.

That negativity quickly came to the surface in my conversations with Martha, an advertising agency account manager, and Randy, her artist husband. Randy works an additional job as a waiter in the evenings to help bring in the money they need to complete renovations on their sprawling farmhouse, purchased far below market value because of its desperate need for repairs.

"I feel like I'm the primary caretaker of our two-year-old son," the very pregnant Martha told me, wincing as an early contraction hit her. Our interview served as a distraction while she waited for her second child to arrive—and he did, a strapping boy, just a few hours later.

"When Brandon was born, Randy and I suddenly had a gender issue. Until then I was taking care of the financial aspects of the house and home and Randy dealt with the physical—like repairs and housework. I'm not sure what Randy's expectations were when we had a child. He just never seems to think about him. Randy's got things to do, so Brandon's more of an afterthought."

She sighed. "I feel like I have to say, 'Hello, can you watch Brandon? I'm leaving the room.' I just don't think that's fair."

When we met again nearly a year later, Martha pushed her grinning younger son, Robbie, in a stroller while Brandon ran ahead, chattering happily. It was a sunny Saturday afternoon and Martha had taken the children on an outing so that Randy could have time alone at home to work.

"I know he loves the kids, but it seems like it just never occurs to him that they need his attention," she said. "Look, here we are out as a family—but not as a family. When Randy has something else to do, the kids are just not in the picture. It would never occur to him to give up his time doing something else to be with them.

"I'm not saying he's not a good father. I think he is—he plays with the kids and he enjoys being with them. But they're my responsibility when I get up in the morning and I'm the one who puts them to bed. He's got other things to do."

What is Randy's perspective on this issue? I spoke with him on several occasions, sitting at the dining room table in the couple's house while Brandon—and later Robbie—played within sight in the living room. "I would prefer to spend more time with my children," he told me. "I see them maybe three hours a week. However, the child care arrangement we have is fine with me. They're in day care during the day and I think those people do a great job."

He shook his head. "But it's my responsibility as a parent to raise them, not someone else's. Our arrangement is an economic necessity. We can't afford to have one of us at home."

A traditional man with the non-conformist trappings of a studio artist, Randy's greatest wish, I discovered, was that Martha become a full-time mother and give up some or all of her breadwinning responsibility. Of all the husbands I interviewed, Randy seemed the least comfortable with his wife's breadwinning role. "The long range plan is that if I can make 50 percent more, Martha could work part-time and stay home a great deal. That would make her happy," he noted.

Martha, on the other hand, expressed no such desire. "I am mostly contented," she said. "I do wish that Randy made more money; we could do more things then. But it's more important that we spend a greater amount of time together as a family. If that means that I must continue working and make the money, that's fine. With me doing that, Randy has more time and we can do more things together as a family."

She thought about this for a moment. "What I really want is not to have to spend twice as much time thinking about where the children are and what they might be into, because I know that Randy isn't thinking about it at all," she said. "I'd like to feel that the children are at the top of his consciousness the way they are mine. That's just not how it goes."

Martha was not the only wife I interviewed who found herself in this double-time scenario. The husbands who spend the least amount of time with their children or who bear the least daily responsibility for their care, take their wives' or outside caregivers' attention to their children very much for granted. They don't see themselves as active participants in the child care role—and clearly, they never have. Even though they live in nontraditional relationships, with their wives carrying the breadwinning load, these husbands tend to see child raising in the most traditional terms: women's work.

How did they reach this conclusion? Perhaps through their own upbringing, as we discussed in chapter 5. The vast majority of these men were raised in traditional homes with a stay-at-home mother and a father whose attention was perfunctory at best. However, the breadwinning wives who have accepted total responsibility for child care have done themselves and their children an injustice—they have not actively worked to break through their husbands' conventional points of view. They have not brought them into the child care picture as equal partners who share in decision making and take on responsibilities. Breadwinner wives who parent alone have lowered their expectations of their husbands' commitment to child care...and their husbands have willingly gone along.

The plight of the working father

On top of this, pressure to perform at work can limit the amount of time and energy working fathers feel they can give to child care. This pressure magnifies if the men are uncomfortable with their wives' positions as top wage earners and they feel the need to get ahead so that they can take over the family breadwinning role.

In his book, *Working Fathers: New Strategies for Balancing Work and Family*, James A. Levine discusses the dynamic of fatherhood and career: "For the majority of American men, an internal shift in values has created what I call the *invisible dilemma of Daddy Stress*, a largely unrecognized conflict between their double duties of work and family that they feel they should not expose."[3] Levine, director of The Fatherhood Project at the Families and Work Institute, leads seminars at corporations across the country to help break down the barriers between working fathers, their drive to succeed at work and their need to spend more time with their families.

Another recent study by the Families and Work Institute examined major corporations that now offer work-family balance programs for their employees. The 1998 Business-Work Life Study revealed that 88 percent of companies surveyed allow workers to take time off work to attend school and child care functions, and 81 percent permit employees to return to work on a gradual basis following childbirth and adoption. More than two-thirds of these employers have programs for flextime and more than half allow employees to move back and forth between full-time and part-time positions and to work at home occasionally.[4] All of these trends are good news for working parents of either gender.

The percentage of employees—especially male employees—taking advantage of these programs, however, is significantly low. In *The Time Bind*, Arlie Hochschild postulated that working parents do not choose these programs, because they actually want to escape the stresses of their families, rather than spending more time with them.[5] However, James Levine notes in *Working Fathers* that there are many other reasons for men's low enrollment in family-friendly work programs—not the least of which is that the corporate structure expects *women* to want additional time with their families, but does not expect this of *men*. Men can significantly compromise their career objectives in some companies by demonstrating a high commitment to their families—and a perceived lower commitment to the job. Levine reports, "One man told me he can't bring himself to ask for a change in the weekly staff meeting that ends at 5:30 P.M., even though he needs to pick up his daughter at day care by 5:30. Why not? Because at work he'd seen an excellent temp lose the opportunity for a permanent position by saying she wanted to get home in time for dinner with her large family each night. 'I live in fear,' this man says, 'that speaking out about my domestic responsibilities could work against me as well.'"[6]

Two-parent systems begin at home

If we're going to break down the barriers that keep working fathers from equally participating in child care, we have to stop thinking in terms of gender. We need to concentrate instead on considering the family as a unit—two parents who are of equal importance to the children, who need both parents' care and love.

What can breadwinning wives do to engage husbands in parenting as equal partners?

Start early. If you are currently expecting a child or even planning your first child with your husband, this is the time to lay the foundation for dual parenting. As the spouse who actually bears the child, you are deeply aware of your child's development. You know at every moment that a child will soon be in your life—but your husband can't physically share this part of the experience. It's up to you to share this phase with him, by involving him in the preparations for your child's arrival, from reading books on child care to inviting him to the baby shower (have one for couples, so that he and "the guys" can attend). Make him part of the focus at every opportunity.

When the baby arrives, involve your husband in every way you can. Whether or not he chooses paternity leave, give him responsibilities for the baby's care. Dr. Robert Frank, author of *The Involved Father*, recommends leaving your husband alone with the baby on occasion, even when the child is a newborn. "Spending time alone with the newborn is an entirely different experience for a father than spending time with his wife and newborn as a threesome," he writes. "It is an essential experience of discovery, during which dads come up with their own unique way of doing the same child care 'tasks' moms do, including bathing, feeding, rocking, taking the baby to the pediatrician and more."[7]

This is not to say that if your children are past toddler age, it's too late for your husband to be more involved in their care. Every child needs a father—and every breadwinning wife needs her husband to be a partner in the child care scenario. It's never too late to begin implementing a plan for co-parenting.

Treat your husband as your co-parent. He's not your assistant and not your gofer. He's the father of your children, essentially your partner in the parenting enterprise. Give him the opportunity to take responsibility for your child's care and be clear that you want him to be an equal part of the process.

This means that you will involve him in as many of the tasks and activities associated with child care as you can. He can't breast-feed, but he can give the baby a bottle filled with your expressed breast milk or formula. He can and should be included in choosing between a nanny, day care, family care or at-home parent care for your child. He can take on specific tasks or activities he does with the child, both while the child is a baby and as he or she grows. Or he can split responsibilities with you—so that either parent can act quickly to perform whatever task is at hand.

If your husband does not take an active role now, you need to begin by helping him understand that you *want* him to be involved. Our society has long been the proponent of the mother as the dominant provider of care to her children. Many men truly believe that they don't belong in the child care role, that this is a feminine pursuit and that they won't know what to do with their children. When they understand that they are welcome as your partner, they may surprise you with the strength of their "paternal instincts."

Make your husband part of the routine. If you both work, split the evening responsibilities with your husband. Maybe one night your husband makes dinner while you see to your children's needs and the next night you switch roles. Establish a schedule that works for both of you, with the clear understanding that you each play an equal part in the overall care and happiness of your children. When you have guidelines and a clear set of expectations, it will be much easier for your husband to act accordingly—and much less likely that you will become frustrated, overburdened and angry.

This can be especially important in the mornings, when children need to be fed, dressed and taken to school or a child care provider at the same time you're preparing to leave for work. When both parents share the responsibility for getting the children ready in the morning, both will understand the challenges involved and will be able to make schedule adjustments or changes in the routine.

Give each other breaks. Schedule one night each week when he takes the kids and you get time for yourself—and one night a week for him to do the same. This is *not* the time for you to do the family grocery shopping, attend an association meeting or run errands. This *is* the time for you to go sit in a coffeehouse with a good book, get a manicure or a massage, visit with friends or enjoy your favorite hobby in or out of the house. The same goes for him: On your husband's night to himself, it's up to him to do something he enjoys as well. You both need breaks; when you share equally in achieving them, you both have opportunities for a few hours of real relaxation knowing your children are well cared for.

Do not give lists. Your husband's time with the children is time to share activities with them. Resist the urge to micromanage this time by providing a list of ideas—or worse, actually scheduling something for the kids so that he becomes little more than transportation for them. If Saturday morning is Dad's time to take the children out or even to stay in with them, let him decide what they do together. It may be drastically different from what you would choose—but that's the whole point! Keep in mind that a father's involvement has strong positive influences on a child's ability to take initiative and direct his or her own actions. Diverse activities will hold your child's interest and help him or her learn new skills.

Discuss, don't criticize. I heard a discouraging refrain from the husbands of breadwinning wives who are not especially active in their children's upbringing: "She doesn't like the way I do it, so I just don't." As wives with responsible jobs, we often find ourselves in positions of supervision. Would we simply grab a project away from a staff member and say, "Never mind, I'll do it myself"? Would we stand a few feet away, saying, "No, not like that...that's no good...that won't work..."? Of course we wouldn't—we are professionals and we trust the people we hired to do their best work or to ask for help when they need it.

Our husbands, the fathers of our children, deserve the same respect. We know from the experience of supervising others (or from being supervised ourselves) that they probably won't do everything perfectly the first time. We need to bite back the fast criticism, refrain from over-supervising and allow our husbands to find their own rhythm with our children. They are adults and they understand the significance of caring for a child. Given the opportunity, they will work as hard as we do to get it right.

The flip side of this is that if you criticize and correct, your husband eventually will avoid the situation altogether. This leaves you with the full responsibility of caring for your children in every waking moment that you're not at work. As a friend once said to me, "I didn't get married to raise children as a single parent." If you want your husband's support, you will need to be supportive of him as a parent, praising the small acts and making him feel comfortable and confident about his parenting skills.

Communicate, communicate, communicate. Make time every day for you and your husband to touch base on child care issues. You both should express your needs clearly and without anger and listen to each other's needs without judgment. The more you both understand about each other's styles, expectations and issues with parenting, the better parents you will be together—and the happier your children will be.

Full-time fatherhood

One of the most important and visible developments resulting from the breadwinning-wife marriage is the opportunity for fathers to play an equal or even dominant role in the care of their children.

Many of the couples I interviewed spoke at great length of their belief that children should be raised by their own parents, not by day care workers, nannies or baby-sitters—but at the same time, the wives also seek stimulating work, a sense of personal accomplishment outside the home and a better-than-average income. Enter the father, the parent whom society does not expect to share in raising his kids—but often, the parent who yearns for the opportunity to be more involved in his children's lives.

In past decades, the possibility that a father might give up his job to stay home with his children was little more than the subject of high comedy. The most memorable is the 1984 film *Mr. Mom*, in which Michael Keaton plays a bumbling, inept father forced into unemployment and full-time fatherhood, while his reluctant wife takes on the breadwinning responsibility. Keaton's character nearly destroys the house in his botched attempts at cooking and cleaning, lures the neighborhood mothers into poker games, brandishes a chain saw before his wife's boss to prove his masculinity and generally makes it obvious that this dad shouldn't be home setting an example for his children. By the end of the film, he returns to employment...while his wife lays the groundwork to cut back hours in favor of child care.

Today, at-home dads (AHDs) are not common, but they are far more prevalent than they were as recently as five years ago. Some full-time mothers regard them with suspicion or cool tolerance, so many AHDs across the country have found one another with the help of the Internet and *At-Home Dad*, a newsletter published by Peter Baylies, a Massachusetts full-time father. Now several Web sites offer anecdotal information and advice to and from these men, encouraging them to master the art of child raising and to embrace their role as primary child caregiver.

Even a summer replacement television series, *Daddio*, boldly moved to approximate the AHD role, using the character of a strong, masculine, involved father to illustrate the point that full-time fathers are not a bunch of sissies. *Daddio's* message is summed up well by an editorial in the *Providence Journal* by James Sulanowski, himself a full-time father to his four-year-old daughter, Emily: "Most modern-day AHDs have chosen to stay home. I am not between jobs. I have simply chosen a new one."[8]

What could make a man give up his career—even temporarily—to stay at home with his children? Many of the AHDs who spoke with me were eager to tell stories of their own fathers, men who worked in industry, medicine, law or a dozen other professions that required their virtually undivided attention from early morning until long after their children were asleep. "My dad worked himself into an early grave," said Stan, an accountant who scaled back his employment by half to spend more time with his two children. "He was gone at fifty-two. I barely knew him and I hated that. I want a real relationship with my children. I want to be part of their lives."

Others gave a much simpler answer. When asked, "Why did you become a full-time dad?" they replied, "Because I could."

The fact is that these men had the opportunity to make a *choice*, thanks to their wives' roles as principal family breadwinners. In nearly all cases, they made this choice with their wives' encouragement and full support, putting an end to the cycle of guilt, fear and day care expenses that plague so many two-income families. Because they have the opportunity to choose—and choose their children over work—at-home dads are more likely than any other group of husbands to participate in other household duties traditionally assigned to women: house cleaning, grocery shopping, laundry and much more.

This is a gift that breadwinning wives can bring to their husbands—the chance to give up a job that does not offer them the level of fulfillment they believe they will find at home with their children. And this is the gift that at-home fathers bring to their wives: the peace of mind that their children's caregivers are those who cherish these children as much as their mothers do.

Even in the realm of the at-home dad, I found that the work-family conflict played a critical role. Despite their willingness to give up a steady paycheck for diapers and the Discovery Zone, many of the AHDs I interviewed used a layoff, unwanted promotion or other turning point in their careers to help them make the bold move to house-husbandry. Encouraged by their wives and stunned by the high cost of quality day care, these men were ready for the change...but less ready to take on the societal criticism and pressures that accompanied it. "I still get that comment—'What are you, some kind of deadbeat, sponging off your wife?'" said Ray, a forty-eight-year-old AHD and former documentary filmmaker, whose wife is a cardiothoracic surgeon. "People can't figure out that I really like being home with my daughter. I have a special relationship with her I could never have otherwise. But they think I'm just unemployable. What the heck is that about?"

Sulanowski summed up this non-validation in his *Providence Journal* commentary. "I wish we were accepted as run of the mill, but I'm confronted daily with subtle reminders that we are not. The life insurance application that won't let me put 'dad' in the employment space, but will allow me to check the 'unemployed' box.... More and more of the household accounts which require proof of employment or income are in my wife's name (the phone, the cable, the gas, etc.). I never gave it a second thought until I tried to make a minor change in our phone service the other day and was told that I couldn't, since the account was not in my name."[9]

This mind-set lives even outside of corporate employers and public utilities. In an April 2000 issue of *Fast Company*, writer Tony Schwartz makes this observation about his own brother-in-law. "It was in the midst of talking with my sister's husband, a stay-at-home dad for thirteen years, that I had an attitude adjustment. For the first time, I understood that Michael's choice to stay home was not his way of avoiding work, but rather a conscious, difficult and ultimately courageous decision to do what he felt was best for his son."[10]

The men who have left work for full-time fatherhood, who have embraced work-family balance programs or who have made alternate arrangements one-on-one with their employers, are those who are not afraid to express higher commitments to their families than to their jobs—or who have swallowed their fears to act upon their needs to be with their children. I spoke with a selection of these men—fathers who put their careers on hold to become primary caregivers to their children, fathers who cut back hours or rearranged work schedules to take on more responsibility as parents and fathers who work hard to squeeze more time with their children out of their daily work lives. What they have achieved is a new balance in their homes. They have the opportunity to build stronger relationships with their children, while relieving some stressors of the breadwinner role from their wives.

Getting on the right AHD track

Beyond the problems of outside influences and criticism, couples in which the husbands assume full-time child care responsibilities meet with their own unique sets of joys and pitfalls, smooth roads and stumbling blocks.

Mark and Teresa were such a couple—she held a tenure-track position as a professor with a university, while he was on the way up the corporate ladder as a top salesman for a contract sheet metal fabrication company. Mark, whose income surpassed Teresa's until recently, received a promotion that put him on the road four days out of every week. "When I started, there were forty-seven salesmen and my territory was just the neighboring counties," he said. "But then they expanded my territory. It required so much traveling and it was just too far away from home."

Yet the irresistible pull of high income drove Mark to accept the additional responsibility, leaving Teresa as the sole parent available to their two young children, aged five and two, four nights of every week. "It's tough when you leave Monday morning and you get back Friday afternoon, that is tough to do to your wife and children," he said. "I can't tell you how much I missed them."

"It was so hard," Teresa recalled in a separate interview. "During the week I had full responsibility for the kids all day, even while I was at work. We had a day care situation, but you get calls and some days they need to come home early. They were mine when I woke up and again when I went to bed. On the weekend, I would hand them over and say, 'Here, they're yours.' But he had a week's worth of work around the house to do on the weekends. So it got even worse."

Then something happened to change Mark's perspective on life and work: His forty-three-year-old supervisor died unexpectedly of cancer. "He had two young kids," Mark said. "That was a real reality check for me. I thought, *I have two young kids, too. Life is too short.*"

Teresa well remembered the day they decided to change their lives. "He was lonely," she said of Mark. "He said, 'I am the kind of father who wants to be with my family. When my daughter is in a play, I want to be part of it. I'm going to stay home and take care of the kids.'"

Mark cut his hours and responsibilities at work by more than half to take on the role of primary child care provider. He and Teresa maintained a relationship with their former in-home day care worker, a woman down the street, so that Mark could take occasional assignments that required road trips or office time. "My boss was dead set against it—he tried to talk me out of it," he said. "He thought I was crazy. My brother also thought I was nuts to quit a day job with nice benefits and good pay."

A decisive man with little regard for other people's opinions, Mark forged ahead to do what he felt was best for himself and his family. Teresa had always wished that one parent could be home with their children, but knew that she was not the parent to do it. "I could not stay home with my kids all day," she said. "I have to be challenged mentally. I have to have the camaraderie with other people in an office environment. I love my kids more than anything, but I am not the kind of person to stay home. But I have so much admiration for Mark that he can. They have a ball together. They're fixing the motorcycle or planting the garden or playing games. It's always something."

As a nearly full-time father, Mark established himself as the parent in charge, seeing changes in his children's behavior in the first few months. "I've seen a lot of modifications in discipline," he said. "They listen to me like there's no tomorrow. Not so much to Teresa—they listen to her, but they push her and test her. If she tells our son to come over to her, he will look at her and he knows he's supposed to do it, but he won't. I'll tell him to come over and he will get right over. He is very, very attached to me."

Their daughter's behavior has also improved, Teresa noted with no hint of jealousy. She spoke of her husband's relationship with their children with real admiration in her voice. "Since Mark has been home, Renee has been a lot less whiny," she said. "Her attitude toward everything is much better. I know it's because she has her father all day. She walks all over me, but she respects her dad."

The payoffs for full-time fatherhood are enormous, Mark noted—but he received little recognition or encouragement for this from his extended family or former coworkers. Mark's sisters were the only ones to help him make peace in the family. "They thought I was crazy, too, but they also knew it was the right thing for me to do," he said.

Dad's the caregiver—so what's Mom?

Mark and Teresa make observations about their children's responsiveness to each of them as parents, noting that their son does whatever his father tells him, but "tests" his mother. This poses an important question about the gender reversal in parenting: Do breadwinning wives whose husbands become stay-at-home dads sacrifice their own relationships with their children?

My research points to the contrary. In fact, an argument could be made that wives who make more put as much time into forming meaningful relationships with their children as they do into their careers. They battle against the example set by the stereotypes of working fathers in the 1950s and 1960s, who came home from work and distanced themselves from their children by retreating into sports, television, workshops or additional work they brought home from the office.

Most of the breadwinning wives I interviewed described in detail the activities they shared with their children at the end of the workday and throughout the weekend. Wives of working husbands talked of joining their husbands wholeheartedly in taking care of the young children from dinnertime until bedtime, carving out both commonplace and special things they would do together. Wives of AHDs described relieving their husbands of the child care responsibilities at day's end, supervising their children's homework and playtime while their husbands did household chores or took time for their own pursuits.

Many researchers point to the phenomenon of working mothers taking over child care at the end of the workday as if this were a negative in the parenting balance. They refer back to Hochschild's concept of the "second shift," noting that stay-at-home fathers hand over the kids at day's end as if their job is done, while the mothers take on the process of dinner, bath time and bedtime as if these were just additional chores.

However, as we look back on those 1950s husbands, we know that their aversion to child care at day's end was hardly the reaction of involved parents who wished to form meaningful bonds with their children. Would we recommend the same behavior for breadwinning wives who have stay-at-home husbands? Absolutely not! These wives' engagement in child care in their hours at home is what we wished of fathers in the days of "traditional" families. Rather than chastise today's AHDs for sharing or relinquishing their parental responsibilities at the end of the workday, we should praise both parents for their shared involvement with their children.

The temptation is there, however, for some breadwinning wives to cast their at-home husbands as helpmates and full-time homemakers, subjugating them to a stereotype more commonly reserved for women at home.

Linda, a cardiothoracic surgeon and the wife of Ray, mentioned earlier, makes a point of handling bath and bedtime every night for her four-year-old daughter, Ashley. Ray put his career as a documentary filmmaker on hold until Ashley enters school full-time and now spends the entire day with his precocious child. On weekends, he and Linda share parenting. Linda takes Ashley shopping, to the playground, to swimming lessons or to the park or plays with her at home. In the evenings, while Linda looks after Ashley, Ray makes dinner, finishes household chores and spends time on his computer, developing Web sites for others.

"This is all a work in progress," Linda told me. "Some days it's great and some days it's frustrating." Torn between her need to support their lifestyle—a modest house in a pleasant neighborhood and the best possible preschool for her gifted daughter—and her desire to spend more time with Ashley and Ray than an hour-long commute to and from her practice permits, she made the tough decision to cut out Saturday morning office hours in favor of family time. But the subsequent dip in income created new tensions, even as the change alleviated a great deal of Linda's overall stress.

"Sometimes Ray picks up some weekend or evening work, shooting commercials or non-profit fund-raising films," she explained. "That's fine, except for the times when I'm on call. Then I have to hire a baby-sitter to just sit here with us, in case I get paged and have to leave the house to deal with a patient. Ray tends to leave the responsibility for getting a sitter to me—as if it's not his problem. That can be really irritating. Plus, it's expensive—especially when I don't get paged and the baby sitter was here all evening for nothing."

Ray understands the dilemma, but is firm in his own position. "Linda's out with adults all day," he said. "She interacts with people. I can take Ashley to the park or to a playgroup, but mostly we're here alone, the two of us. There's just so much Barney and Candy Land an adult can take. I need a break, so when Linda is here, I take my break. And when I get work, I take the work. There's no real money in these jobs, but there's certainly enough to cover the sitter."

"I am so grateful to Ray for making all of this possible for us, but we have our moments," Linda continued. "I can do the thing I love doing—which is being a doctor—while we have the pleasure of bringing up this wonderful child. She has so much energy and every day she develops something new—she adds a word to her vocabulary or she seems to understand something in a new way or she jumps ahead in motor skills. It's a remarkable thing to watch a little person take form. But I see other parents and I can't imagine how they manage it—juggling day care and schedules."

There's a lot going on here where role reversal is concerned. On the positive side, the power of ritual—special times with children—gives Linda the opportunity to connect with Ashley on a daily basis. Her evening bath and story at bedtime are activities Linda reserves for herself with her daughter, giving Ashley a dependable time to ask questions, share her thoughts and just be a kid with Mom. Linda and Ray have found a way to share in their care of Ashley on a fairly equal basis, even with the occasional rocks in the road.

Ray, meanwhile, tells of experiences that are common to many AHDs—loneliness, the need for adult conversation, long days with no intellectual stimulation, barriers in joining play groups filled with mothers, all of the problems discussed at length throughout the Dad-to-Dad Internet network and on the Web site created specifically for AHDs. He struggles to break up his days with evening work when he can, adding marginally to the household income while providing the mental and physical challenge he craves. Linda balks at this, but catches herself—as an aggressive professional used to having her orders followed, she knows she could boss him into the role of "housewife," which would ruin their arrangement.

"Sometimes I do wish he would just stay home and take care of Ashley, so I don't have to think about it," she said. "But I also know that Ray is a thinking person and needs to be productive. I couldn't be here all day, the way he is. I just have to keep reminding myself of that."

"He's just a *dad*."

Where some wives of stay-at-home dads falter is in believing that their at-home husbands have usurped their motherly places in their children's lives. With Dad as the primary child care provider, some mothers feel left out, even *pushed* out of the parent-child relationship. The quest for equal time with children can turn some breadwinning wives into score-keepers, counting the hours or days they spend with their children while discounting their husbands' contribution to the child's upbringing.

Elaine, a corporate executive with a Fortune 100 company, rushes home after work to relieve her husband, Tim, from his day-long stay-at-home shift with their two children, three-year-old Nancy and Gary, who is not quite a year old. Before their second child was born, Elaine worked days while Tim worked nights at the same corporation. "I came home and he went to work, so we saw each other for five minutes," Elaine explained. "We did that for two and a half years and then, with the birth of my second child, we just couldn't keep up that schedule any-more. Too much stress on the kids and too much stress on the marriage."

Then the ax fell at the corporation and Tim found himself with-out a job. "Honestly, it was the best thing that could have happened," Elaine said. "He was never too happy with his job. We still had great benefits, because I was still employed. And then I started getting pro-motions."

Tim agreed that the circumstances turned out to be fortuitous. "When I was working, each of us had a different schedule, so we were both able to work full-time without day care. Occasionally we'd have to drop off one of the kids at a friend's house or a baby-sitter for an hour or two if I had to go in early. But it just wasn't worth it. We were running on empty. And at that point, we just didn't feel we could afford day care. "

Tim's full-time parent status relieved most of the pressure in their relationship, at least as far as scheduling was concerned. "We had better communication and we saw each other a lot more, instead of for just five minutes," Elaine said. "I don't have to start conversations with, 'Remember last Tuesday, when you did this?' I stopped holding things in. We resolve things faster and more easily."

However, Elaine replaced the frustration she'd felt with a new conflict—a competition with her husband to be an equally effective par-ent in her own eyes. She finds herself keeping a running mental tally of the hours she spends with her children, versus Tim's time with them.

"When I come home, I feel that it's my job to take care of the kids from that point forward," she said. "That's when Tim will do more laborious things, like vacuum and clean. When I'm home, I'm very focused on the kids. I want to do more with them. Before, I did it because he wasn't here in the evenings, but now I want to get my time in,"

She admitted that Tim doesn't demand a break from his child care provider role. "It's not because I *have* to, but because I *need* to for myself," she explained. "But he doesn't really need the break. After all, the kids napped for two hours, so he was really only with them for five hours. I was with them for five *and a half* hours today."

Rightly or wrongly, Elaine considers her activities with the children to be somehow more valuable and important than Tim's daylong care. "I'm really good at developmentally playing with the kids," she said. "I ask my children challenging questions. It's the natural teacher in me. Tim's home with the kids all day, but there is a part of me that says I know what the kids need better than he does, because, you know, he's just a *dad*. The kids aren't in a child care center with certified teachers all day. He does a great job with them and everything, but I'm always picking out books for them that will be developmentally challenging or finding games that will teach them.

"Tim will do that stuff with them during the day," Elaine added after a moment, "but my doing it at the end of the day, *that's* what makes the difference. I know that the kids are stimulated the right way at some point that day. I can say, 'All right, Nancy and I played a color game today and she loves to play with colors. She learned her colors.' So I know she got something of real quality. I'm sure they do get some of this with Tim, but I wasn't there to see it."

Like all the husbands I interviewed, I spoke with Tim separately, without sharing any of his wife's comments. He was quick to describe Elaine's different style in taking care of the children and freely volunteered his point of view. "I'm probably a lot more lenient than she is," he said. "I'm a lot more laid back and relaxed about things. She probably does a lot more book-type stuff with them, where I do a lot more fun things. That can really be a problem for Elaine. When she gets home from work, she doesn't have the time to take the kids to the museum or see them with other kids. So I do a lot of the fun stuff, while she does a lot of the bathing and nighttime reading and that sort of thing."

He sighed. "Sometimes I wish she'd just relax and have fun with the kids. They're not machines and neither is she. Not everything has to be a lesson."

Elaine, however, continued to tally up her contribution. "I get up with the kids in the morning and feed them breakfast. Then Tim gets up about fifteen minutes before I leave. So I'm out of the house for seven hours a day, total. I took a $5,000 pay cut to work one hour less a day, so I can be home by 4:30. Then the kids are up until 8:00 or so. When I'm with the kids, Tim can go down into the basement and work on his own projects.

"Except, of course, he only does that once in a while —usually he makes dinner and cleans the house," Elaine remembered, pausing for a moment to consider this. Then she rushed on, "But that whole time, I'm with the kids."

Determined to retain her role as primary child caregiver and mother, Elaine worked hard to convince me that her contribution was greater than Tim's was. She acknowledged that Tim had made a great sacrifice in giving up career and income to stay home with the children, but to her, his shift as father is a time of play and fun, not the important, meaningful time with the children she initiates at the end of her workday.

Does Elaine truly see her husband's participation in such trivial terms? Not at all—in fact, she is painfully aware of exactly what Tim has given up and what his long days at home mean to the family. Elaine suffers from the guilt and fear of many working mothers—guilt about being away from her children all day at work and fear that she will lose her connection with them. While Tim's AHD role makes her career possible, it also poses a threat to her—the threat that her husband's sacrifice and his active interest in their children may make him appear to be a better parent than she is.

So when Elaine arrives home, she relieves Tim of parent duty and takes over with a structured plan, a timeline and goals. No doubt Elaine approaches her career in much the same way—she believes that effective parenting, like effective management, requires objectives and strategy. Tim's free-form style may be exactly what attracted her to him in the initial stages of their relationship—but now, when he applies this as a parenting approach, she perceives this as weak and chooses to single out his laissez-faire attitude as fundamentally flawed. She leaps in to take up the slack.

There is no right or wrong here and certainly the children benefit from a measured dose of daily play and evening learning, if that is truly what's taking place. The real danger lies in whether or not Elaine can allow herself to fully appreciate Tim's contribution to their parenting or whether she will continue to minimize his efforts so that she herself will feel less diminished.

How do wives and husbands in this predicament end their competition over which one is the better parent? First, by realizing that parenthood is *not* a competition and that each participant has his or her strengths to contribute to the relationship. Tim's style may be the opposite of Elaine's, but the children learn different things from him than they learn from her—lessons that are just as important. In *Working Fathers*, Levine noted that children with involved fathers have stronger abilities to manage stress, higher senses of competence in technical subjects, better problem-solving skills and greater abilities to take initiative.[11]

Second, wives who feel challenged by their husbands' roles as full-time fathers or displaced from their children's lives because of the husbands' more active roles, may actually be feeling the conflict of work/family balance. Elaine had already adjusted her schedule to accommodate her need to be with her children, but this extra hour each day has only become another point in her favor on an internal scoreboard. If lack of time with children is a source of conflict and stress—or even jealousy—then breadwinning wives may need to make allowances in their own lives so that they, too, can make choices to spend more time with their children. If this means greater adjustments in schedules, flextime arrangements or other changes that accommodate their needs to be with their families, they should explore these options with their employers.

We have seen this problem with other couples at whom we have looked. In chapter 10, Sonia found herself overwhelmed by maternal drive when her son, Jacob, was born, so she and her husband, Donald, worked out a schedule that would satisfy her own need to be home with her baby as well as her husband's. Linda cut back on weekend work, closing her practice on Saturdays when her daughter Ashley turned four so that Linda could spend full weekends with her husband and daughter. Linda retained the breadwinner role, while Sonia returned to work full-time and quickly rose to her professional goals. Each woman found a way to make the choices that would satisfy objectives on both sides of the work-family question.

Recommendations: Making the Most of Life With At-home Dads.
1. Share the responsibility
The husband's role as full-time father does not diminish or eliminate the mother's importance in her children's lives. When the breadwinner mother returns home from work, she should share the evening child care tasks with her husband—bath time, bedtime, play time, homework and all the other activities that fill parents' hours. The mother's participation enriches the children's lives—and hers, as she stays abreast of

the children's constant growth, the lessons they learn, the changes in their perceptions and the adventures they experience every day.

Making the children priorities every evening is important to satisfying the breadwinner mother's need for parenting. At the same time, it satisfies the husband's needs as well, by showing respect for his role as an at-home parent. Breadwinner mothers should avoid relegating their husbands to the ultimate housewife role, expecting them to "keep the kids out of the way" in the evening while the breadwinners relax or work on projects brought home from the office. Save these other activities for when the children are in bed, using the time after work to take part in their lives.

2. Create rituals

Choose regular, predictable, daily or weekly activities that reserve time with the children: reading bedtime stories, taking evening walks or bike rides, playing favorite games, even chatting over late evening snacks. When these activities become part of the children's routine, they can look forward to sharing their special time with their mother—and moms will look forward to it as well, especially on days that seem especially taxing or frustrating at work. Rituals can help breadwinner mothers maintain healthy perspectives on the balance between work and family life, while they serve as tools for achieving and maintaining that balance.

3. No contests

Child raising is not a competition! Accept that the at-home husband has time with the children that doesn't include the breadwinner mother and that she has time with the children in which he is not involved. Allow him to develop his own routines and build his child care skills without indignant scrutiny. He won't do it your way—he'll do it his way, which has just as much validity.

If it seems like the kids always run to Daddy with their scraped knees or their hurt feelings, remind yourself that this is a *good* thing—because these demonstrations of their love and trust in their father are important, positive signs that he is doing a great job.

Know that even though you are the breadwinner you are still the mother and your role as comforting, loving parent is no less important just because your children may be more accustomed to their father's constant presence. Find ways that you can contribute to your children's development and well-being in the time that you spend with them, either through the rituals you create with them or through regular, daily interaction.

    Never force children to choose one parent over another or give them reason to believe that one parent's attentions have more value than the other's. Every child benefits from having two parents; be grateful that your children have the opportunity to enjoy, appreciate and learn from both of you.

4. Express appreciation

As Linda said earlier, her husband makes it possible for her to do the work she loves, because he is willing to stay home and care for their child. We can only hope that she tells Ray on a regular basis how much she appreciates his role in their partnership! Every healthy human being responds positively to praise. Your husband is no exception—and he deserves recognition for his efforts in taking care of your children and maintaining a smoothly running household. Tell him how much you respect and appreciate his contribution. This will go a long way toward quelling any misgivings he may have about giving up a steady paycheck to pursue his lifestyle.

5. Respect the partner's need for adult time

Many breadwinning wives are not at home with their children because, in their own words, "I would lose my mind." Try, then, to put yourself in your husband's place. He may be a man of infinite patience and exquisite temperament, but he faces long days of some monotonous children's activities and monosyllabic conversations. Whenever possible, give him the room and the support he needs to get out and spend time with adults. You'll get the opportunity to interact with your children one-on-one, without his involvement; he will get chances for different activities and discussions with people of his choice and interests.

6. Be a responsible breadwinning parent

Do your best to be a considerate co-parent, even though your job is important and your income supports the family. If you're going to be late getting home, if you've got an unexpected commitment after work or if you're stuck with a large project that will occupy you at home that evening, tell your at-home husband in advance. Part of your daily routine should be to check in with him about dinner plans or anything out of the ordinary the children may need from you in the evenings. When your children are involved in special events and expect you there as a spectator or participant, be there as often as you can. These acts are more than gestures—they reinforce your parental role in your children's eyes, showing them that they are every bit as important to you as your profession and income.

At the same time, you're sending your husband the same message about his importance in your life. You're acknowledging that his job is challenging, difficult and often frustrating and that you will do your best to be part of the solution, not part of the problem. Don't allow inconsiderate acts to demonstrate to your husband that you think his contribution is insignificant when compared to yours. Instead, show him your appreciation for his co-parenting and making the children his highest priority.

7. Recognize your needs as a mother

There may come a time when your own need to be home with your children will overwhelm your need for job satisfaction. Should that day arrive, don't deny yourself the pleasure of spending more time with your family. Discuss your needs with your husband, so you both can make the changes in your lives that support your family financially and emotionally, but give you the flexibility you need to be a greater participant in life at home. Talk with your employer about flex-time arrangements, shorter work hours, telecommuting or even a sabbatical, so you can enjoy your children while they are still children.

CHAPTER 12

BREADWINNING AT FIFTY
When Role Reversal Comes Late

When the opportunity came to Phyllis to take a higher-paying job in a new city, she was ready to go—even though she and her husband, Cliff, were both fifty-one years old and their home mortgage was almost paid off.

"I went back to work in the mid-1980s, when my children were in first and third grades," Phyllis said. Her return to the workforce after full-time motherhood involved a position as an administrative assistant to a corporate vice-president at a large Des Moines food processing company. "When I decided to go to work again, Cliff was a controller with a local company. I hadn't finished my degree, so before I started to work full-time, I went back to school, finished my undergraduate degree and got my MBA. Right away, I started getting promotions. That was when my salary began to grow."

In seven years, Phyllis moved from support staff to positions of higher and higher responsibility, finally taking on the marketing management for a division of the corporation. "Then I was offered a new position that involved a move," she said. "In all honesty, I never saw it coming. I never considered the possibility that I would be the one to uproot the family for more money."

The new job took Phyllis and Cliff across the country to Atlanta: a warmer climate, a bigger city and a big boost in Phyllis' income. It was the chance of a lifetime for Phyllis—but for Cliff, her husband of more than twenty-five years, the move meant letting go of a secure position to venture into the unknown.

"I gave up my job to come here," said Cliff by phone from the couple's Atlanta home. "We sold our house and everything. I thought I'd have no trouble finding a job here." He chuckled. "Shows what I knew. I looked for close to a year unsuccessfully."

In that year, Phyllis found herself less satisfied with the new position than she had expected to be—not because the work was unfulfilling, but because she had become the lone breadwinner in the family, a responsibility she had never sought nor desired. "I think for a while I was angry," she said. "After all, now I was working because I had to, not because I wanted to. That's completely different from what had been going on for the twenty-five years we'd been married. We thought Cliff would get a job here in Atlanta, but he didn't. I really wanted to quit working. I'd been working for a while and I began to feel like it was enough."

Happy to be home with her children for the first half of her marriage and happy to have the extra income her earning power added to the family pot, Phyllis had enjoyed her profession and excelled at work. But when her income became the family's sole support, her pleasure in professional achievement waned. "I had a lot of trouble with the whole idea," she said. "I kept thinking I would stop working. Not to retire, just not to have to work."

Finally, a year after their move, Cliff found a position with a local company, doing the financial work he knew well. However, even though his salary closely matched his Des Moines earnings, the money just didn't go as far in Atlanta—so Phyllis' income remained paramount to the family's quality of life.

"I would say the amount of time I work now is sort of part-time," Cliff said. "I travel every other week, so it seems like one week is pretty heavy and the following week will be a little lighter. I'll probably continue this way for a while. But I want Phyllis to retire in a few years. She'd like to do it tomorrow if she could, but she has a very good position and they treat her well—and she's putting a lot of money into our retirement funds. That's a big kicker. And her job provides our medical benefits."

For the sake of practicality—combined with his love of golf, which he can now play all year—Cliff has adapted to Phyllis' higher earning status. While he was quick to tell me, "Sometimes, she really only makes about 10 percent more than I do, you know," he also noted, "I am not money motivated. It comes from where it comes from. The rest just isn't that important."

Phyllis and Cliff both grew up in the 1940s and 1950s, an era when men supported their families and women stayed home, raised the kids and kept the house in perfect working order. Neither of them encountered role models for their current situation anywhere in their lives—certainly not their parents and not any of their friends. "My father worked," Phyllis said. "He was the breadwinner and mom was a stay-at-home mom. She did all the housework, cooking, shopping, everything. My dad did nothing except go to work, come home and putter in the garden. So it was hard for me to grow into this new role, when I had no frame of reference for it.

"I decided not to think about it," she continued. "I just did it. Cliff encouraged me to go back to school—he never stood in my way. Not like my dad—Dad was very protective, so I didn't have a lot of confidence. But Cliff always said, 'You can do whatever you want to do.'"

Cliff did more than talk the talk—he walked the walk as well. "He watched the kids while I was in school at night," Phyllis said. "He was really very supportive of my getting more education. He could have said no and made it more difficult—in fact, I expected him to do that. I'd heard about other women whose husbands didn't approve of their going to school. But Cliff was never like that."

How did Cliff come to believe that his wife should do whatever was required to make herself a success? Like so many men in his age group, he knew better than to accept the "traditional family" icon as the only option, because he'd lived through both its idealized myth and its reality. "My father was the breadwinner," he explained, "and back in the old days, he worked a lot of hours—he was a machine tool maker and he often put in a twelve hour day. My mother stayed home and watched the kids. When we were teenagers, the family moved to the suburbs. It was a nicer house, but my father was still working very hard, a lot of overtime and a lot of night work. We didn't see him much.

"Then, in 1954, I was in the eleventh grade and my father died. My mother had to go to work to keep things going. We had a little insurance, but it wasn't much, so my brothers and I got jobs and we contributed to the running of the house."

Seeing his mother keep the family together and hold onto the house without a husband's help made Cliff understand early on that *everyone* worked hard—women as well as men—just to make enough money to feed the family. "That was typical in those days," he said. "Then came the modern era. Things change and change continually.

The marketplace today is nowhere near what it was even fifteen years ago. I think, though, that people still really work hard—certainly Phyllis does. I wish we could go back to Iowa and retire and I wish Phyllis could quit. But the fact is that right now, she can't and we can't. So while we are here for a few more years, it's up to me to help Phyllis enjoy her life."

When the time came to do what had to be done to maintain their comfortable lifestyle, Phyllis and Cliff swallowed their discomfort and surged forward. Consciously discarding the gender roles they had grown up with and practiced in their own marriage, they discovered what so many breadwinning-wife couples demonstrated throughout my research: There are more ways to support your family than with money.

"Housework? I'm good at it," Cliff laughed. "I probably don't do it as well as Phyllis would like, but it gets done. I clean up after meals and we both do the laundry and the grocery shopping."

Phyllis smiles when she talks about the day she let go of her "supermom" responsibilities. "When I started working full-time, I just couldn't seem to get the meals on the table," she said. "One day my oldest daughter came home and said, 'Why aren't you cooking regular dinners anymore?' I just snapped at her. I said, 'I've resigned from cooking and cleaning.'"

During their daughters' last years in high school, Phyllis encouraged them to cook and handle their own dishes. Now that the girls are in college, however, there's no one but Phyllis and Cliff. "Cliff doesn't cook, except on the grill. So I still get something together when I get home," she said. "But he does all of the housework; he will vacuum and clean the bathrooms. And he cleans up the dishes. I like that deal."

Practicality over position

Total role reversal beginning after husband and wife have spent decades in gender roles demonstrated for them since birth is not a situation I expected to discover in very many couples. I had not expected to find so many older couples in which the wife became the principal breadwinner in her fifties, especially when these couples had been together for twenty years or more. However, I soon realized that many wives do find themselves taking over the higher earning responsibility at this age. Some may re-enter the workforce in their late thirties or forties after raising children, because their husbands retire, get "downsized" by corporate change or begin a new career. And many professional women suddenly surpass their husbands' steady earnings by moving up the corporate ladder or see their newly founded businesses take off, catapulting these wives into the primary breadwinning positions and changing their family's lives and the marital dynamic.

I thought these older husbands, steeped in tradition and long established as family breadwinners, would balk at the idea of relinquishing their positions to their wives. Instead, many of these men spoke with relief, expressing gratitude for the respite from long years of responsibility as sole breadwinners and pleasure at having more opportunities to enjoy some of the other joys they had been denied in decades of hard work.

In none of these discussions did I hear anger or embarrassment over the men's step down from breadwinning status. Their words came instead from innate senses of practicality: Whatever was best for the marriage was A-O-K with them. If their wives' incomes could make positive differences in the couple's overall lifestyles, these men were ready and willing to get comfortable with their partners' higher earning status.

"Downsized" doesn't have to mean disaster

Even husbands who became the victims of corporate layoffs found solace in their wives' abilities to maintain the families' lifestyles without the men's customarily higher incomes. While we commonly expect to find that men are demoralized, depressed or even incapacitated by unplanned job loss—especially in their older years, when statistics tell us that it's tougher for men to find new positions at comparable pay scales[1]—men whose wives had high earning potential were only too happy to accept the secondary breadwinner position at this stage of their lives.

Change came late to Gloria and Don, when they had both reached their fifties and their children were nearly adults. "I changed jobs on Halloween and the company Don worked for let him go right about the same time," Gloria explained. "They were folding. He had recently come home with a twenty-five year pin. He thought he was staying there until he retired and then the news was that he had no job."

Suddenly, after nearly thirty years of a fairly traditional marriage in which Gloria had assumed the role of housekeeper and primary child care provider even as she worked full-time, Gloria and Don traded places. Gloria, an engineer, made the move from public works to the private sector and saw her income skyrocket almost overnight. Meanwhile, Don searched for a new job in tool and die making—his career trade—and found that no other company could match the inflated salaries of the large corporation for which he'd worked since before he was thirty.

"It became obvious that I would be making more than my husband," Gloria said. "Don tried to make a career change. He went to school for two years, but he didn't last in his new field for nine months.

Finally, he got back into the tool and die business, but he never could command the salary he had been making. That's partly why that company had gone under—their rate of pay was so inflated. Don knew that and he knows he's now making the wages he should have been making all along. That means that anything I do, I will make more than he does."

"You would think this would crush someone's ego," Gloria continued. "At first, I had guilt feelings. I would come home late and I hadn't made any supper. But he said, 'Hey, I didn't marry a home economist.' Now my job involves some travel and his reaction is, 'I'm a big boy. You don't have to take care of me.' We have a lot of strength in our marriage."

We might expect to find that wives who suddenly become breadwinners at midlife create such a disruption in their households that they risk losing everything they've created over the last twenty to thirty years. After decades of making their homes and families their primary focus, now these wives pour their energies into work outside the home—work that might make it impossible for them to continue in their traditional roles of homemaker, child caregiver and chef.

Once again, the truth shows us another side to this story. Census statistics tell us that there are more divorced people in the forty-five to sixty-four age bracket,[2] but other studies indicate that the actual divorces take place much earlier, when couples are in their mid-thirties.[3] Many wives who become breadwinners at fifty do indeed turn the household upside down as chores shift and responsibilities change, but my research showed that these families hold together and make the necessary adjustments.

Why do these older couples take this fundamental change in stride, while the younger couples we've met—presumably the more flexible group—often struggle to accept their circumstances? Studies tell us that the longer a couple stays together, the more the overall quality of their marriage improves. Fundamental relationship characteristics become more important to marital stability as couples grow older together. In a recent study published in *Current Psychology,* commitment to the spouse as a person turned out to be the strongest and most consistent predictor of the quality of an older couple's relationship. Couples with higher reciprocal commitment to each spouse reported fewer problems in their marriage.[4]

If a husband agrees to follow his wife across the country so that she can take a new job with greater responsibility and higher income—even if it means selling the house, pulling teenagers out of their high school and giving up his own job—he demonstrates a high commitment to his wife. If at the same time, the wife takes the new job so that she can provide an improved lifestyle for her family, even though she would prefer an easier assignment at this stage of her life, she demonstrates an equally high commitment to her husband and family.

The older couples I interviewed measured the length of their marriages in multiple decades. Each couple had weathered storms, faced obstacles and worked their way through good times and bad, so this new stage, when the wife's income surpassed her husband's, seemed like just another switch back in their long journey together.

"I just took a new job that doubled my salary again," Gloria said. "I checked this out with my husband. I said, 'Hey, you can quit your job now if you want.' He said, 'No, I feel good. I want to work until retirement.' I said, 'That's great, because we'll have the money to take more trips and do more stuff.' He liked that."

Remarkably unperturbed by the chain of events that led him to become the lower-earning spouse, Don continues to do the "man's work" around the house: lawn mowing, snow shoveling and repairs. He always participated in raising the children, because his manufacturing workday ended at three o'clock, so he'd be home by 3:30, just as the three children arrived home from school. "He would take care of getting the babysitters," Gloria explained. "He often had to take the kids to the doctor and everywhere else they went after school, because I wouldn't get home in time. He always made the appointments in the late afternoon and went to work extra early, so he could get off in time. So we shared a lot of responsibilities."

So much for *Ozzie and Harriet*

Those of us who were children in the 1960s and 1970s witnessed the shift from the so-called traditional family to the dual-income household, while younger people are aware only through television reruns that "tradition" has been something different. Yet we were led to believe that this celebrated structure was the absolute natural order intended for the American family: a suburban house, a hardworking father, a full-time mother at home, two or three children, the pets, the lawn and the barbecue.

For couples now in their fifties and sixties, the traditional family goes well beyond myth. These wives and husbands actually lived the phenomenon, perhaps seeing fathers come home from war to enjoy the benefits of the GI Bill and build on that American dream, while mothers raised children, kept house and established ties with the neighborhood.

Despite all that has come since—*The Feminine Mystique*, the realization that many traditional wives were bored and miserable, the eventual dominance of two-income families and the exponential growth in the number of wives who make more than their husbands—much of our society clings to the idea that in the 1940s and 1950s "true" families reigned. They continue to revere the image of the self-sacrificing, full-time mother; they assume that all men strive to be family leaders; they hold fast to the belief that children are best raised in their own homes by their own mothers—and that the problems with "these kids today" come from children who do not receive this mega-dose of traditional family values.

What we do not realize, until we begin to talk to couples who grew up in these supposed idyllic times, is that the "ideal" American family existed more vividly on television than in most homes. Today's older wives describe their mothers as "frustrated" and "forced to stay home," while husbands sigh as they talk about fathers whose long work hours prohibited family relationships or drove their fathers to early graves.

"Not only was the 1950s family a new invention," writes renowned historian Stephanie Coontz in her landmark book, *The Way We Never Were*, "it was also a historical fluke, based on a unique and temporary conjuncture of economic, social and political factors." Before World War II, Coontz notes, poverty had placed considerable emphasis on the value of the extended family, but "in ways that were experienced by most people as stultifying and oppressive."[5] During the war, family separations and housing shortages forced millions of American families into shared housing, causing conflicts between generations living in the same home.

By the 1950s, amid the prosperity of postwar America, young newlyweds marched in droves to the suburbs, where they purchased new homes at a great distance from their parents' scrutiny. This "modern" move away from the extended family and into single-family housing launched what moralists, politicians and traditionalists point to today as the "real" American family. However, much of this family structure was entirely new to American culture. Even the concept of women doing the housework while the husbands worked was unique to this period.

"Beneath a superficial revival of Victorian domesticity and gender distinctions, a novel rearrangement of family ideas and male-female relations was accomplished," writes Coontz. "Nineteenth-century middle-class women had cheerfully left everything to servants, yet 1950s women of all classes created make-work in their homes and felt guilty when they did not do everything for themselves. The amount of time women spent doing housework actually increased in the 1950s...(and) child care absorbed more than twice as much time as it had in the 1920s."[6]

How many American families actually shared in the middle-class existence we see on *Leave It To Beaver* and *Ozzie and Harriet*? The fact is that more than 25 percent of Americans were poor in the 1950s—in a time before food stamps and other social programs were commonplace. Sixty-five percent of older Americans had annual incomes below $1,000 in 1958, well below the middle-class level of $3,000 to $10,000 for that time. A quarter of the population had no liquid assets and one-third of white families could not get by on the income provided by the household head—in nearly all cases, the father."[7]

Did all married women freely adopt the housewife role? Not only do historians say otherwise, my own interviews point in the opposite direction. "My mother was fired the week she got married," Gloria told me. "She had a good job, but her boss told her, 'Now that you've got your MRS, this job is going to someone who needs it.' They didn't want women to work in those days even when their families needed the money."

We all know the stories of the thousands of women who filled factory jobs throughout World War II, only to find themselves back home as soon as the men returned from overseas and claimed the jobs. "Although 95 percent of the new women employees had expected when they were first hired to quit work at the end of the war, by 1945 almost an equally overwhelming majority did not want to give up their independence, responsibility and income, and expressed the desire to continue working," Coontz discovered.[8] The role of women in postwar America became abundantly clear over the next fifteen years, as they launched the baby boom that produced the single largest generation in our nation's history.

These were the years during which women hardly dared admit that motherhood and housework did not fulfill their dreams and ambitions. Those who instigated the first murmuring of feminist concepts were labeled perverted, neurotic and even schizophrenic. More than a decade would pass before women could speak freely about their discontent with the homemaking life, yet countless women felt that ennui and complained of it to their daughters—girls who would grow into women who would later embrace the new ideal of the working wife and mother.

"My mother raised us alone," said Dorothy, now seventy-three years old and a breadwinning wife since 1972. "There were four children in our family and I was the youngest. One night, my father came home in a rage and started breaking the dishes. It was one of many nights like that and Ma did something very brave, especially for that time. She called the police and she threw him out. He never came back to the house. I honestly don't know how she kept food on the table after that—my father owned a business and he was supposed to give her money, but most of the time he didn't. She took little part-time jobs and my older brother and sisters worked, so I guess everyone contributed."

She paused, considering. "Not exactly the typical model of the great American family, huh?"

Not exactly.

Dorothy and Abe: Feminism's hidden pioneers

In an expansive Miami condominium on a high floor overlooking the Intracoastal Waterway, Dorothy, a trim, attractive redhead, relaxed in a chaise on her screened patio and admired the spectacular view. "Isn't it nice here?" she asked, waving her arm as if pulling back a grand drape. "It's so pretty. And the weather is gorgeous, every day, all the time."

Inside, her husband, Abe, sat in an easy chair in the Florida Room (the rest of the country would call it the den) and read the paper. At an astoundingly healthy and nimble eighty-four years old, he'd seized a much-needed day off after the Christmas rush, during which he doubled his usual schedule as a department store floorwalker and worked five or even six days weekly. Now, for the first time in his life, he had begun to consider retirement.

"I just don't want to be on my feet all day anymore," he said. "It's time to enjoy just being with Dorothy. We have things to do."

Abe's crazy-quilt career in retail sales had seen him in all kinds of environments: on the road selling specialty papers; at car dealerships, where he'd topped the charts with annual deals closed; in fine women's shoe stores, learning the fashion industry; and in department store management, where he'd been particularly successful with sporting goods. In the late 1960s, Abe and Dorothy decided to capitalize on Abe's specialized knowledge and open a sports store of their own, in a suburban area outside their native Cleveland.

"The store was very successful," said Dorothy. "We thought we were going to be rich. We bought a nice house in the suburbs, in the affluent area so our daughter could go to the good schools there. We thought we had it made."

Caught up in their own focus, Dorothy and Abe didn't see the biggest retail trend of the twentieth century heading their way: the advent and eventual dominance of suburban malls. The grand opening of the first big mall in the neighborhood spelled disaster for the family sporting goods business.

"There was nothing to be done," said Dorothy. "In that mall

were *four* sporting goods stores. We couldn't compete. We were wiped out in a couple of months."

With a son in college, a daughter in junior high and no savings left, Dorothy knew there was only one thing for her to do: Get a job and get a good one.

"Abe was home for seven months, just sitting in a chair and reading books," she said "I could see we weren't going to make it if I didn't get moving. I had two kids to put through college and we weren't young kids ourselves. I had to build retirement funds and get us health benefits. I needed a good, corporate job."

A highly skilled professional with the self-confidence to face male executives and speak her mind, Dorothy had held significant administrative positions in her younger years, including service at the Pentagon in the last years of World War II. She quickly turned a temporary assignment into gold and landed a position as an administrative assistant to a corporate vice-president in a growing manufacturing company. As her substantial paychecks began to eliminate their remaining debt, Dorothy set up deductions from her compensation so that she could accumulate funds for retirement and college tuitions and she took over the mortgage and utility payments at home.

"Then I came home one day and there was Abe, sitting in his chair," she said. "He looked so sad, so defeated. I couldn't stand it anymore. I said, 'Get the hell out of that chair and start looking for a job. You can work; there's nothing wrong with you. Just do it already. You're making all of us nuts.'"

Some men would have balked or panicked or lashed out in return. Abe, however, was a different kind of man. "I got up the next morning and went out," he said. "I got a job right away. I was good; I had skills. I had a good reputation; everyone knew me. I just needed a kick in the pants."

Abe took a position as manager of a sporting goods department in—you guessed it—a mall store. While he earned a substantial living by 1970s standards, he knew he could never match Dorothy's corporate-scale paycheck.

"You're going to ask if that bothered me," he said. "You know what? It never did. She worked hard, she worked damned hard. She was good at what she did. And I never cared about money, even though I always worked in sales. I always brought home my pay, took twenty dollars for myself for the week and gave her the rest. She paid the bills, I never asked questions. We always had what we needed."

He sat forward, jabbing his index finger in my direction. "You know what's really important? Love. If you don't have that, you've gone *stones*. Nothing. We always had love in the house. We never fought..."

I looked at him dubiously.

"Okay, so we fought," he corrected himself. "Who doesn't fight? She even took the kids and walked out a couple of times. But she always came back the next day, because we loved each other. That's what keeps people together. That's *so* much more important than money."

Even with the outstanding moral and emotional support she received from her husband, Dorothy found her breadwinning status a tough route to travel. "Remember, it was the 1970s," she said. "Women were still second-class citizens then. I tried to get a credit card in my name and the bank wouldn't give it to me. They wanted my husband to co-sign. I said no! It was my money and I deserved my own card. But the bank wouldn't hear of it."

It took a call from Dorothy's employer—who happened to be a friend of the bank vice-president—to secure a card in her own name. "He told the bank, 'I assure you that Dorothy is gainfully employed and will be for some time,'" Dorothy said proudly. "It was still a man who had to do it, but it was on a professional level, not as if I couldn't support myself.'"

While she assumed that some of her close friends guessed her higher earning power, Dorothy never told a soul that she made more than her husband. "Eventually Abe went back into car sales and he became the top salesman at the dealership," she said. "Anyone would think he made more than I did, because people think car salesmen make a lot of money. They should only know. The agency owners make the money."

When they would go out for an evening with friends, Dorothy would remove money from her wallet and pass it to Abe under the table so that he could pay the bill. "I didn't like it and neither did he," she said. "He just thought it was stupid. But I didn't want anyone to think less of him. I wanted them to think nothing at all." Caught between the desire to keep up appearances and the reality of maintaining her traditional role while working full-time, Dorothy was one of several women I interviewed who announced to her family her total resignation from cooking and cleaning. "Abe did the grocery shopping and our daughter was old enough to make dinner for herself," she said. "Abe usually worked late— most days the store and then the agency closed at 9:30—so he didn't expect a big dinner. But I cooked for the first twenty years of our marriage and I always hated it. Once I was working full-time, it was absurd to come home at 7:00 at night and start dinner. We also ate out a lot. That was before we knew everything we know now about nutrition. We don't eat like that anymore."

Abe did his best to support Dorothy's work by helping at home, keeping the house neat and occasionally dusting and vacuuming. "In truth, I hired a cleaning service," Dorothy said. "For one thing, I *could*. But Abe kind of...pushed the dust around, if you know what I mean. He was very sweet and he helped in other ways. But he grew up with three sisters. He never really had to do much housecleaning."

Abe said only, "She hired someone to clean, thank God."

Now, thirty years later and on the verge of complete retirement, both Dorothy and Abe recall no specific gender conflicts between them. "Men, women, who does what, who cares?" said Abe. "This is now. I didn't care then and I don't care today. I just want to be with my wife and have a good time. The rest of it, they can stick it."

Making marriage a safe place

What echoes through the stories these couples tell is a familiarity with one another, a comfort level that allows each partner the freedom to speak his or her mind, voice concerns and bring up issues without fearing the loss of the other's love. Their many years together do not act as a prison, in which routine and habit demand that each spouse carry out a certain set of behaviors without deviation. Instead, these long relationships become the safe haven from which wife and husband can venture out, gather new ideas and information, try new experiences and develop new skills, as long as they return home and remain constant in their affection for one another.

In their book, *The Good Marriage*, Judith Wallerstein and Sandra Blakeslee describe a series of life challenges all couples face in building strong and happy marriages. Of these challenges, several become critical if a couple is to accept the wife's breadwinning role when it emerges later in life: creating both intimacy and autonomy within the relationship; strengthening the marriage bond in the face of crisis; creating a safe place to hammer out conflicts even as they nurture one another.

Such couples know when to fight, when to let things go and how far they can push each other when the going gets tough. An example would be Dorothy, who came home one day ready to face her husband Abe's long depression over the loss of his business. She pulled no punches in ordering him back out into the working world, taking an approach outsiders might find cold and harsh. Yet Dorothy's thirty years with Abe gave her the experience to know that he would hear the truth in her words, because they were spoken by his loving—albeit frustrated—life partner.

With their roles in one another's lives as well established as their mutual affection for one another, couples in their fifties and sixties realize new priorities in their lives. No longer are they jockeying for territory and position in their homes, dealing with children's issues or facing down tyrannical in-laws. Gender roles are long since established in dozens of ways that go well beyond breadwinning status: conceiving and raising children, tending to the household and making major decisions that affect the entire family.

So when the wife's career success begins to outpace her husband's earning potential, older couples are far more likely to take this in stride than are their younger counterparts.

Irving, a sixty-year-old bank loan officer whose wife is a hospital administrator, put it this way: "When you get a little older, an awful lot of stuff just doesn't matter anymore. You get kind of philosophical about it. What matters is that everyone should be healthy, have time together, get to enjoy the things they have. That's all. Who cooks, who does the dishes, who matches the socks, who makes the money—that's not so important."

CHAPTER 13

IT'S NOT FOR EVERYONE
Why Some Couples Can't Make the Breadwinning-wife Marriage Work

Not more than ten minutes into my interview with Lloyd, the truth about his supposedly happy relationship with Priscilla began to reveal itself.

"We don't actually live together right now," he said. "We're not separated or anything—we just don't share the same house."

"But you live in the same city?" I asked.

"Oh, yeah," Lloyd replied. "Most of the time."

A fund-raising consultant who manages capital campaigns for non-profit organizations nationwide, Lloyd's job required him to become part of his client's staff and work full-time with that organization until the campaign reached a predetermined interim goal—a process that often lasted as much as a year. Sometimes, his assignments took him to other states for months at a time—and once he'd hunkered down and begun his work, his grueling schedule permitted only occasional weekend visits with his wife.

Priscilla had become accustomed to functioning as a single woman in a married relationship, running the thriving chain of bakeries she'd founded when she and Lloyd were married for two years, more than ten years before. When she'd first met Lloyd in 1987, she had romanticized about traveling with him from client to client. "But the upheaval was just too much to deal with—and when you came down to it, he didn't want me there while he was working," she explained. "He worked eighteen, sometimes twenty hours a day. What was I supposed to do—sit in his apartment? I had my own aspirations."

Lloyd hit the road for several months out of every year, coming home for short periods in between assignments, while Priscilla opened her first store and built a solid enterprise. For most of their marriage, they had lived together for no more than a few weeks at a time, until Lloyd's employer hit a dry spell and he found himself in town for longer than expected.

"I was home for maybe four months," he said, "and we realized that we would probably be better off not living together. In order to maintain our relationship, we really should not cohabit."

"It's just because of our schedules," Priscilla insisted, sipping coffee and offering me a slice of freshly baked bread. We were in the tiny sitting area of one of her most popular bakery sites, during the lull of business in mid-afternoon. "When he's in town he goes out a lot in the evening and I need to not have him come in and wake me up—and he doesn't need to hear me getting up at five in the morning. So we live separately, but we still maintain a marriage."

I chose to swallow my skepticism and continued to ask questions, probing gently for the rest of the story. "When did your income begin to exceed Lloyd's?"

She considered, munching on a thick slice of cinnamon swirl. "You know what? I don't know, exactly. We were probably pretty close to earning equal amounts when I was starting my business and he was getting established in consulting. It's interesting; I never gave it much thought.

"You have to understand," she said, leaping to the heart of the problem, "I spent a lot of time trying to pretend that money didn't matter. I grew up in this really dysfunctional family. My parents didn't get along at all—we were very financially strapped. My mother worked and I was a latchkey kid from day one. She was really resentful and bitter, always working menial jobs. There were tremendous power plays in our house over money, every day. My business, the success of my bakeries, was my way of showing that I could do better and not have to worry about money. But it was all at my own expense. I drove myself into the ground making money, as opposed to asking for it or having someone share the responsibilities. I made money a big deal in my marriage by *not* making it a big deal. And not having an equal partner—it's a bigger deal than it needs to be."

Priscilla paused. "This is going to be like therapy," she said with a small, rueful smile. "Now I see it. When the money shifted, so did our relationship. When the first store took off."

"And what happened?" I asked. "How did you know things were changing?"

"Simple." She put down her coffee cup. "Lloyd had an affair and got caught."

Ah. There it was.

"It was a power play on his part," she continued. "Right when the money increase became really obvious. All of a sudden I was bringing home six figures. It's funny now that I'm talking to you about it. It was the worst part of my life. I was so busy at work that I just put it out of my mind at the time. But I came home one day—to the house we lived in, the house *I* owned, that I'd bought with my money—and caught Lloyd with this woman. Fortunately or unfortunately."

"Then I was in charge for a while," Priscilla said, sitting back with a cool smile and smoldering eyes. "So we came up with this deal that he would come off the road and he would have to focus on being responsible in the house and share some of the household duties. If he couldn't contribute financially, he'd have to do other things. For instance, one summer, he didn't have to work, so he painted the house. That saved us a lot of money. The point is, he had to be accountable—he couldn't just keep doing what he wanted whenever he wanted to do it."

The smile vanished. "But I was angry! Here I was, pulling this house together and doing all this stuff. I'd put in new carpeting and wallpaper to surprise him, but when I got home that day, he had the biggest surprise of all for me, now, didn't he?"

In our conversation alone, Lloyd told me none of this, providing only the most circumspect responses about the change in his relationship with Priscilla. "Boy, that ties into a long theory I have," he said, "about people changing. I just think that people change in general. As people grow, they change. Whether or not they change at the same rate and in the same direction is questionable. I think we are just experiencing normal growth, as people and as individuals."

"If you could change one thing about your relationship now, what would it be?" I asked.

He laughed. "What do you think? I would change the financial imbalance. I would like us to make the same amount of money so that there would be no imbalance. I think that would put less stress on the relationship."

When I contacted Priscilla again some time later, as this book neared publication, I received the news I'd fully expected to hear. She and Lloyd had divorced just a few months after my conversations with each of them.

"It was the best thing to do, the only thing to do," Priscilla said by phone from the Midwest, where her bakeries were expanding into new cities. "We're still great friends. Lloyd moved to the West Coast. We preserved a lot between us, but we just don't need to be together. I'm seeing a man now who actually makes as much money as I do."

Was it Priscilla's breadwinning status that drove the wedge between Lloyd and her...or was it something else? The complexities of this relationship reflect what I found in all of the damaged, disintegrating or destroyed marriages I encountered in my research.

In no case did I find a relationship that ended simply because the wife's income exceeded her husband's. In every case, I found multiple influences that compounded at the same time that the wife began to make more.

"It's the leading cause of divorce."

When I first began my research, I consulted a well-established research specialist whom I had known for most of my life. A former political science professor and an expert in the development of research methods and data analysis, he had a working familiarity with many of the sociological issues about marriage I was about to tackle.

"You know, of course," he said, "that the wife making more than the husband is one of the leading causes of divorce."

Fascinated, I began an in-depth search for this revealing statistic. I contacted dozens of sources, pored through periodicals, examined the journals, searched the Web...and guess what? I never found it.

The fact is that there is no truly useful data on the leading causes of divorce. A whopping 80 percent of all divorce filings cite the familiar catchall, "irreconcilable differences," as their cause, while another 4.2 percent are attributed to economic problems, according to Divorce Magazine.com.[1]

Plenty of sources tell us that the leading cause of divorce is connected to whatever service, method or product they advocate or sell. A survey conducted by Citibank suggests that 57 percent of divorced couples break up over financial disputes.[2] Literature published by Alcoholics Anonymous notes that substance abuse is one of the leading causes of divorce. Financial planners, banks and insurance companies who offer debt reduction services tell us that financial problems and debt play a leading role in divorce, while religious Web sites speak of spiritual differences, sexual incompatibility and psychological abuse as divorce's primary causes.

"I am not sure there is any such list of the leading causes of divorce," said Henry Gornbein of Divorce On-line in an E-mail correspondence with me. "Examples of leading causes of divorce include lack of communication, growing apart, infidelity, control and power issues, physical and psychological abuse (and) problems with alcohol and drugs, just to name a few."

As we sift through the claims, the self-serving diatribes, the anecdotes and the analytical studies, one point becomes especially important to breadwinning-wife couples. There is no evidence out there to support the claim that husbands automatically leave their marriages when their wives begin to outearn them. Nor do wives dump their husbands the moment it becomes clear that these men will not be the families' primary breadwinners.

In fact, the truth is entirely the opposite. A study published in a sociology journal in spring 2000 asks this question: Do husbands see their wives' high earning ability as a threat to their marriages or as a benefit? Using longitudinal data collected over twelve years, researchers Jiping Zuo and Shengming Tang discovered that the lower the husband's income in relation to his wife's, the more he is likely to adopt an egalitarian attitude about marriage, sharing of household responsibilities and his wife's breadwinning status. In addition, when the husband's income is markedly lower, the wife tends to view marriage as a more equitable partnership as well. The researchers determined that these husbands see their wives' elevated income as a *benefit* to the relationship, not as a threat.[3]

In 1999, a study reported by the *New York Times* found that 66 percent of men surveyed said they would be perfectly happy to have a higher-earning wife. Yet 53 percent of women said they thought there would be problems in their marriages if they earned more than their husbands did.[4] Men are moving to a more welcoming view of their wives as principal breadwinners, while we wives still wait with bated breath for our husbands to explode over this issue.

Some studies in the 1970s put forth the theory of the independence effect—a hypothesis, proven by actual research of the era, that wives' employment and divorce were causally related. Circumstantial evidence and historical trend data both suggested that this was true: women's income actually destabilized marriage, by reducing the benefits husbands received from their wives: household management, child care, cooking and so on. "The enhanced leverage of the wife may exact increasing levels of investment in housework or child care by the husband, thus further reducing his benefits from marriage," one report noted.[5]

That was the 1970s, when women made their first permanent entrance into the workforce in large numbers and tossed gender ideologies to the winds. Three decades later, researchers Sayer and Bianchi threw out the theory of the independence effect, finding only the weakest correlation between the wife's income and divorce rates. "Although evaluations of marital relationships undoubtedly include financial considerations, the decision to exit or remain in an existing marriage is a very complex process, one that probably hinges much more on non-economic factors than on whether a wife works for pay or earns a lot compared with her husband," they concluded.[6]

An interesting study by S.J. Rogers suggests that while increases in wives' incomes have no significant effect on levels of marital problems, marital problems definitely contributed to wives' increased earnings.[7] In essence, wives who believe their marriages are on the rocks may work harder to earn more money, so that they will have resources at their disposal to help them through their divorces.

This observation can hardly be parlayed into an indictment of breadwinning wives as marriage-busters. However, there's no question that some marriages fail when the wife's income grows while her husband's does not. Do they fail simply because the wife makes more money, robbing her husband of his breadwinning role? Or is there more at play, a greater issue—or series of issues—that intersect at the central point of a husband's self-esteem, gender identity and closely held beliefs about his role in the marriage?

As I talked to couples who claimed to be happy or unhappy, I began to see dangerous patterns emerging that acted as signposts for potentially major issues. Every marriage is a unique entity, but many couples face similar challenges and make the same missteps, not realizing that they've set themselves on courses that, if left unchecked, could lead to the end of these relationships.

Here are the most prevalent patterns I encountered.

The competition

No single component stood out more as the greatest danger to the breadwinning-wife marriage than the husband and wife who see their individual earning power as a competition with one another. When a competitive, employed husband discovers that his wife's income has begun to exceed his own, he usually responds with one or more in a series of uncomfortable options:

- He sets his sights on a promotion or a new profession and redoubles his efforts to remain the breadwinner, working harder than ever. This may mean long hours and additional shifts on the job, taking him out of the house for lengthier periods.

- He minimizes his wife's accomplishments by belittling her or needling her, pointing out her faults and turning every conversation into a conflict.
- He undermines her efforts in subtler ways, leaving home projects undone or refusing to help with housework or child care, thus producing a second shift at home for his wife.
- He spends money ostentatiously on himself and his own interests, leaving his wife to make ends meet with her own earnings.
- He salves his own masculinity by looking outside the marriage for female companionship.

It is no secret to a wife that her husband is a competitive man. Nor is competition within the relationship always unhealthy—on the contrary, some couples thrive on opportunities to outdo one another in benign ways. However, many men who regard their professional accomplishments as paramount also assume that their earnings will be enough to secure their breadwinning status at home. These men see their ability to support a family as a key element in their assessment of their own success...so when wives surpass them in income, competitive husbands simply have no way to reconcile this with their own self-images. Caught off-guard and without solutions, they may go so far as to insist that their wives give up the higher earning positions to "save" the marriage.

If the wife of a competitive man agrees to relinquish her professional stature for the sake of the marriage, however, what is the likely result? Almost immediately, resentment and anger on her part will begin to erode the relationship this wife endeavored to save.

I spoke to many couples who encountered the conundrum of the competitive husband. In not one case did the wife choose to give up her higher income position to save the marriage. In nearly every case, the wife chose to leave a marriage that threatened to rob her of her identity and her accomplishments.

Olivia and George met while they were both in medical school. Several years older than Olivia and chief resident at the teaching hospital, George took Olivia under his wing in her first year as an intern and guided her through the rigors of thirty-six hour shifts and life-and-death diagnoses. "I looked up to him so much," Olivia said. "He was my mentor, my friend and the more accomplished of the two of us. It was a hero worship situation."

When they married, as George completed his residency and moved into a university research position, Olivia still saw George as her great teacher, her superior...and her savior.

"He was the professor, the more sophisticated one," she said. "I was the starry-eyed student. That was clearly the basis of our relationship."

George had a dream, however. He wanted to be a well-recognized specialist in his area of expertise, one of the chosen few whose medical opinion would be sought by patients and colleagues far and wide. He chose research first, to make his name in the world of science and discovery, leading a team of technicians to find the cure for a menacing illness.

Meanwhile, Olivia completed her own education and moved quickly into an attending position at a nearby hospital. Her bedside manner, winning personality and superior skill quickly brought her to the attention of the hospital administrators, who began to accelerate her growth within the health system. In a few years, she had risen to a chief's position in her specialty.

"George was stricken by this," she said. "Here I was, getting the recognition he thought he deserved and receiving opportunities he had always wanted. He accused me of being carried away by the glamour of it all, of being a cold businesswoman instead of a compassionate doctor. And then, he put me in the worst position of all."

An opening in George's specialty surfaced at the hospital where Olivia served as a department chief—a staff appointment that would report directly to Olivia. George made the decision to apply for it.

"I begged him not to do it," Olivia said. "I pleaded with him not to put me in that position. I told him that it wasn't my decision; there was a panel of physicians involved and they would make the decision by majority vote. And I knew that, even going beyond the fact that he had been in a laboratory all those years and had not seen patients, there were things in George's personality that would just keep him from being selected. It was never going to work and I knew it would hurt our relationship."

Olivia was right. The panel rejected George, choosing a doctor with much more clinical and diagnostic experience and George took his anger and frustration out on his wife.

"He accused me of ruining the opportunity for him, of asking them not to hire him," she said. "Never mind that he didn't have the qualifications for the position. That was not relevant to him. It was all my fault for succeeding, instead of his responsibility to put his time and energy into pursuing his dreams. After that, it all just started to fall apart between us."

Olivia remembered well the moment that she knew her marriage had deteriorated beyond repair. "We were in bed watching television and the cat jumped up on the bed. I started cuddling the cat and talking to it in a baby voice. George turned to me and said, 'I wish you'd talk to me the way you talk to the cat. You're never affectionate with me anymore. You've become so cold.' Suddenly I realized he saw me as unfeminine, unloving. I had stolen his dream and he couldn't forgive me for that." Their divorce was inevitable.

Now, remarried to a man whose income exceeds her own, Olivia sees marriage from a new perspective. "Jack, my current husband, is a completely different kind of man," she said. "All of a sudden I'm going to ball games and hanging out in sports bars with him and his friends. I never did any of those things before. And Jack leaves it to me to take care of all the housework and the cooking, even though I still have my hospital position and I work six days a week. He works hard, too, in a corporate position that actually nets him more per year than me, by a lot. But he's a traditional man, much more so than George. It's a new kind of life."

Successful, exceptionally talented, well-respected and high earning, Olivia nevertheless found herself the target for jealousy, anger and disrespect from her first husband. Her higher income was not the core issue—it was her success in a field he had chosen for himself. George had positioned himself as the teacher, mentor and leader in his relationship with his wife, but when the student began to surpass the teacher, he saw her not with a professor's pride, but with a rival's wrath. Olivia's success made George a failure, *ipso facto*.

Was a more equitable resolution possible here? Olivia could have chosen to downgrade her position with the hospital, passing up promotions to keep her marriage sound...but such a sacrifice could have caused her to harbor bitter regret and new hostility toward George. George, meanwhile, found it impossible to accept Olivia's growth. He could not find it within himself to become comfortable with her visibility and respected position.

Some marriages run up against insurmountable obstacles. This sad end to a promising relationship reminds us that not all conflicts can be resolved and not all partners are suited to the breadwinning-wife arrangement—especially when the wife's position is one the husband cannot accept, because it flies in the face of his own failure.

Overcoming the competition

One particularly remarkable case I encountered in the course of my research was that of Lewis and Val. This husband and wife so loved the spirit of competition that they planned a full day of team sports for their wedding weekend, in which all guests participated in volleyball tournaments, swimming races and canoe-tilting contests. When Lewis realized that his wife's higher income was more than short-term issue, he chose to take the steps necessary to move beyond his own competitive nature, resolve his issues and preserve his relationship with his wife and their preschool-aged daughter, Robin.

Lewis and Val had survived a fairly tumultuous series of break-ups and make-ups before they married in the early 1990s, when they were in their thirties. College friends and pals living in San Francisco, they danced around the subject of commitment while Lewis determined whether or not Val could be "the one" for him. "We finally made the decision to live together and be together," Lewis told me by phone, intermittently putting me on hold as he fielded incoming calls to the technical assistance hotline he manned for a New York City technology company. "We moved to Kansas City, because Val's father owned several businesses and wanted to involve Val in fixing them, making them work financially. We worked there together for nine months and when I realized that we'd been there and working together all that time and we hadn't killed each other, I concluded that we were probably good candidates for marriage."

Yet one concern plagued Lewis, even then. A gifted salesman with an easy charm and superior technical knowledge, Lewis never worried that he would struggle to make a living. He expected to succeed in business, earn the primary income for his family and lead his wife and eventual children to the comfortable, even luxurious lifestyle to which he planned to become accustomed. However, in choosing Val as his wife, he'd chosen a woman of independent means—she made more money than he did, even before they were married.

"When we went to Kansas City, Val was the vice-president of the business for which we both worked, her father's business," Lewis explained. "I was just a hired gun. My salary was about $50,000 a year and she was paid substantially more than that. That ticked me off. But it didn't tick me off to the point where I said, 'Val, forget it.'"

He put me on hold for a moment, then returned. "All right, let's be honest. I was furious about it," he said. "But I also had to acknowledge that we came from two different places in our lives. I was frustrated by it, but encouraged. No, not even encouraged. Motivated."

"So rather than turning you off on the situation, Val's higher income actually made you want to succeed more?" I asked.

"Absolutely," Lewis said. "It gave me a goal to shoot for."

When the Kansas City business had stabilized, Lewis and Val moved on to reorganize another of Val's father's holdings, a medical imaging company in New York City. Once again, Lewis was assigned to a sales and quality assurance position, while Val became company president. "Val was the senior member of the team and I was the junior. I had to live in that context," he said. "The real difficulty I found was keeping the separation between our relationship at home and our relationship in the office. If I didn't keep that separation between Val and the business, we never would have survived this long."

This ability to compartmentalize, to separate his love for Val from their financial situation, made it possible for Lewis to stomach the idea that his substantial income did not match his wife's. "I do the same things with finances at home that I did at work with Val," he explained. "At home she's the mommy and I'm the daddy and we enjoy our beautiful daughter. But when we're discussing finances, everything goes into one pot. And Val does the books. She has the skills; she has the talent; she has been in financial management all of her life. And I do not question that. I deposit my paycheck in our joint account and she handles it from there."

Ever independent and self-reliant, is Lewis truly comfortable relinquishing control of his own money to his wife? "I made a decision and I stuck with it," he said. "I *decided* that I am perfectly comfortable with her handling the money. When a situation comes up, we talk about how we are going to address it. Then we do what we discussed. I trust Val's ability to see what is most important at the moment."

He chuckled. "I hear other men saying to their wives, 'No, I have to control the finances and you have to give me the check.' But with us, that would blow everything up, because it's an alpha thing that becomes stronger than the relationship itself. It's like saying, 'I am top dog and so I'm going to get top billing here.'"

"You made the conscious decision to avoid that," I said, ready to congratulate him for this.

"Right," Lewis replied. "And guess what? It is frustrating as hell."

He clicked off to take a call, then returned. "There are times when I would like to say that I'm going to the bank and taking out three hundred dollars and I'm going to spend it on drinks and strip bars in the city. Not really my style, but there it is. And it has happened a couple of times—when I did stupid things with a hundred dollars, just to establish that I'm still in charge. But those occasions are few and far between now."

Lewis excused himself once again. When he returned to the call, I could detect another person on the line.

"Here's Val," he said to me. Then, "Val, I'm talking to Randi Minetor. About our marriage."

A beat. "I'll close my office door," Val said finally.

"I'm not going to put you on the spot," I interjected quickly, but Val was ready to talk and characteristically frank, she addressed most of her comments directly to Lewis.

"Okay," she began, warming to the subject instantly. "A generic description of when you are not comfortable is when we need to make decisions as a family about how to spend my money," she began.

Lewis laughed out loud. "Right there!" he said. "It's difficult for me to bring up the subject, so I'm glad you did."

Val had no difficulty with the subject. "About 90 percent of the time, that's when you express your discomfort with our income difference—when the money is coming from *me*, not us." To me, she said, "He gets angry. He gets quiet. And then he turns it into, 'I don't care.'"

"Which means that you *do* care?" I said to Lewis, but Val responded.

"Right. And then I raise my voice," she said, doing so. "I say that this argument is ridiculous. I say, 'This is for us. How many times do we have to go over this? The money is for us to use for things to make our lives better.' I also remind him of the other discussions we are going to be having. Are we going to have this argument when we choose a private school for our daughter? We need to resolve this disagreement and find out why it is still a problem. And he says, 'Because it is. I can't help it.'"

"Scary, huh?" Lewis interjected.

Clearly it was scary for Lewis, but a lot less scary than the idea of leaving Val to find a wife who would achieve less, earn less and need more. "I hate to think of us breaking up or divorcing," he said, "but you have to think about that rationally today. One out of two marriages ends in divorce. And if you're a woman and you think about it happening to you, then you have to say that you need money to survive the first two or three years." Lewis had had a relationship like this. Years before he and Val were married, he found himself in a romance with a woman whose divorce had left her nearly destitute. "In Val's case, maybe having her own work, having so much involvement in her father's businesses, maybe that helps—because I know that she is set. It's not all about me. I'm more comfortable, because I know she is solid. If I go under a bus, I know she will be okay and she will be able to take care of Robin. That's really important to me."

Lewis could see the advantages of sharing his life with a high-earning spouse...to a point. "Ultimately, that's still what drove me out of the family business," he said. "I moved to this job, knowing that I'd have a better chance of advancing my income. This may be the opportunity for me to eclipse Val's income in a year or two."

Lewis had the self-awareness to understand his own consternation. He was professionally successful, he commanded a high income and yet he still found himself earning less than his wife. However, he had no intention of allowing his wife's success to dampen the pleasure of his marriage to her, even if it meant swallowing his own pride. "We have a full and rich life," he said. "Val is a lot of fun to be around. Val is sophisticated. We know each other really well. We don't need to go too far from our backyard to be comfortable. What keeps our relationship going is that we have experienced a lot together already and we are still together."

"When things get really tough between Lewis and me, I always go back to the fact that he really does care, despite what we are fighting about today," Val concluded. "He really has my interests at heart."

Is this a convoluted way of saying that love conquers all? The answer here is not so simple, but lies in Lewis's strength of character and his long history with Val. While he takes the secondary breadwinning role involuntarily, Lewis is frustrated, but he is not jealous. He doesn't turn his home into a battleground over petty issues. He feels that he and Val being together has greater value than their being apart and does his best to conquer his own competitive spirit and his need to be the "top dog."

Val, meanwhile, helps minimize the situation by handling all the family finances as well as her personal investments. Lewis is well aware of the total income picture, but does not deal with the details of dollars and cents. He has no opportunity to make daily comparisons of his contribution versus his wife's, so he need not be reminded with every bill paid that he contributed 30 percent, while she contributed 70 percent.

The traditionalist

A man whose belief system dictates that his wife should be home raising the children will probably find that marrying someone with breadwinning status will rock his world.

Even at the dawn of the twenty-first century, we still encounter plenty of men who long for the traditional family structure. Many of these men will accept the overall concept of working wives in theory, knowing that today's economy often requires two incomes per family to maintain comfortable lifestyles. They may tolerate their wives' working at low-income jobs that provide grocery money or discretionary spending money—cash for their wives' clothing and cosmetics, for example. But there is *no way* that a man who believes child care is "mother's" work and expects his dinner on the table in a spic-and-span house when he gets home will enjoy being the husband of a breadwinning wife. If a traditional man "allows" his wife to make more than he does, her success indicates that he has failed as a provider, as a husband and as a man.

Virginia and Dale dated for nine years before they were finally married, when Virginia was twenty-eight and Dale had turned thirty-two. They met while Virginia was in high school, when handsome Dale was the answer to her dreams: a strong, attractive college man with a big car and a football star's social circle. Dating on and off throughout Virginia's college years and finally choosing one another exclusively, they had high hopes as they settled down to raise a family.

Three weeks after they were married, Dale stunned Virginia one evening. "We had dated for almost a decade and for the last couple of years before we were married, we saw each other almost every night. However, on this one evening, he turned to me and said, 'When are you going to start acting like a wife and cook the meals? Not once in nine years had I ever made a meal for him. He knew I hated cooking. He expected some sort of domestic transformation to take place once I had a ring on my finger."

In all those years, Dale had stuck to his assumption that wives did the cooking and cleaning, even though all the evidence told him that Virginia would never be one of those traditional wives. At the time, however, Virginia had clung to her own assumption would provide primary support for the family. If he dis would warn her about his earning potential or his ignored them.

Soon after the cooking incident, attitude about work didn't match his fer the football field. "For all his sports ba competitive guy," she said. "He just wante struction masonry—and come home. He didn't want to be in charge or climb the ladder or challenge himself. Oddly enough, money didn't seem to make any difference to him. So if we were going to have a decent home or any nice things, I decided I would have to be the one to go out and make money to have those things.

Virginia did just that. With a business degree and several college internships under her belt, Virginia landed a position in the financial department of a large corporation. In two years, she moved from clerk to manager, taking over entire functions and landing the company's conversion to a faster, more reliable computer accounting system. Her successes brought accolades from the highest executives in the organization. Clearly, Virginia's advancement would outshine Dale in short order.

"Now here's where it got weird," Virginia said. "Even though Dale had no interest in getting a better job or making more money, he still expected me to live within his means and settle for what he was willing to bring in—less than $30,000 a year. He just couldn't get his mind around the idea that I could make more money or that we could have a better life because of my income. When he saw my salary numbers on paper, he just couldn't deal with it. He actually barely spoke for weeks."

His wife's larger income was only the secondary blow for Dale, however. The real problem was far more crushing to his masculine identity. For three years, he and Virginia struggled to conceive a child.

"We went through the whole fertility thing, from the pills to the injections to artificial insemination," Virginia said. "He got tested, I got tested. It became the single greatest obsession in our lives."

Finally a child arrived, a healthy baby girl. Dale assumed that after all that effort, Virginia would quit her job and become a full-time mother and wife. Virginia, on the other hand, had no such plans. By now the couple had moved into a comfortable suburban home, made possible by Virginia's income.

"I did stay home for a short while," she said. "Then we hired a nanny, so Beth was home all day, in her own space and with her own things. I was pretty happy with that, but Dale just couldn't understand it. Although," Virginia added, stopping for ironic emphasis, "he was perfectly happy to have the money I made and the things it could buy."

Dale's frustration with Virginia became more and more obvious over time. He made plans with his male friends three or four nights every week, leaving Virginia alone to take care of their daughter even after her toughest workdays. If Virginia planned an evening out with her friends, Dale insisted that she ask his permission and see if it would fit into his schedule first. "The result, of course, was that I never went out," she said. "No matter what I planned, he'd have plans for that night. Of course, he knew that I couldn't leave the baby at home by herself. He tried to force me to act like a mother—the wife and mother he thought I should be."

This behavior reached its climax during a family trip to Las Vegas when Beth turned five. On the fourth day of the weeklong trip, Virginia asked Dale to take Beth out for a couple of hours so that she could have some time to relax. "It's just exhausting there, with so much to do and your child running everywhere," she said. "And every night, we'd get back to the hotel and Dale would announce that he was going out to gamble or to one of the bars. He'd leave me in the hotel room with Beth. He never even invited me to join him or suggested we use one of the baby-sitting services."

Dale obliged Virginia that afternoon, taking Beth on a brief visit to one of the hotel amusement areas so that his wife could sit by the pool with a magazine. "They were gone about two hours," she said.

"Then, that evening, I asked Dale if he would keep an eye on Beth while I took a shower. He said, 'Okay, if you'll take her tomorrow afternoon so I can get some time to myself.' He went out every night and left me with Beth, but I asked for two hours and he expected minute-for-minute reciprocity."

That vacation was the last straw for Virginia. "I told him I couldn't live like this. When we got back, I filed for divorce." She considered for a moment. "Throughout our relationship, I'd matured, but Dale had not. He still wanted to be the attractive, twenty-one year old guy with the cool car and he wanted me to be his adoring fan. Never did he want a wife who was his equal. That was our downfall."

Studies tell us that many men now believe in a more egalitarian marriage structure, in which working husbands help with household tasks and participate in child care, while their wives earn substantial incomes and share the home responsibilities with their husbands. Yet a significant number of men still cling to the traditions in which they were raised, expecting their wives to do the "women's work" and accept whatever living their husbands bring home for them.

Both Virginia and Dale faced a battle between their traditional beliefs and the realities of their marriage. Dale thought that somehow, despite all indications during their long relationship, his new spouse would turn into the perfect housewife and mother moments after she said, "I do." Virginia, meanwhile, made an equally dangerous assumption, not realizing that her husband had no career aspirations, even though his lack of progress could impede his family's standard of living.

Virginia took what seemed to her an obvious route, using her skills to bring more money into the family. The fact that she could do this, however, became a slap in the face to her husband, who chose to punish Virginia for her success, instead of either supporting her efforts to improve the family's quality of life or working to match or surpass his wife's income. In his eyes, Virginia's actions were simply *wrong*—unfeminine, unwifely. Apparently, it never occurred to Dale that his comparative lack of ambition didn't gel with his wife's plans for her own life.

Men with such traditional beliefs are unlikely to change. Fundamental beliefs form in us at a very early age, often because we observe certain behaviors in those close to us. While we cannot turn today's traditional men into modern thinkers, we can begin to demonstrate more equitable behavior to our children by sharing responsibilities in our own homes. The child whose parents do not discriminate between "men's work" and "women's work" will not know that such divisions existed. We can end gender-specific expectations by setting no such boundaries in our homes and by showing our children that all tasks are appropriate for all people.

The meddling mouths

When a breadwinning wife begins to see her husband through the eyes of disapproving friends, relatives or coworkers, her marriage may end up on the rocks.

Well-meaning individuals with strong opinions can be the most destructive influences on our marriages, especially when it's critically important to us to gain their approval. Parents, siblings, employers, supervisors and close friends feel comfortable sharing their views with us, even when these views are uninvited, inappropriate, uninformed or just plain wrong.

Recently, I found myself the confidant of an elderly mother who observed her daughter's hard work in preparing Easter Sunday dinner, while her son-in-law—an at-home dad with primary responsibility for the couple's two preschool-age children—chatted with my husband and played Candy Land with the kids in the living room. The grandmother shook her head as she pulled me aside, "That one—he's got the life, eh?" she whispered to me. "All he has to do is play with those kids and gab with his friends, while my daughter makes all the money *and* takes care of the house. How'd she get herself into this?"

Grandma had it wrong, of course. Carl, the at-home dad, did indeed handle all the housework responsibilities during the week, but since his mother-in-law lived out of town, she never saw this effort. Arriving only for holidays, she saw Gretchen, her daughter, knocking herself out in the kitchen in a desperate effort to please her judgmental mother by preparing her favorite dishes. She would never witness Carl changing diapers, cleaning up after the kids, vacuuming the house, washing the windows or making dinner every night to have it on the table when Gretchen arrived home from her surgical practice.

"Mom never says anything to me, but I know what she thinks and I know she doesn't approve," Gretchen told me later. "She says it in other ways, like when she bugs me about saving for retirement. 'How are you going to do that on your salary alone?' she asks me. She can't understand that I make more then $100,000 a year. She assumes that I'm a woman, so I don't make much—even though she made a nice living of her own in her day. So I see her watching Carl with one raised eyebrow."

She dried her hands as she finished the dinner dishes and turned to me. "Some days, I actually wonder if she's right and I'm crazy.

But I look at the ledger sheet and I see our children's happy faces and I think, no, I'm right. She just doesn't get it."

The influence of a disapproving parent or close friend often has one of two effects: Ill-chosen words from an outsider can drive a wedge into an already eroding marriage or these comments can cause a couple to circle the wagons, bringing them closer together as they battle a common foe. Such was my own experience when my mother and friends insisted to me that Nic's income would be inadequate in bringing me the life my mother had always planned for me: an upscale, protected, suburban existence.

The more my mother pressed the point, forcing me to defend my choice of Nic over the high-earning professional men who would forever see my achievements as second to their own, the harder I fought the battle. Eventually, after a knockdown verbal skirmish that ended when I slammed down the phone and refused to call her for days, Mom gave in, even apologizing for her harsh words. "I guess I have to see that Nic is good for you," she said. "He's not what we expected, but he's a very good man."

Why do parents and friends equate being a "good man" with being the better or even sole provider of household income, even now in supposedly enlightened times? Tradition runs deep, especially in the case of gender roles. Many have cited the women's movement as the fastest and most total revolution to take place in recorded history—a transformation that altered thousands of social mores and upended numerous closely held beliefs in its wake. Yet not everyone participated in this revolution and not everyone lives by its new ideals. The recent success of the best-selling book *The Surrendered Wife*, a volume suggesting that women abandon their own identities to keep peace in their homes, provides more evidence that plenty of women still reject feminist principles and plenty of men continue to reject the idea of gender equality.[8]

Every day, breadwinner wives run up against people who feel they have a right to comment on the women's marriages and positions as breadwinners. It's up to us to filter out the noise and make intelligent choices about others' opinions, taking to heart those ideas that help us create healthy relationships with our husbands, our children and the other people who are most important in our lives.

Respect-me-not
What happens when a husband doesn't live up to his wife's expectations—even when the breadwinner wife expects him to make less than she does?

People can disappoint each other in many ways that go well beyond earning power. If your husband has difficulty remaining employed because of skill deficiencies, personality conflicts or other challenges, you may begin to see him in a less than radiant light. If your husband lets you down at home by leaving projects unfinished, repeatedly forgetting to pick up the kids from dance class or ignoring accumulated chores, your respect for him may crumble. If your husband spends money too easily, bounces checks or ruins his credit with late payments, your constant attempts to bail him out and set him on a straight course may seriously damage his creditability with you.

By the same token, your breadwinning position can trigger a whole set of stimuli that can change your husband's impressions of you as well—especially if he finds himself the involuntary secondary breadwinner or non-earning spouse.

"I've been on my own most of my life," said Wanda, a fifty-three-year-old research chemist in San Diego, "so when I decided that maybe I would give marriage a try, I thought I was much more interested in companionship than in the financial end. I was more interested in finding someone to share my life with than to worry about money. I figured that someone around my own age would be making decent money and that it would be okay. I wouldn't marry anyone who was a deadbeat. I just made some assumptions." She swallowed. "They turned out to be wrong."

Married for the first time on her fiftieth birthday, Wanda chose Dwayne, who served as receptionist and handyman for the landscaping firm she hired to remove some trees on her property. Her many telephone conversations with him led to coffee, then dating and finally marriage—a long-awaited union that Wanda approached with as much trepidation as hope.

"One of the things that was not clear to me until after we were in the marriage a while was the fact that Dwayne is really an underachiever," she told me. "He had held a series of jobs that he liked for the content of the work, but he didn't have the right skills to do the work. He'd worked a lot in retail, so I assumed he was a great salesman. Well, he's not. He's very personable and outgoing, the kind of guy who will sit down and have a cup of coffee with you and you'll be divulging your entire life within ten minutes. But he was never going to be a real contributor to our combined income."

She shrugged. "What could I expect? At this stage in life I pretty well figured out that it would be rare to find a man who was going to be my age, successful in his own right and looking for a new wife that wasn't a trophy. Let's face it, the demographics are fairly clear. Men in their forties and fifties are looking for young women in their twenties. Men that age are not looking to marry women who are more like themselves."

After a few years of marriage, Wanda found herself disappointed, disillusioned and convinced that she had settled for whatever she could get. Worse, she'd decided that Dwayne was far from the cream of the crop, mostly because he was not a success professionally or financially.

Is Wanda being realistic or is she undermining her marriage by placing her husband in this diminished light? Time will tell whether or not their marriage can survive. Respect for one another is absolutely key in sustaining a happy marriage. When one spouse loses that respect, the relationship could shatter.

Her big change

When the conditions of a husband's employment change overnight—because of a layoff, a job dismissal or, worse yet, an accident that leaves him unable to continue in his current profession—the wife may become the breadwinner in an instant. If she never intended to hold this higher earning position, especially in lieu of any income from her husband, the change can shake the marriage to its very core.

By no means is it absolutely certain that a husband's job loss will result in disaster. As we've seen in previous chapters, I spoke with many couples who saw such big changes as opportunities. Facing life with exorbitant day care bills for small children or with a newly purchased fixer-upper home, these couples made the decision to take the husband's job loss and turn it into the solution to a knottier family problem: The husband takes a turn as an at-home dad, uses his expertise and free time to renovate the house or brings his skills into the business his wife owns.

However, many families face the losses of husbands' incomes with the knowledge that this will mean compromises, cutbacks and potential deprivations, even when the wives have the abilities to earn sizable salaries of their own. Job loss, after all, affects far more than a family's wallet—emotional distress, psychological disturbances and diminished self-esteem become dominant factors as husband and wife grapple with the enormous changes in their lives.

"I guess when we got married, I always thought that Arthur would be the one bringing home the paycheck," said Tricia, a twenty-seven-year-old biochemist in Austin. "But he was laid off right when I was finishing my degree, so we were both unemployed at the beginning of our marriage. Then to top it off, I got pregnant right away."

Arthur had taken a position in the genetics lab of a large bio-engineering corporation, but the company dropped the project in which Arthur was involved, leaving him with no job and no immediate prospects. "We just had to take some time and live with my parents while I had the baby," Tricia continued. "Then he decided to go back to school, to take some classes and kind of retool himself. One of his professors convinced him that this was the perfect time to get his Ph.D."

Maybe it was a perfect time for Arthur, but for Tricia, the timing couldn't have been worse. With a new baby, her first job after college and a burning desire to get out of her parents' home and start her own household, Tricia felt that Arthur's unilateral decision to return to school left her with all the responsibility in the relationship—and none of the control. "I have come to realize that Arthur is much more of a dreamer than I am," she said. "I am more practical. I will do whatever I have to do for forty hours a week if it will bring home enough money to keep us happy. Right now, even though Arthur gets a stipend, I am making 80 percent of the household budget." Tricia noted that at the time of our conversation, her annual gross income was about $32,000. "But Arthur has to do something that's more fulfilling, a job that will make him feel like a whole person. Which means right now, he is almost unemployable—and with the type of degree he's working on, he's really going to be even more unemployable."

Tension tightened Tricia's voice. "We have really struggled with this problem. I feel that he's just hanging us out on a line. If I ever lose my job, we're going to be in real financial trouble. We can't do any long-range planning, because we don't have a whole lot of financial security. The field I'm in is pretty volatile and there are a lot of ups and downs in the job market. I could lose my job, too, so it's a big source of stress."

How do Tricia and Arthur cope with this? "We yell at each other," Tricia said frankly. "We have a lot of pretty explosive fights. They're not destructive fights—just blowing off steam. But I've decided that I can't worry about whether I'm going to get laid off in six months. I have decided that we need to take it day by day. We'll try to do our daily things and be happy as a family."

Compounding Tricia's stress is her impression that Arthur doesn't respond quickly to her requests for help with their baby and the housework. "I ask him to do things, but not anything regular," she said. "With the addition of having the baby, it's made me realize that I am way overloaded. I've asked for help a number of times, but he hasn't done it as fast as I would like. We went round and round on this and I decided that I have to just let go and let him do things on his own

schedule rather than nagging." She sighed. "But I do feel like I am ultimately responsible for everything that happens."

When a husband makes a major change in his career path,
either voluntarily or because of job loss, the time between his decision
and his eventual success can place crushing stress on the wife who supports him financially. In the case of Tricia and Arthur, their frequent
arguments gave way to more open discussions over time—talks that
helped them begin to reconcile their opposing points of view and
helped them find ways to cope with their compromised situation.

"We have a lot of discussions about our financial condition and
what Arthur wants to do with his life. These have been kind of an energy
drain for me," Tricia said. "But I feel that we have worked through a lot
of issues and have made peace with them. I wish we had some financial
security and I wish that we didn't have student loans and credit cards
and medical bills hanging over our heads. If we didn't have the debt, I
think that the decisions we made about our careers, or at least my career,
would be a lot different. I would love more time with my son. I would
love to have more time doing things at home. But that will come. It has
to come."

Once again, we can see that Tricia and Arthur's conflicts go well
beyond the simple fact that Tricia makes more money than Arthur does.
Differences in outlook, opposite ideas about supporting the family, an
inequitable sharing of household chores and the couple's compounding
debt contribute to the overall stress in their relationship, so that Arthur's
lowered earning position becomes just one in a series of obstacles to
Tricia's happiness in the relationship. While Arthur declined to be interviewed, we can guess that he is more comfortable than Tricia with their
compromised household income, because he is executing a chosen
course of action that he believes will change their situation. The problem
here is not that Arthur dislikes being the secondary breadwinner. If anything, the problem may be that he does *not* dislike his temporary lack of
income.

Her big chance

What happens when a breadwinning wife doesn't want to be the breadwinner anymore?

We have discussed extensively the pressures that come with taking the breadwinner household position—for either spouse—and the need
to leave room in a couple's life to make choices that benefit the entire
family. Yet many couples find themselves boxed into corners, either by
design or by circumstances, limiting opportunities for breadwinning

wives to accommodate their own needs when a life change turns a high-paying job into a prison.

This is especially poignant if the wife's desire for change comes with the arrival of a child. When a mother's instincts tell her that she should have more time with her children, she should have the opportunity to seek that time through work-family balance programs and whatever other methods she can put into place. For breadwinning wives, however, this flexibility can be virtually impossible without seriously compromising the family's well-being. This situation is far more than a dilemma—it can lead to conflict in the home that jeopardizes an otherwise happy marriage.

"We have two children, ages one and four," said Chrissy, a Rhode Island attorney with an associate's position in a rising law firm. Chrissy's husband, Cameron, is a freelance writer working out of their home, so he is able to raise the children and tend to household activities. "I get to work around 7:00 A.M. and I've scheduled everything so that I can leave by noon. But I usually stay an hour or two after that to meet with clients, at lunch or whatever, or to finish up paperwork. I get home around 1:00 P.M. or so."

Chrissy worked with her employer to create this truncated schedule so that she could spend afternoons with her children, allowing Cameron time for his own work as he finishes a novel. "I'm supposed to attend two conferences a year of my own choosing, to keep up with new points of law," Chrissy said. "But I am restricted, because I won't go overnight. I won't be away from my kids that way. I try to find things that are presented locally, so I can get home that evening. Sometimes I feel guilty about that, but I look around and see that a lot of people at these conferences are doing the same thing—attending locally, so they can get home to their young kids."

Balancing work and home became far more important to Chrissy with the arrival of their second child, she told me. "I really don't like the idea of children in day care a lot of time," she said. "Even when the kids are just with a neighbor down the street and she's a wonderful caregiver, I think they should be home with their parents. It's great when our kids are home with their dad. Everyone at work is jealous that I have only taken one 'sick kid day' in the last three years. He's there, so I don't have to worry about them."

However, Chrissy's part-time arrangement had begun to wear thin at work and her abbreviated income barely made ends meet for the family, especially as Cameron came closer to completing his book and took on less freelance work. "We've had a lot more late night discussions recently," Chrissy said. "I think Cameron has really taken over the house and the kids, so even though he may not be making money, he balances it by making sure that I have a lot more time. But we have plenty of talks about whether or not he is happy. And I'm not sure that I'm happy."

Chrissy knew that she couldn't expect to advance to a partnership position at the law firm where she worked while she maintained part-time status, but when we spoke, she had come to the conclusion that partnership might not be so important to her anymore. However, Cameron's current income, less than $15,000 annually, simply did not fill the gap left by Chrissy's move from full-time to part-time. "If we are going to have another year with the amount of freelancing Cameron's been doing, I think I would have to go back full-time," she said. "And that would mean I wouldn't get home until six o'clock or later every night and we would have to pay a lot more for child care. I don't like either of those ideas at all."

When I spoke with Cameron several days after my conversation with Chrissy, he knew well his wife's unrelenting pull between her job and her children and how this measured up against the inevitabilities of supporting the family. "Up until two years ago, I was with an advertising agency and I had a steady paycheck," he said. "It used to be that my income would cover all of our household expenses and groceries and Chrissy paid the mortgage. Now, I get a check if I work and I don't get a check if I don't work. Chrissy was very supportive of my leaving to write my book, even though we knew it would mean financial hardship. But the last couple of years have been very hard for her."

Chrissy specializes in family law, so she faces a constant barrage of divorce cases, custody battles, child abuse issues and other disputes that affect her deeply. "It's very high pressure and very stressful where she works," Cameron acknowledged. "It's put the pressure on me, too, to bring in more income so that she can at least entertain the idea of taking time off from her work. I know that she does feel like she'd like to take a break, but right now, we just can't afford it."

A man who laughs easily and who is quick with a clever comeback, Cameron dismissed his own discomfort as he jokingly described Chrissy's many positive influences on his life. "I tell her often, if I hadn't met her I would be living in a cardboard box somewhere," he said. "There are so many ways she's been a great influence. I'm a much better dresser. I shower more often. And I cut way down on dating, which is definitely for the best." More solemnly, he continued, "I do my best to try to make an equal contribution. I wash dishes, I take out the garbage, I do the laundry and the shopping. I cook breakfast and lunch for the kids. I do the lawn mowing and shovel the snow."

He paused, considering his next statements carefully. "The truth is that I have never in my life been very good at making a lot of money. Dealing with the fact that my wife makes more than I do, and probably always will, is tough to swallow. The male ego—it's a subtle skirmish. But I have also decided that it's really important that I be here, with my children, and that I have this time to make my own dream happen. If I could work at something that I really liked and make lots of money, I would love it, because Chrissy could quit her job. But if it meant my doing something that I wasn't happy with just to earn a lot of money, I would only be..." He hesitated. "Well, moderately pleased, I guess."

Chrissy didn't hesitate at all in her assessment of her family's income situation. "I push Cameron on this," she said. "I ask him, 'Do you think you are going to be more aggressive about getting more freelance work or will you investigate other advertising firms about whether there are openings?' I think he is sorting out his feelings about going back to work full-time."

"I would be very pleased if our situation were reversed and if Cameron made enough money for me to stay home with the children," she continued. "But only if he did it willingly, happily and if it was something he really wanted to do. I don't want him to go back to work just to please me or just to make money. That would be the same problem I'm dealing with now, all over again."

Considerate of one another, well aware of the conundrum they face, but also aware that they must find a way to accommodate all the family's needs, Chrissy and Cameron travel the same loop every day. They know that one thing is certain: They can only fulfill one dream at a time. Right now, they've agreed that Cameron's dream ranks first. However, this unofficial contract between them leaves Chrissy to deal with the reality of a job she daily finds less enjoyable, complicated by the desire to spend her children's earliest years with them as a full-time mother.

As in so many marital challenges, there are no easy answers. Both Cameron and Chrissy can take comfort in the fact that while they may not meet all of their personal needs, they are working together to provide a secure home for their children, in which the kids see both their parents for extended periods every day. Whatever sacrifices they have each made to create this environment, they have made the family unit their first priority. The solution has not been perfect for either of them. But Chrissy and Cameron continue to work together to make it better.

The Free Ride

Are there men out there who victimize their wives by allowing them to bring home the family income while they contribute nothing?

I did not meet any of these men, although I did speak with wives whose husbands seemed disinclined to earn a living at all. You may recall Liesel and Dan in chapter 5—he agreed to become an at-home father when he couldn't find work, but after only two months he placed their child in full-time day care and spent his days on his own pursuits. This couple came the closest to the Free Ride concept of any I interviewed, making them stand out in a field of hardworking, devoted men and women.

There seems to be no question that there are men who take advantage of their breadwinning wives, even though they didn't show up significantly in my research. At the very least, we know that these men might be found in the ranks of alcohol or drug abusers or those who have behavioral or personality challenges that prevent them from maintaining steady employment. Studying these issues, of course, was not the focus of my research.

However, if you are a breadwinning wife whose husband takes advantage of your earning ability—by refusing to work, by contributing neither money nor effort to the household, by spending your money freely and confounding your efforts to support the family or by using your money to fund his addiction—then I strongly urge you to seek guidance outside of the family. Talk to a counselor, a clergy member, a social worker or another advisor who can help you understand your situation and find ways to improve your circumstances. No human being, male or female, should be forced to support a spouse who gives nothing in return and who frustrates every effort to build a comfortable life.

— CHAPTER 14 —

SINGLE AND SUCCESSFUL
Could You Marry a Man Who Makes Less?

Some women who purchase this book may be single, successful professionals in their late twenties, thirties, forties or more who have not yet discovered the right man for the long term.

If you are one of these successful women with a promising career ahead of you or a career that's well under way, the possibility exists that you will marry a man who earns less than you do.

Stop, right now, and pay attention to the way that statement made you feel. Did your stomach tighten? Did you groan aloud? Did you shake your head and inwardly curse the forty years of feminism that brought you to this moment?

Or did you feel your muscles unclench as you relaxed into the idea?

Your initial reaction is critically important, because it tells you something about your needs and your expectations about marriage. So many of us are still wound up in the Cinderella Complex, the idea that someday, somehow, a prince on a white charger will come and whisk us away to a secure, protected life with every imaginable advantage. Deep down inside many women still think the men they eventually marry should "save" them from the horrors of self-reliance, potential deprivation and loneliness.[1] Even women who are otherwise self-sufficient, living comfortably within their own means and enjoying the fruits of their professional accomplishments, often still believe what those fairy tales they learned as children told them: Someday, their prince will come. Someday, every woman should "marry up."

Here's the big secret the fairy tales never revealed. Princes *do* come—but they're not all rich and they don't all come with the trappings and finery of royal life.

Princes are men who treat you well, who celebrate your accomplishments and who love you even when you're having the worst—or best—day of your life. They are men whose wealth and value comes in forms other than money, as ideas or laughter or an ability to understand you in ways no other man ever has. These princes may not sweep you away to Monte Carlo for the weekend or buy you diamonds for your anniversary, but they will know what pleases you and what doesn't and they will make it their personal mission to do everything in their power to make you happy.

Some women spend so much time looking for the fantasy princes—the ones with castles and riches—that they don't even see different kinds of men, men who will contribute to their future wives' quality of life in less ostentatious, more subtle ways. These men may never make more money than you do, but they may never see that as an obstacle to your combined happiness, either.

The question is: Will you? Are you prepared to be a breadwinning wife?

And if you believe you are, where are these alternative princes?

Are you cut out for this?

For some of us, the breadwinning wife role comes naturally. Not every woman expects the financial support of a man to change her life one day—in fact, many women chafe at the idea of *ever* asking another person for money, be it a husband, friend, parent or even a bank loan officer. To a woman who craves and cherishes her self-sufficiency, it makes no difference who else brings money into the household. She will always do whatever it takes to maintain her own financial independence.

Other professional women take a more moderate stance when they consider sharing household funds. They know that they will bring in substantial incomes that will enhance their future families' quality of life and they expect to share the burdens of supporting their families with the husbands they eventually choose. These women may plan to take time off to raise children or they may expect to foot the bills for day care while they continue to work. Whatever the case, they know their incomes will be part of their families' pots.

Some women continue to assume that their future husbands will earn more than they do—and that's the condition they find most desirable, the one that fits into their overall life plans. Even women with high-level positions in corporations or other organizations may hope to find those elusive princes, the men who will take them away from all this and make their lives easier by earning even more substantial incomes.

Whether you fall into one of these three categories or somewhere in between, you need to ask yourself some tough questions and answer them honestly before you consider a relationship with a man whose earnings are lower than your own.

1. What do you believe is the "natural order" of the family relationship?
Think carefully before you answer this and go down below the surface to find your real expectations.

In your heart of hearts, you may believe that your husband should bring home the bigger paycheck, because that's what men are supposed to do. If that's the case, you have your answer: Your life as the family breadwinner may lead you to resent your husband's lesser earning position. You may find yourself feeling unappreciated, taken for granted or even feeling that your husband takes advantage of you. The breadwinning wife arrangement will pose challenges you may not have an interest in tackling.

If you answered that you believe a husband and wife are partners and should share the responsibility for household finances and management, you have a better chance of finding happiness as a breadwinning wife. Your husband may not participate as an equal partner—his income could be significantly lower than yours or he may not become the housework helpmate you expected. However, your breadwinning status will give you the opportunity to seek his help and work out ways for him to participate more fully in your relationship.

If you responded that there is no natural order in the family relationship and that roles should be defined based on what's best for the individual family, you are likely to succeed as a breadwinning wife—so long as your husband agrees with your views.

2. What is your relationship with your own money?
Yes, you and your money have a relationship, one that has its roots in your earliest understanding of money and its impact on your life to date.

Maybe your money is critically important to you. Having money means that you have a firm hold on your independence and self-sufficiency—you owe nothing to any individual and you never have to ask a soul's permission to spend your money the way you choose. You know your checking account balance to the penny on any given day; you monitor the progress of your investments on a regular basis; you keep a constant, running tally of your income versus expenses both in your own head and on the computer. You can't imagine ever asking a husband for a nickel, especially under any condition that would mean you'd have no income of your own.

While none of the wives I interviewed would say that they actively sought men who earn less than they do, such men certainly fit into their life plans. At no point did these women expect to be supported by someone else—in fact, they abhorred such a concept.

But perhaps you see money from a different perspective. Maybe you see your money as a means to an end, rather than as an end in itself. Your current income may simply be a necessity borne of circumstance, reflecting the fact that you are single and must support yourself in a manner that makes you comfortable. Once you find a life partner, you will be ready to cut back your hours or take a lesser position, continuing to bring income into the household, but preparing for the eventual arrival of children. You fully expect your future husband to pull his own weight as well as some of yours and you assume that he will be the primary provider for your children's needs.

If the previous perspective matches your viewpoint, chances are you would find yourself uncomfortable as a breadwinning wife. Your husband's lesser income would interfere with the future you picture for yourself, potentially requiring you to stick with your job so that you can continue to bring substantial income into the family. Cutting back could mean making sweeping changes in your lifestyle, unless you have been frugal and saved for these changes.

Or you may view your own money in another way, giving it little weight in your life and keeping its value in perspective when compared to the quality of your relationships with others. You make a decent living; that's great! A future husband may match or exceed your income—even better! More money in the household means more for everyone. If your husband makes less than you, then so be it. The important thing is that you find the right man with whom you will spend your life; his income compared to yours is not important in the grander scheme.

Women who can be happy as breadwinning wives tend either to see money as the most important element in their personal security or they see it as a pleasant by-product of working, a reward for their accomplishments and an opportunity to do more for themselves and their families.

As a breadwinning wife in the money-equals-independence category, you may find yourself choosing a man whose income is truly limited, so that he never has the opportunity to suggest that you let him
support you. As a wife to whom money is only an element in the larger
picture, you may find the greatest happiness with a man whose income
comes close to yours, but does not exceed yours. By the same token,
should your circumstances change and your husband take a turn as
breadwinner for a while, you will not find this new situation uncomfortable or unnatural—in fact, you may hardly notice the change at all.

*3. How important is a diamond engagement ring to your overall happiness as
a wife?*
This is not the superficial question it appears to be. I'm not asking if you
like jewelry; nor am I suggesting that diamonds are indeed a girl's best
friend. On the contrary, I point to what the engagement ring represents:
an outward indication of your future husband's success, his willingness
to demonstrate this by providing you with the traditional expression of
his romantic love and your own need to wear this symbol for all the
world to see.

Our society assumes that the larger the diamond, the greater your
husband's ability to provide for you and your family. Here are some of the
assumptions I've heard about this supposedly romantic symbol: The
absence of a diamond leads others to label your husband a cheapskate, a
lesser provider—or worse, a man who doesn't "really" love you. A tiny diamond chip or an alternative stone indicates that you've chosen a man
who is trying, but is already delinquent in his duty to you. These may be
the judgments we face as we choose a man to marry, whether or not the
diamond ring has any meaning to each of us individually.

The assumptions don't stop with the diamond, however. The
ring is the first in a series of purchases that signify accomplishment,
success and a husband's ability to provide for his family: the suburban
home, the wardrobe, the car, the extended vacations and on and on as
your marriage continues and your possessions accumulate.

As a breadwinning wife, you may eventually acquire all the
things your heart desires—but you may buy them with your own money
or with funds from the family pot, the majority of which came from you.
If you have always assumed that your husband will pay for these things
as a function of his male role, this reality will jar against your fundamental beliefs.

Before you become involved with a man who earns less than
you do, consider this basic question. If he gets down on one knee and

proposes, but is in no position to offer you a diamond ring...how much will that matter? Will it cast a pall on the entire relationship? Will you be ready to share the acquisition of material possessions with your husband on an equal or even dominant basis? Or will it make no difference whatsoever?

4. How do you define "success"?
We're talking about your personal success here—not your husband's. What elements in your own life make you feel that you are a successful, accomplished woman?

Many of us work against the definitions of success set for us by the generation that preceded us. We hear the messages from our mothers and other family members and from friends whose aspirations didn't necessarily link to careers: A successful woman is a *married* woman.

A few years ago, I joined the committee to plan my twenty year high school reunion. As some of the committee women gathered in the kitchen of one classmate's suburban house to catch up after the meeting, family pictures began to spring from wallets. Portraits and snapshots of happy children, smiling husbands and comfortable homes circulated throughout the room, each of us exclaiming over the other's "accomplishments." No one asked what anyone did for a living—in fact, many of these women were full-time wives and mothers. Yet over and over I heard women exclaim, "Wow, you've done so well!"

After a time, I noticed that one ordinarily gregarious woman, Nancy, had stepped out of the circle. One by one, my former classmates turned as if they'd suddenly noticed Nancy and asked, "So, you're not married yet?"

Nancy shook her head, smiling ruefully.

"Oh well," the classmate invariably responded, "It'll happen for you someday." Each woman then turned away, physically cutting Nancy out of the group. Their body language said it all: Nancy wasn't married, so Nancy must be a failure.

I, too, hung outside the circle slightly, a childless anomaly in this celebration of traditional womanhood. The more I heard these abbreviated conversations with Nancy, however, the more appalled I became. Finally, I turned to her and asked, "What do you *do*, Nancy?"

Instantly, she brightened. "I'm the director of a series of elder living centers across five counties," she said. She launched into an enthusiastic description of her job and its rewards. The room went quiet. Others in the group turned to look at Nancy with new respect. "Wow," said one. "That all sounds really...responsible."

Here I stood in a roomful of people I'd known since I was fourteen years old and I'd never seen them clearly before. Every one of them
considered marriage the ultimate achievement, with bearing and raising
children as the second accomplishment on their success criteria list. Not
one of them had given a moment's thought to professional achievement
as an indication of self-worth, even though some of these women worked
outside the home.

The happiest breadwinning wives are those who extend their
definitions of success far beyond their marital statuses. Rather than
seeking to place their senses of identity in the hands of their husbands—considering themselves successful *because* they've married high-
earning men—breadwinning wives look to themselves and to their own
abilities as indications of their success. Significant income, the plea-
sures of doing good work and the ability to provide for the family are all
part of a breadwinning wife's self-image and self-worth. Within such a
definition of success, there is no pressure to marry a high-earning man
to prove that she can hook a "good catch."

Do your identity and your sense of personal achievement come
from within or are you waiting for the opportunity to define yourself
through the man you marry? The answer to this question will tell you a
great deal about your potential comfort level as a breadwinning wife.

5. How do you approach the concept of the working mother?

There's a basic fact that comes with the role of breadwinning wife: If
you someday plan to stay home and raise children, you may seriously
compromise your family's lifestyle by giving up your job. Your place as
breadwinner means that your income will be the primary support for
your family. Knock out that support and you will be left with your husband's income—which may be substantially lower than yours.

If you're considering marriage to a man who makes less than
you, you must take into account the impact this decision will have on
your additional role as a mother.

Some working women know well in advance that the extended
child care role is not for them. They expect that after six weeks' maternity leave, they will be more than ready to return to work—so they make
arrangements for alternative child care well in advance and keep close
tabs on their children's daily experiences with nannies, in others'
homes or in day care centers. These women are prepared to balance the
demands of motherhood with their work responsibilities—and they
build their husbands' participation into the master plan so that the burden of child care does not fall exclusively to either parent.

Certainly these women are well suited to the breadwinning wife role. However, what about all the other potential mothers—those who hope to spend greater amounts of time with their children, especially in their youngest years? What about wives who believe children should be raised at home, in the care of a full-time parent?

Nearly two million at-home parents are fathers. If you are willing to consider this option so that your children can be raised in their own home, you could find the breadwinning wife scenario well-suited to the fulfillment of your parenting dream. If *you* hope to be the primary child care provider in your home, however, and you maintain the breadwinning role as well, you face a conflict that can lead to years of guilt, remorse and anguish over missed milestones and events. Inevitable conflict will surface when you blame your husband's lower income for coming between you and your children.

As you consider your plans for a family within the context of your potential breadwinning wife role, leave room for the possibility that your plans may change. Today you may feel that you would rush back to work as your standard-issue maternity leave came to a close, but once you have a child in your life, you may experience the transformation many new mothers encounter. You may find that your new baby has stolen your heart and changed your outlook on life forever. Look for ways to accommodate your own needs as a mother while continuing to provide primary support to your family—flex time, work-family balance programs, split child care shifts with your husband. The breadwinner role need not become a tender trap when a new baby arrives.

6. What would happen if you broke with your relationship pattern?
How vividly I remember my dating years! One after another, I'd become attracted to men who lived for each moment in the spotlight. Desperate to be center of attention and center of my universe, these flamboyant, ostentatious men overwhelmed my comparatively reserved nature with their big voices and big personalities. At parties, friends commented admiringly to me, "He's really fun to be with, isn't he?" I basked in the residual glow of my man's aura, just pleased to be with someone who shed such a happy light on me.

Behind closed doors, however, beyond predictably passionate sex and occasional grandiose romantic gestures, these men were moody, self-involved, dark, brooding, busily constructing walls of mystery for the express purpose of forcing me to climb them. Each came with his own fascinating set of neuroses and social dysfunctions, the products of questionable choices made by questionable parents.

Invariably, these relationships would deteriorate as I grew weary of building each man's confidence and catering to his need for attention, while he allowed my needs to languish, unmet and unimportant to him. (One three-year boyfriend went so far as to tell me, "You will never be a spotlight personality. You just don't have what it takes. You'll always live in my shadow." Sheesh!)

So committed to this pattern was I that when I met Nic, I nearly passed him by entirely. Days after we were first introduced, I realized he had begun to seek me out at work, suddenly appearing at my office door or catching up with me in the hallway. Quiet, respectful, unendingly sweet and considerate, he matched none of my usual guidelines for the men in my life. There was no mystery to solve—and this became the grandest mystery of all, with me as Agatha Christie, scrutinizing every detail to find the reasons I so enjoyed Nic's company.

Nic shattered my relationship pattern into thousands of irretrievable pieces. It was only by breaking with my own traditions that I found happiness—by abandoning the need for the "star" relationship and trading in the tinsel and glitter for sincerity, comfort and honesty.

What is your pattern? What would happen if you threw it out? As women with expectations of professional success, we are born and bred to "marry up," to find a man whose professional aspirations and drive exceed our own. All too often, those admirable traits are coupled with others that can work against our own success: competitiveness, egocentrism, self-involvement, a need to be seen as the family leader and provider, insistence on traditional family roles. When we marry these men and we succeed in our own right, we can find ourselves enmeshed in conflicts we never would have predicted.

Could you be attracted to a man who may always make less than you do? Try this: Make a list of the character traits that mean the most to you in a relationship—not the physical characteristics of your dream man or his rank and position in the world, but the more basic elements of personality and ethics and the way he would approach the world. Now take a hard look at this list as you consider your past relationships. Are these the traits you find in the men you usually choose?

If not, it may be time to break your past pattern and consider an entirely different kind of man.

Breaking your relationship pattern may mean changing the way you present yourself to friends who could introduce you to potential men, "I did the fix-up thing with my friends setting me up," said Yvonne, a forty-two-year-old divorcee. "They assumed that because I have a corporate job, I would want to meet only men who make more than I do. Frankly, I didn't click with any of those guys—they were too much like my first husband."

A middle manager with an income exceeding $60,000 annually, Yvonne surprised herself when she placed a personal advertisement and received a call from Stuart, a divorced man who told her on the first date that he "didn't make much money."

"He works in manufacturing," Yvonne said. "His first wife left him because she wanted a man who made more and could give her more. I have to say that if someone had just described him to me for a potential fix-up, I would have said, 'Nothing doing.' But he was so nice on the phone that I had to meet him. On the second date, he brought me flowers and he had a little gift of some kind for me every time he saw me. Who does that anymore?"

Had Yvonne stuck to her friends' assumption—and her own—that she needed to be with a man whose income topped hers, she might never have met Stuart. "Now we've been together for almost a year," she continued. "He's sweet and funny and cute as a button. He kids me about wanting to do everything myself—but he doesn't tell me that I can't. He's a whole different kind of guy."

Where are these guys?

If you've determined that you could indeed entertain the idea of becoming the breadwinning wife of a supportive man, now you want to know where you can find the new man of your dreams.

Look behind the scenes. Move your focus from the man in the spotlight to the man who aims the beam. Behind every supervisor, CEO, executive director and high-earning professional is a hardworking staff of intelligent, accomplished people who do not necessarily seek the responsibility of the top spot.

In high technology organizations, look to the programmers, developers and integrators who create the systems their bosses dream up. In large corporations, look to the field personnel, the financial staff, the people who keep the organization running but who may never receive the recognition their higher-ups get. Look to the research laboratories of a medical facility or the product development or fabrication team at a manufacturing company. You'll find men of high intelligence and advanced education, applying their skills in practical ways that rarely receive public credit or acknowledgement.

Outside of big companies, look to small business owners—the tradesmen, shop managers, restaurant owners and countless others who combine management expertise, business sense and professional skills with an ability to deal with the public. Some may have inherited the family business, while others are entrepreneurs who hope to grow their ideas into large, profitable enterprises. In the meantime, at an early stage in their growth, they may earn a lower income. This may change as their success grows.

The enormous world of non-profit organizations holds thousands and thousands of men who have traded high incomes for opportunities to do something important in the world—create great art, help the underprivileged, raise money to cure diseases, save open spaces, change society for the better. Fulfill your own need to make a difference on a grander scale by volunteering for one of these organizations or by seeking membership on a non-profit board of trustees. Not only will you do some good for your community, you will have close interaction with staff members and other volunteers. You may meet someone who shares your passion for a cause as well as your desire to create a home and raise a family.

If you are a business owner, look to men in related professional associations who may be starting home businesses or who work as freelancers. Slow-growth income or intermittent work schedules may limit their earning potential, but these men may be especially open to at-home fatherhood if your lives move together in that direction.

These men are not hard to find—but they *are* hard to see. We are so often dazzled by the men who lead, we can't see beyond them. Rub your eyes, refocus your lens and turn your scope past the male songbird with the bright feathers. The real find may be the subtler thrush in the background, the one who hides in the brushy undergrowth of the forest, but whose more melodious song makes you stop and listen with delight.

CHAPTER 15

WHAT'S NEXT?
The Future for Breadwinning Wives

Will a day come when breadwinning wives are commonplace?

Indeed, that day has nearly arrived. With one in three wives out-earning their husbands and all trends pointing toward the continued advancement of women in the workplace—coupled with a decline in men's overall achievement—it's conceivable that we could reach the fifty-fifty mark, with wives as breadwinners in half of all married couples, within the next two decades.

What happens then?

As we have traveled through the many characteristics of marriages in which the wife is the principal breadwinner, we've seen that the wife's breadwinning status did not immediately indicate an egalitarian marriage. In fact, in many cases, wives continue to handle the greatest share of so-called "women's work"—cooking, cleaning, child care—even though they also brought in the higher paycheck.

We are closer than we have ever been to achieving true equality between men and women in the workplace and at home. Many individual couples already have reached this goal—a challenge that seemed insurmountable even twenty years ago. Now, how do we move the marker the rest of the way? What do we require—from ourselves, from our spouses and from society—to truly discard gender ideologies and create the right environment for equitable marriage?

Work-family balance. Husbands and wives deserve the opportunity to balance their work against the needs of their families. While many companies offer balance programs, many more do not—and even those who offer them may curtail the careers of men and women who actually take their employers up on the offer. Until these programs are ubiquitous, one working parent is forced to carry the greater share of child care responsibility—or one parent must stay home with the children. While this may be the preferred configuration in many households, it should come as a *choice*, not as the only way out of an inflexible work situation.

Employers must recognize that parents can still be excellent employees, that the "mommy track" is not a given when a baby enters the family picture and that fathers are devoted parents—many of whom want to correct the inequities in their own childhoods by spending as much time as possible with their children. When more employers accept the fact that parents who do not worry constantly about their children can perform more effectively on the job, they will see the potential for a win-win situation in improving their work-family balance offerings.

Equity at home. Decades of social pressure and demonstration tell us that women do housework and men do not. Yet already, 51 percent of my male respondents believe that they are the primary housekeepers—and they were proud to tell me so! Wives must ask for, encourage and accept their husbands' assistance at home by working with them to divide up responsibilities. Especially we who are breadwinner wives must take it upon ourselves to make this happen and stop waiting for our husbands to "notice" that we need their involvement in handling our homes.

In a fifty-fifty partnership, each partner does half. That's the definition! Full role reversal, in which the husband becomes the household manager and child care provider while the working wife has no role in household tasks, is as unworkable as it was when women were expected to take on this role in earlier generations. Breadwinner wives cannot expect to turn their spouses into househusbands without recognizing that they will feel just as taken for granted, just as victimized and just as trapped as women did when this was their only available role.

Partnership means that both spouses participate, working to divide up responsibility in equitable ways. If your husband washes the dishes and the laundry and you wipe down the kitchen counters and put the folded clothes away, you've split the chores between you. That's how partnership works. When you wipe down the counters, this act is *not* another example in a long line of demonstrations of your husband's inability to complete a task—"the 98 percent project," as one wife called it. The sooner we understand that we must all be participants in our own households, the sooner we will find satisfaction in a truly egalitarian relationship.

The next generation. Breadwinner wives have a golden opportunity to end the passing down of gender roles to another generation. Your children can see parents who are happily sharing the responsibility for funding and running their home—with no regard for "women's work" and "men's work." If you teach your children that there is no such thing as a gender role, they will grow up to believe that they can structure their own homes in any way that works best for them as individuals. It's up to you to pass on your value system and to put a stop to the role stereotyping we battle every day.

Normalize your relationship. Don't complain to your parents and friends about your husband's lower income. Don't make it an issue at work, telling your boss you need a raise, because your husband makes less than you do. Don't play the martyr or the victim, because you're a breadwinning wife. Each time you turn your status into an issue, you make it an issue for everyone around you—and you reconfirm the idea that men must make more, while women make less. Not only does this undermine your own relationship—it's the same insidious philosophy that keeps the Equal Rights Amendment from becoming law and keeps women's wages from becoming equal to those of men in equivalent jobs. You are the breadwinner; that's a responsibility, not a punishment.

Should you choose to tell others about your financial role in your marriage, treat your disclosure as if it's normal, not an aberration. You are on the cusp of great change and great victories for all women, today and for generations to come. Celebrate and enjoy!

My own dream is this: In ten years, I hope that this book will be a quaint little treatise that recognized a trend before it became commonplace. I hope that a decade from now, none of you will need this book, because no one will think twice of women making more money than their husbands.

Breadwinner wives, I hope to meet you at the top of that hill.

The view will be spectacular.

Share ideas and insights with other breadwinner wives and find more information and resources for working women at the official Web site for **Breadwinner Wives and the Men They Marry:**
http://www.breadwinnerwives.com.

ENDNOTES

Chapter 1

1. Kim Clark, "Women, Men and Money," *Fortune* 134, no. 3 (August 5, 1996): 60.
2. Current Population Survey, Bureau of Labor Statistics and Bureau of the Census. "Chart FINC-08. Earnings of Wife By Earnings of Husband in 1996—Married Couple Families by Work Experience, Age, Presence of Children and Race, Hispanic Origin of Reference Person" (U.S. Bureau of Labor Statistics, Washington, DC, 1997).
3. Amy Goldstein, "Breadwinning Wives Alter Marriage Equation," *Washington Post*, February 27, 2000, sec. A, p. 1.
4. Matt A. Towery, *Powerchicks: How Women Will Dominate America* (Marietta, GA: Longstreet Press, 1998).

Chapter 2

1. Richard B. Freeman, "The Feminization of Work in the U.S.: A New Era for (Man)kind?" *Gender and the Labor Market: Econometric Evidence on Obstacles in Achieving Gender Equality*. (Cambridge, MA: National Bureau of Economic Review, Harvard University, April 1999).
2. The Employment Situation News Release. "Table A-1. Employment Status of the Civilian Population by Sex and Age" (U.S. Bureau of Labor Statistics, Washington, DC, January 2001).
3. Freeman, p. 2.
4. Joann S. Lublin, "Playing 2nd Fiddle Tough for Many Men," *Wall Street Journal*, reprinted in *Rocky Mountain News*, May 19, 1993.
5. Michelle Ingrassia and Pat Wingert, "The New Providers," *Newsweek* (May 22, 1995): 36.
6. Peggy Orenstein, "Almost Equal," *New York Times Magazine* (April 5, 1998): 42-48.
7. Goldstein, p. 1.
8. Joan R. Rose, "Med-school Enrollment is Approaching 50 Percent Female," *Medical Economics* (March 6, 2000): 29.
9. "More Women Go to College" and "Women, College and Careers," *Monthly Labor Review*, U.S. Department of Labor (July 1999): 2 and (December 1999): 44.
10. "Where the Boys Aren't," *US News and World Report* (February 8, 1999): 46.

11. Dave Curtin, "New BMOC: Barely Men on Campus. Fewer Males Head to College, Officials Say," *Denver Post,* August 21, 2000, Rockies edition, sec.A, p. 1.
12. Paul A. Strassman, "Women Take Over," *Computerworld* (February 1, 1999): 47.
13. Laura DiDio, "IS Women Near Parity with Men," *Computerworld* (June 30, 1997): 41.
14. Ibid.
15. Strassman, p. 47.
16. Sharon Gaudin, "Women, Minorities Could Fill More High-tech Jobs," "Table: The IT gender gap," *Network World* (July 17, 2000): 16.
17. "1999 Catalyst Census of Women Corporate Officers and Top Earners" (http://www.catalystwomen.org/press/factsheet/factscore99.html).
18. Shelly Coolidge, "When Wives Transfer, Husbands Trail," *The Christian Science Monitor* (January 12, 1998).
19. "Women Making It to the Top," Catalyst INFOBRIEF: *Women in Corporate Leadership, Progress and Prospects* (1996).
20. "Women-Owned Businesses Top 9 Million in 1999," Research summary, National Foundation for Women Business Owners (May 11, 1999, http://www.nfwbo.org/LocLink/BIZC/RESEARCH/Link To/5-11-1999/5-11-1999.htm).
21. Ibid.
22. Betty Friedan, *Beyond Gender: The New Politics of Work and Family* (Washington, DC: Woodrow Wilson Center Press, 1997), 2.
23. Cheryl Russell, "Find the Missing Men," *American Demographics* (May 1995).
24. *The AAUW Report: How Schools Shortchange Girls,* American Association of University Women Educational Foundation, Washington, DC, 1992.
25. *Gender Gaps: Where Schools Still Fail Our Children,* Executive summary. American Association of University Women Educational Foundation, Washington, DC, 1998.
26. Kathleen Parker, "Schools Discriminate Against Boys," *Denver Post,* December 9, 1998, Rockies edition, sec. B, p. 11.
27. *The State of Black America 2000: Blacks in the New Millennium* (New York: National Urban League Publications Unit, 2000), 5.
28. Christina Hoff Summers, "Fair Treatment for Boys," *The Washington Post,* August 22, 2000, Final edition, Editorial page.
29. Lionel Tiger, *The Decline of Males* (New York: Griffen, 1999), 21-27.
30. Susan Faludi, *Stiffed: The Betrayal of the American Man* (New York: Perennial/Harper Collins Publishers, 1999), 27.

Chapter 3
1. Rhona Mahoney, *Kidding Ourselves: Breadwinning, Babies and Bargaining Power* (New York: Basic Books, 1995), 219.
2. Current Population Survey, Bureau of Labor Statistics and Bureau of the Census. "Chart FINC-08. Earnings of Wife By Earnings of Husband in 1996—Married Couple Families by Work Experience, Age, Presence of Children and Race, Hispanic Origin of Reference Person" (U.S. Bureau of Labor Statistics, Washington, DC, 1997).
3. Anne E. Winkler, "Earnings of Husbands and Wives in Dual-earner Families," *Monthly Labor Review* (April 1998): 42-48.
4. Ibid.
5. Cheryl Russell, "Find the Missing Men," *American Demographics* (May 1995).
6. Robert O. Blood, Jr. and Donald M. Wolfe, *Husbands and Wives: The Dynamics of Married Living* (New York: Free Press Paperback, 1960), 12.
7. Ibid., 12-13.
8. Candace West and Don H. Zimmerman, "Doing Gender," *Gender & Society* 1, no. 2 (June 1987): 125.
9. Ibid., 137.

10. Veronica Jaris Tichenor, "Status and Income as Gendered Resources: The Case for Marital Power," *Journal of Marriage and the Family* 61, (August 1999): 638-650.

Chapter 5
1. Christina LeBeau, "'It Sounded Like Prison.'" *Rochester Democrat & Chronicle*, December 14, 1998, sec. F, p. 5.
2. Arlie Russell Hoschchild, *The Second Shift* (New York: Avon Books, 1989).
3. Susan J. Wells, "What Happens if Harriet Makes More than Ozzie?" *The New York Times*, August 1, 1999.

Chapter 6
1. Anne Kohn Blau, *The Sex of the Dollar* (New York: Simon & Schuster, 1988), 12.
2. Colette Dowling, *Maxing Out: Why Women Sabotage Their Financial Security* (Boston: Little, Brown & Company, 1998), x.
3. Carolyn Vogler and Jan Pahl, "Money, Power and Inequality Within Marriage," *The Sociological Review* (Oxford, UK: Blackwell Publishers, May 1994), 272, Table 2.
4. SRI Consulting Business Intelligence, "Report Reveals Why Women Are Increasingly Valuable as Financial Consumers," (February 10, 1999, http://future.sri.com/BICPR/CFD.PRO299.html).
5. Joan Raymond with Robbie Woliver, "For Richer and For Poorer," *American Demographics* (July 2000).
6. Christopher L. Hayes and Carol A. Anderson, *The Women Cents Study*, Executive summary (National Center for Women and Retirement Research, New York, January 1995, http://www.agingfocus.com).
7. Raymond with Woliver.
8. Jan Pahl, "Household Spending, Personal Spending and the Control of Money in Marriage," *Sociology: The Journal of the British Sociological Association* (February 1990): 119-138.
9. Veronica Jaris Tichenor, "Status and Income as Gendered Resources: The Case for Marital Power," *Journal of Marriage and the Family* 61, (August 1999): 640.
10. Vogler and Pahl, "Money, Power and Inequality Within Marriage," 278-279.
11. J. Treas, "Money in the Bank: Transaction Costs and the Economic Organization of Marriage," *American Sociological Review* (October 1993): 732-734.
12. Carole B. Burgoyne, "Money in Marriage: How Patterns of Allocation Both Reflect and Conceal Power," *The Sociological Review* (November 1990): 638.

Chapter 7
1. Current Population Survey, Bureau of Labor Statistics and Bureau of the Census. "Chart FINC-08. Earnings of Wife By Earnings of Husband in 1996—Married Couple Families by Work Experience, Age, Presence of Children and Race, Hispanic Origin of Reference Person" (U.S. Bureau of Labor Statistics, Washington, DC, 1997.
2. U.S. Department of Health and Human Services, Office of the Assistant Secretary for Planning and Evaluation. "The 1998 HHS Poverty Guidelines" (http://aspe.hhs.gov/poverty/98poverty.htm).
3. Michelle Singletary, "Pressure to Spend on Valentine Needs Relief," *Rochester Democrat & Chronicle*, February 11, 2001, sec. E, p. 1.
4. Raymond with Woliver.

Chapter 8
1. Hochschild, *The Second Shift*.
2. Christine Delphy, *Close to Home: A Materialist Analysis of Women's Oppression* (Amherst, MA: The University of Massachusetts Press, 1984), 38-39.
3. Julie Brines, "Economic Dependency, Gender, and the Division of Labor at Home," *American Journal of Sociology* (November 1994): 663-664.

4. Ibid, 664.
5. Ibid, 682.
6. Hochschild, *The Second Shift*, 221-222.
7. *The 1997 National Study of the Changing Workforce*, Executive summary by the Families and Work Institute (http://www.familiesandwork.org/nationalstudy.html).
8. David W. Moore, *Today's Husband More Involved with Household Duties than Post WWII Generation*, Report by The Gallup Poll (http://www.gallup.com).

Chapter 9
1. Brines, 682.

Chapter 10
1. Harriet Johnson Brackey, "Mr. Mom Furor Fuels Case," Knight-Ridder wire, *Rochester Democrat & Chronicle*, January 24, 2000, sec. F, p. 5.
2. Ibid.
3. Esther Wachs Book, *Why The Best Man for the Job Is a Woman* (New York: Harper-business, 2000), xii.
4. "Mothers Can't Win," *New York Times Magazine*, April 5, 1998, pp. 42-48.
5. Arlie Russell Hochschild, *The Time Bind: When Work Becomes Home and Home Becomes Work* (New York: Metropolitan Books, Henry Holt and Company, 1997), 44.
6. Laura Schlessinger, *Parenthood by Proxy: Don't Have Them If You Don't Want to Raise Them* (New York: HarperCollins, 2000).
7. Labor Force Statistics from the Current Population Survey, US Bureau of Labor Statistics. "Table 5. Employment status of the population by sex, marital status, and presence and age of own children under 18, 1998-99 annual averages" (http://www.bls/gov/text_only/cps_cont_txt.htm).
8. The National Institute of Child Health and Human Development. "*The NICHD Study of Early Child Care,*" (http://www.nichd.nih.gov/about/despr/cohort/index/htm).
9. Beth Azar, "The Debate Over Child Care Isn't Over," *Monitor on Psychology* 31, no. 3, (March 2000).
10. *Morning Edition*, National Public Radio. "Daycare Kids More Likely to Become Bullies," Report on information released by the Society for Research in Child Development (April 21, 2001).
11. Ellen Galinsky, *Ask The Children: What America's Children Really Think About Working Parents* (New York: William Morrow & Company, 1999), 4.
12. Ibid, 27-44.
13. Ibid, 37.
14. Ibid, 49.
15. Ibid, 41-44.
16. James A. Levine and Todd Pittinsky, *Working Fathers: New Strategies for Balancing Work and Family* (New York: A Harvest Book, 1997), 97-102.
17. Whirlpool Foundation Study, *Women: The New Providers*. Whirlpool Foundation Study by Families and Work Institute, conducted by Louis Harris and Associates, Inc., (May 1995), 28.

Chapter 11
1. Martha Farrell Erickson, Ph.D., "Research Confirms What Dads and Kids Tell Us: Fathers Are Important in the Lives of Their Children and Children Help Me 'Grow Up,' too." *Seeds of Promise* 3, The Child, Youth and Family Consortium at the University of Minnesota (http://www.cyfc.umn.edu/Parenting/Seeds/volume3.html).
2. *1997 National Study of the Changing Workforce*, Executive summary by the Families and Work Institute 5 (http://www.familiesandwork.org/nationalstudy.html).
3. Levine, *Working Fathers: News Strategies for Balancing Work and Family*, 17.

4. *The Families and Work Institute's 1998 Business Work-Life Study.* Executive summary, 2 (https://swww.igc.apc.org/fwi/pubs/worklife.pdf).
5. Hochschild, *The Time Bind.*
6. Levine, *Working Fathers,* 29.
7. Robert Frank, Ph.D., *The Involved Father* (New York: The Phillip Lief Group, 1999), 138.
8. James Sulanowski, "Pan It If You Want, but Sitcom Makes Me Feel Less Alone," *Providence Journal,* June 18, 2000.
9. Ibid.
10. Tony Schwartz, "Full-time Dads Often Struggle with Respect—Getting It from Others and Having It from Themselves," *Fast Company* (April 2000, http://www.fastcompany.com/online/33/tschwartz.html).
11. Levine, *Working Fathers,* 41.

Chapter 12
1. "Job Loss and Older Men." *Monthly Labor Review* 122, no.6 (June 1999): 40.
2. "Marital Status and Living Arrangements of Adults 18 Years Old and Over, March 1998," Table B, From Unpublished Tables: Marital Status and Living Arrangements, March 1998, U.S. Bureau of the Census.
3. "U.S. Divorce Statistics," Divorcemagazine.com (http://www.divorcemagazine.com).
4. Richard Clements and Clifford H. Swensen, "Commitment to One's Spouse as a Predictor of Marital Quality Among Older Couple," *Current Psychology* 19, no. 2 (Summer 2000): 110.
5. Stephanie Coontz, *The Way We Never Were* (New York: Basic Books, 1992), 26.
6. Ibid, 27.
7. Ibid, 29-30.
8. Ibid, 31.
9. Judith Wallerstein and Sandra Blakeslee, *The Good Marriage: How and Why Love Lasts* (New York: Warner Books, 1996).

Chapter 13
1. "U.S. Divorce Statistics," Divorcemagazine.com, (http://www.divorcemagazine.com)
2. Michele Morris, "Yours, Mine and Ours," *Ladies Home Journal* (October 1996): 52.
3. Jiping Zuo and Shengming Tang, "Breadwinning Status and Gender Ideologies of Men and Women Regarding Family Roles," *Sociological Perspectives* 43 (Spring 2000): 29.
4. Susan J. Wells, "What Happens if Harriet Makes More Than Ozzie?"
5. Liana C. Sayer, and Suzanne M. Bianchi, "Women's Economic Independence and the Probability of Divorce: A Review and Reexamination," *Journal of Family Issues* (October 2000): 906-943.
6. Ibid.
7. Stacey J. Rogers, "Wives' Incomes and Marital Quality: Are There Reciprocal Effects?" *Journal of Marriage and the Family* 61, no. 1 (February 1999): 123-132.
8. Laura Doyle, *The Surrendered Wife: A Practical Guide to Finding Intimacy, Passion and Peace with Your Man* (New York: Simon & Schuster, 2001).

Chapter 14
1. Colette Dowling, *The Cinderella Complex,* (New York: Pocket Books, 1981).

BREADWINNING WIVES
Survey Questionnaire

The following questionnaire was used in interviewing the 120 respondents who participated in the research for this book.

Use this questionnaire to explore your own experiences as a breadwinning wife. Should you wish your husband to participate as well, each of you should record your answers privately and then come together to compare your responses. The results may tell you a great deal about your individual perceptions and whether or not you see your marriage challenges in the same light.

1. Respondent's Profession:
   Provide a brief description of your job responsibilities:

2. Professional activities outside of job responsibilities (i.e. boards, professional associations, volunteer work, etc.):

3. Average hours/month spent on work and professional activities combined:

4. Primary leisure-time activities (hobbies, sports, etc.):

5. Number of hours/month spent on these activities:

6. Number of children living with you:
   Ages:

7. Number of non-adult children in other living situations:
   Ages:

8. Number of adult children (including children in college):

9. Do you provide financial support for these children?

FINANCIAL SITUATION

1. Primary residence is:
   ____ Single-family house
   ____ Multi-family house
   ____ Apartment
   ____ Townhouse
   ____ Condominium
   ____ Co-op
   ____ Mobile home
   ____ Own   ____ Rent

2. Which spouse holds primary responsibility for the following financial tasks:

TASK	WIFE	HUSBAND	BOTH
Management of checking account			
Management of savings account			
Management/choice of investments (stocks, mutual funds, etc.)			
Paying household bills			
Day-to-day household expenses (groceries, cleaning supplies, etc.)			

3. Which of the following monetary arrangements describes the situation in your marriage? (check all that apply)

_____ Joint checking account

_____ Separate checking accounts

_____ All joint bank accounts

_____ All separate bank accounts

_____ A mix of joint and separate bank accounts

_____ Husband receives allowance

_____ Wife receives allowance

_____ Monthly budget established

_____ No monthly budget established

_____ All joint investments

_____ All separate investments

_____ A mix of joint and separate investments

_____ No investments

_____ We have discussed and agreed upon a plan for saving money

_____ We do not have an established plan for saving money

_____ Household expenses paid entirely from wife's income

_____ Household expenses paid entirely from husband's income

_____ Household expenses split between spouses

_____ Other financial management options not listed here that apply to your situation (describe)

4. How did you establish your plan for management of your household's income and expenses?

YOUR RELATIONSHIP

1. Whose income was higher on the day you married?

2. What were your professional circumstances at that time? What were your spouse's?

3. How long were you married when the wife's income exceeded the husband's?

4. What were the circumstances in which this took place?

5. Did your relationship change when the wife's income began to significantly exceed the husband's? (If "yes," describe the change.)

6. Did your child care situation change? (If yes, describe.)

7. Did your relationship with your children change? (If yes, describe.)

8. If your parents are living, are they aware of the income difference between you and your spouse?

9. Did your relationship with your parents change? (If yes, describe.)

10. Are your personal friends aware of the difference in income between you and your spouse?

11. If so, did your relationships with your friends change? (If yes, describe.)

12. Are your coworkers or business associates aware of this income difference?

13. If so, did your relationships with coworkers or business associates change? (If yes, describe.)

14. Describe the role model for marriage and family in which you grew up. What was the family/financial structure in your childhood home?

15. How do you think that model influenced your own definition of marriage and financial position?

HOUSEHOLD RESPONSIBILITIES

1. Which of you holds primary responsibility for the following:

TASK	WIFE	HUS-BAND	EQUAL	CHIL-DREN	HIRED PROFES-SIONALS
House cleaning					
Cooking					
Laundry					
After-meal clean-up					
Lawn mowing and care					
Gardening					
Child care					
Snow removal					
Home repairs (DIY)					
Hiring contractors for home repairs					
Home decorating					
Grocery shopping					
Clothing shopping for children					
Social arrangements					
Family recreational choices					

2. How did you arrive at your current household task arrangement? (Were you entirely in agreement; were there "negotiations," etc.?)

YOUR MARRIAGE

1. Describe one area in which your spouse has encouraged you or influenced you positively (examples: career, raising of children, your relationship, relationships with family, etc.)

2. Are there other areas? If so, describe:

3. Describe one area in which your spouse has discouraged you or influenced you negatively (examples: career, raising of children, your relationship, relationships with family, etc.)

4. Are there other areas? If so, describe:

5. If the situation were reversed and you and your spouse assumed the traditional roles, with the husband as principal breadwinner, would you be:

   _____ Very pleased

   _____ Pleased

   _____ Indifferent (no positive or negative feeling)

   _____ Displeased

   _____ Very displeased

6. If you could change one thing about your current situation, what would it be?